EAT...

... when a book made me more angry. Lawrence's ... be compulsory reading ... Nothing is what it says on the packet' Allison Pearson, *Evening Standard*

'A devastating analysis of the food business' *Sunday Telegraph*

'Challenges each and every one of us to think again about what we buy and eat. It's almost like uncovering a secret state within the state' Andrew Marr, BBC Radio 4's *Start the Week*

'A thorough, complex and shocking insight into the food we eat in the twenty-first century ... Perhaps this should be sold as the most effective diet book ever written' *Daily Mail*

'A brave examination of the calamities caused by a policy laughingly called one of "cheap food"' Jeremy Paxman's Book of the Year, *Observer*

'There are not many books that make you radically reconsider everyday choices: Lawrence's superb and chilling study of the supermarket and its impact on diet certainly will. The facts simply stagger ... This is an excellent book: balanced, polemical and genuinely challenging' *Scotland on Sunday*

'A stark, challenging and compelling book' *The Sunday Times*

'Felicity Lawrence's horrifying account of how the food we eat is produced doesn't make for a good night's sleep but is compulsively readable. It is the sort of book that changes attitudes' *Evening Standard*

'Required reading' *Mail on Sunday*

ABOUT THE AUTHOR

Felicity Lawrence is an award-winning journalist and editor who began writing on food-related issues over twenty years ago. Her previous book, *Not on the Label*, won the Guild of Food Writers' Jeremy Round Award for Best First Book 2005 and a special commendation in the André Simon Awards 2004. She has twice been awarded the Guild of Food Writers' Derek Cooper Award for Investigative Food Writer of the Year, and has twice been shortlisted for Specialist Reporter of the Year at the British Press Awards. She is Special Correspondent for the *Guardian* and lives in London.

Eat Your Heart Out

Why the Food Business is Bad for the Planet and Your Health

FELICITY LAWRENCE

PENGUIN BOOKS

PENGUIN BOOKS

Published by the Penguin Group
Penguin Books Ltd, 80 Strand, London WC2R ORL, England
Penguin Group (USA) Inc., 375 Hudson Street, New York, New York 10014, USA
Penguin Group (Canada), 90 Eglinton Avenue East, Suite 700, Toronto, Ontario, Canada M4P 2Y3
(a division of Pearson Penguin Canada Inc.)
Penguin Ireland, 25 St Stephen's Green, Dublin 2, Ireland (a division of Penguin Books Ltd)
Penguin Group (Australia), 250 Camberwell Road, Camberwell, Victoria 3124, Australia
(a division of Pearson Australia Group Pty Ltd)
Penguin Books India Pvt Ltd, 11 Community Centre, Panchsheel Park, New Delhi – 110 017, India
Penguin Group (NZ), 67 Apollo Drive, Rosedale, North Shore 0632, New Zealand
(a division of Pearson New Zealand Ltd)
Penguin Books (South Africa) (Pty) Ltd, 24 Sturdee Avenue,
Rosebank, Johannesburg 2196, South Africa

Penguin Books Ltd, Registered Offices: 80 Strand, London WC2R ORL, England

www.penguin.com

First published 2008
1

Set in 11/13 pt Monotype Bembo
Typeset by Rowland Phototypesetting Ltd, Bury St Edmunds, Suffolk
Printed in England by Clays Ltd, St Ives plc

ISBN: 978-0-141-02601-5

www.greenpenguin.co.uk

Penguin Books is committed to a sustainable future
for our business, our readers and our planet.
The book in your hands is made from paper
certified by the Forest Stewardship Council.

Mixed Sources
Product group from well-managed
forests and other controlled sources
www.fsc.org · Cert no. SA-COC-1592
© 1996 Forest Stewardship Council
FSC

For Matt, Ellie, Cecy and Anna

Contents

Preface

Four years ago I wrote a book called *Not on the Label* to explain how the food of our modern industrialized diets is made. Like many people I had become disconnected from the processes involved in getting that food on to my plate. It was a revelation then to me as well as to others that a chicken nugget might consist of chopped up skin and fat disguised by additives rather than be made of lean meat, or that the pristine packs of washed, fresh salad I used to buy in supermarkets generally emerged from factory baths of chlorine thanks to hidden armies of poorly paid migrant workers. I found myself exploring a brave new world in which independent shops, local distribution networks and small farmers around the world were being squeezed out with alarming speed to be replaced by increasingly centralized and industrialized processes that are greedy of fossil-fuel energy and that concentrate the money made from food in the hands of a few corporations. Quite apart from epidemics of obesity, heart disease and cancer, the food this system produced just didn't taste very nice.

I was overwhelmed and humbled by the response to that first book. I lost track of the hundreds of letters and emails I received from people kind enough to tell me how they had changed their way of eating and shopping, or even their whole lives, after reading it. For some, change meant considerable personal inconvenience or upheaval – there was the elderly couple from Cornwall who vowed never to shop in supermarkets again having read about the working conditions of migrants; there was the city dealer who decided to reconnect with the land, giving up his lucrative career for a smallholding and a more sustainable life. I heard from dozens of people who had started their own campaigns, dozens more who had joined food co-ops, become part of fair trade towns, sought out farmer's markets, started using breadmakers, or simply gone back to cooking.

In the last four years our understanding has moved on. Concern about the quality of our food and about the wider social and environmental impacts of the way it is produced has at last become the stuff of the mainstream. Celebrity TV chefs have taken up the cause of improving diets and used the all-powerful medium of television to spread the message.

But what has struck me more recently is that while we have become more equipped to chose food that is better for our own health and that of the planet than we were just a few years ago, many of the connections still remain opaque. I find people ask me whether a particular food is all right, whether this brand might be better than that, or one particular retailer better than another, or a new apparently miracle food or technology might be the answer, when what we need for real understanding of the system and what we are being sold is knowledge of how the whole works and why it developed the way it did. What are the forces, economic, political, cultural, that led us down the path of degraded industrialized food in the first place? Where will those forces take us next, if the fundamentals are not changed? How do hunger and migration in one part of the world connect with obesity and ill-health in another? As climate change accelerates, and pressure on resources grows, the answers seem ever more urgent.

This book is an attempt to tackle those questions. When I wrote *Not on the Label*, I was tapping into a vast amount of work done over many years by health campaigners, aid agencies, union activists, environmental experts, and farming and organic producers' organizations. Thanks to their efforts, we have all become far more questioning. Many of them once again provided invaluable help in writing this book.

Professor Tim Lang has given frequent advice and kindly

read much of the manuscript. Professor David Goodman also read chapters and offered insights in to US policy. Professors Aubrey Sheiham, Erik Millstone, Michael Crawford and Jack Winkler have taught me about sugars, fats, and food policy; Professor John Salt steered me through the minefield of migration statistics. Professor John Stein, Dr Alex Richardson, Bernard Gesch, Jo Hibbeln and Ray Cook also kindly gave me many hours of their time.

Bill Vorley, Tim Lobstein, Jane Landon, Kath Dalmeny, Jeanette Longfield, and Andrew Simms have shared their expert knowledge with endless generosity over the last few years.

Patrick Holden, Craig Sams, Simon Wright and Peter Melchett of the Soil Association have all added greatly to my understanding, as have the MEP for the Greens, Caroline Lucas and the original campaigning school dinner lady, Jeanette Orrey.

I am grateful to the many staff at the aid agencies Oxfam, Christian Aid, Action Aid and Banana Link who helped organize trips and provided detailed background briefings. I owe great thanks too to Greenpeace, and John Sauven and his Amazon team for all their help.

As ever, activists on the ground provided the information without which much of the book could not have been written, sometimes at considerable personal cost. Don Pollard, Dave Richards, Miles Hubbard, 'Dan', Spitou Mendy, Binka Le Breton, Edilberto Sena and the late Angela Hale have all been a source of inspiration.

I should like to thank all the officials and press officers at the Food Standards Agency and at supermarket and manufacturing companies who have helped with information and background briefings. I have enjoyed the dialogue with industry thanks to the particular generosity of David Gregory of M&S, Martin Paterson, and Martin Glenn among others.

Much of the work on which this book is based has been carried out in my role as special correspondent for the *Guardian*.

I am incredibly fortunate to work for a newspaper which still invests in investigative journalism and gives its writers such support. I owe an enormous debt to my editors there, to Alan Rusbridger, Paul Johnson, Nick Hopkins, Stuart Millar, Ian Katz, Georgina Henry, Toby Manhire and Katharine Viner, and to many colleagues, including John Vidal, David Adam, Rebecca Smithers, Julia Finch, Ian Griffiths, David Leigh, Nuala Cosgrove and Mary Byrne.

Susannah Osborne not only helped substantially with research but taught me how to organize my files.

At Penguin, Kate Barker has once again coaxed a book out of a manuscript with expert skill; Elspeth Sinclair, Nicola Evans and Sarah Hulbert have somehow kept it to a schedule. Thanks too to Rosie Gailer, Mark Thomson and Robin Shaw. My agent Bill Hamilton as ever helped provide clarity where I lacked it.

My husband Matthew Bullard and my daughters, Ellie, Cecy and Anna, have had to live it, perhaps on occasion more than they would wish, for which the biggest thanks.

1. Cereals

How did it all begin?

It was one of those things that crept up on us and we still can't quite believe it happened. Looking back, we'd been in denial for some time. Then a friend who hadn't seen the family for a while came round and blurted out the bald truth. 'God, Dodi's got rather fat. In fact, you know, I think that might count as obese.'

Once said, it had to be admitted. If you looked at Dodi from behind when he was sitting down, you could see a substantial spare tyre around his thirteen-year-old middle. It bulged out from his hips and flopped down like a muffin rising up and out over its baking case. He had become quite lazy too, preferring to lounge in front of the fire rather than play in the garden as he used to. His excess weight was slowing him down. His joints seemed stiff as he climbed the stairs.

We had already put him on a diet, but he had been hooked on a particular brand of instant meal for ages. We had started giving it to him when it was the easiest option at the end of a long working day.

Guaranteed real tuna! Enriched with omega-3 and -6 fats! The feed was of course not much to do with tuna – 10 per cent minimum, it said in the small print, with the omega-3 and -6 as recent fashionable additions. It was made largely from rendered poultry meal mixed with fillers of corn gluten meal, ground rice, soya oil and dried beet pulp.

Dodi is our cat, and we know cats do not eat carbohydrates such as ground rice or sugar nor corn nor vegetable oils in normal circumstances. Nevertheless that's what we had been feeding him. It said on the packets that it was 'scientifically formulated' after all, though it might better have claimed that it was economically and politically formulated. Beet pulp is the waste from the sugar industry. Corn gluten meal is what's left over from the manufacture of corn syrup or corn starch for a vast range of processed foods and drinks. Rice is both one of the most subsidized and dumped crops in the world. Soya is the ubiquitous commodity that finds its way from the Americas into almost every form of comestible, whether for pets or humans. These are the products of corporate power and agricultural protection, of geopolitics and economic empire, more than any kind of independent science.

While there is every reason for domestic pets to eat waste from human food production, the absurdity of feeding them types of waste they never evolved to eat that actually make them fat and sick ought to be easy enough to see. But we have not apparently been alone in our blindness – feline diabetes has risen dramatically in the last few years in the UK. (Weaning them off this kind of food is another matter. In Dodi's case he had become so used to the flavourings added by the pet food technologists that he sniffed at anything else. And there is something peculiarly shaming about spending good money on diet cat food.)

There is nothing quite like an obstinacy of children around the kitchen table, their food likes and dislikes irreconcilably at odds, for bringing to mind the human parallels. Like many a parent I have often contemplated the paradox: how did Western mealtimes ever become such a source of conflict in an age of plenty? How did we reach the point at which what we eat has become a source of anxiety as much as pleasure? Why are my offspring asking whether it is in fact possible to send broccoli to the starving in Africa and how could we have slipped into such clichéd admonitions? While we're on the subject of the starving, why is food aid to poor countries made up of US corn and soya too? Have we entered an age of decadence, in which developed countries are bloated on a surfeit of choice for which we are biologically unprepared? If we are suffering from a surfeit of choice, though, how come the same small handful of ingredients crop up in everything we eat? Are we too subjects of a new economic empire? Where did I, or rather it, all go wrong?

At a minor domestic level, it is easy enough in one sense to see what the driving forces have been. There is no one moment I can locate at which all the faddiness of modern Britain entered our household, but there is a particular experience that symbolizes our loss of power and confidence over our food. It was the arrival of the health visitor a few months after the birth of our first child.

We had moved just before she was born into a new house whose previous owner, harbouring some fantasy of rural life in inner London, had kept a pig in the tiny back garden. The solicitors' contracts on exchange contained unusual clauses agreeing to white-coated men with long sharp knives being called should said pig not be removed from the property on completion. By the time we took possession in fact all that was left of the pig's occupation were the remains of a sty, a great deal of manure, and tangles of barbed wire lurking in the grass. We had been secretly disappointed. But the health visitor took one look at the garden, drew in her breath sharply, and then warned me . . . that there was a dangerous foxglove growing in the remains of the flower bed which might poison my first-born. Agricultural hazards had presumably not featured in her textbook on child health, though material from the food industry may well have done. I remember being bemused by her priorities on safety but for some reason did not think to take her nutritional advice in similar sceptical vein. Her failure to mention the pig in the garden, the proverbial elephant in the room, later struck me as typical of most current nutritional advice in its determined avoidance of the real point. She told me I should wean my breastfed baby on baby rice from a cardboard box. The traditional foods that I might be tempted to give her – bread, porridge, mashed morsels from our own meals – might induce all manner of terrifying allergies and gastrointestinal problems. So baby rice it was – a smooth pap of almost pure white starch from a grain that had had most of its nutrients removed by processing and that does not even form part of the traditional British diet.

Her advice and my following of it were characteristic of the modern malaise about food. Instead of the distillation of generations of experience, the ease of sharing family meals and a food culture developed over centuries, we have come to defer to the pseudo-scientific instructions of professionals before making the simplest of decisions about what we eat.

My own child was not on baby rice for long – it produced instant constipation. But looking back I can see how easy for the user and how vital to the industry this route to feeding was. Babies retain a liking for what they are weaned on. They also in fact retain their taste for what their mothers ate while pregnant, with studies now showing that the flavours of the maternal diet are transferred to the amniotic fluid. Breast milk, unlike baby milk formula, exposes them to the sensory stimulation of a varied diet, since it too takes on the flavour of whatever the mother has been eating, making children more likely to try a range of foods themselves later. Encouraging them to sample different tastes and textures at the right point is a key part of developing a healthy attitude to food. But for the food business, baby cereal from a packet, a child's palate trained on industrial tastes and textures, graduating to jars of baby food and then to yet more processed foods, is an ideal path.

The ingredients of well-known brands of baby rice tend to have a familiar ring, with a disconcerting overlap with my cat food: rice flour, skimmed milk, whey protein concentrates, sucrose or oligofructose, palm or corn oils, flavouring; and vitamins and minerals to make them acceptable. All those commodity ingredients again, the same division of parts. And in a logical progression, we move from boxed baby rice on to packaged breakfast cereal. The same handful of commodity ingredients wrapped up in yet another form. So it is that 97 per cent of British households today have at least one packet of boxed cereal in their cupboards.

The almost universal hold of breakfast cereal makes a revealing case study of the evolutionary process behind the modern diet. One of the earliest convenience foods, processed cereals represent a triumph of marketing, packaging and US economic and foreign policy. They are the epitome of cheap commodity converted by manufacturing to higher value goods; of agricultural surplus turned into profitable export. Somehow they have wormed into our confused consciousness as intrinsically healthy when by and large they are degraded foods that have to have any goodness artificially restored. As someone who has never enjoyed the experience of breakfast cereal – whichever brand it was, the bits always seemed to me to go from dusty to soggy in the space of a few mouthfuls – I have long been intrigued by how the British breakfast was conquered and what it tells us about the rest of our food. For this is the elephant in the room of course: it is the industrial processing of food that is the real problem, and to understand where not we, but rather it, all went wrong, you have to understand the economic and political structures behind today's food system.

The transformation of the British breakfast in the last 100 years has been complete. Unlike our European partners we have succumbed almost entirely to the American invention. A century ago simple cereal grains, cooked either as porridge or bread, were the staples of breakfast around the world and in this country too, just as they had been in previous centuries.

When the first National Food Survey was conducted on behalf of the medical officer of the Privy Council, Sir John Simon, in 1863 it questioned 370 families of the 'labouring poor' and found that breakfast consisted variously of tea kettle broth (bread soaked in hot milk and salt), bread and butter, bread and cheese, milk gruel, bread and water and oatmeal and milk porridge. In 1901, Joseph Rowntree, collecting the weekly menus of the poor of York, was still finding their breakfast was some bread and butter, perhaps with a little bacon, and shortcake on a Sunday.

Mrs Beeton, it's true, gave advice to the aspiring middle-classes on preparing a breakfast buffet of cold meats and pie, mackerel, sausages, bacon and eggs, muffins, toast and marmalade, butter and jam, with tea and coffee, in her 1861 *Book of Household Management,* but the full English breakfast was, as *The Oxford Companion to Food* puts it, a product of some notional golden era of a more leisured past, usually the world of the late-nineteenth-century country house, and as such an uncommon event. Such meals probably also took place closer to today's lunchtime than any breaking of the overnight fast at first light.

Today, instead, the British and the Irish are the largest eaters of puffed, flaked, flavoured, shaped, sugared, salted and extruded cereals in the world. We munch an average of 6.7kg of the dehydrated stuff per person per year in the UK and 8.4kg each in Ireland.

The Mediterraneans, generally credited with a healthy diet, have so far kept this form of instant breakfast down to an average one kilo per person per year. The French, those cheese-eating surrender monkeys of American opprobrium, have proved culturally resistant to transatlantic pressure in this as in other fields. While the Eastern Europeans, deprived of marketing until the fall of communism and the break up of the Soviet Union, have barely heard of processed cereals yet, being capable of getting through the first meal of the day with no apparent anxiety and only a few grams a year between them.

How can such a radical overhaul of a food culture come about and was there something peculiarly susceptible about the British and the Americans that led to it? To find out, I went to the US, to the Mid-West states that are the heartland of industrial corn production and to the home of the first cornflakes, to try to understand something of the history and economics of the cereal business.

Prepackaged and ready-to-eat breakfast cereals began with the American temperance movement in the nineteenth century. In the 1830s, the Reverend Sylvester Graham preached the virtues of a vegetarian diet to his congregation and in particular the importance of wholemeal flour. Meat-eating, he said, excited the carnal passions. Granula, considered the first ready-to-eat breakfast cereal, was developed from his 'Graham flour' by one of his followers, James Caleb Jackson, for patients at the latter's water cure resort. It was a baked lump of slow-cooked wheat and water that was said to be hard as rock and had to be broken up and soaked overnight to be edible. It was sold at ten times the cost of its ingredients. The business motive for proselytizing by breakfast cereal was established.

Following on from Jackson, the Seventh Day Adventists took up the mission begun by Graham. A colony of them had set up in a small town called Battle Creek near the American Great Lakes in Michigan. There they established the Western Health Reform Institute in 1866 to cure hog guzzling and to their mind degenerate Americans of their dyspepsia and vices. One of their founding elders had a vision from an angel that a better diet was the way to godliness as well as business success, and one of their young men, John Harvey Kellogg, was groomed to take on the institute's leadership. He was sent off to study medicine and nutrition, returning in 1876 to take charge of the operation which he turned into the famous Battle Creek Sanatarium. It was a curious, and curiously spelt, money-spinning mix of health spa, holiday camp and experimental hospital. Kellogg, a sort of early cross between Billy Graham and Gillian McKeith, set about devising cures for what he believed were the common ills of the day, in particular constipation and masturbation. In Kellogg's mind the two were closely linked, the common cause being a lack of fibre, both

7

dietary and moral. Among the tracts for which JH Kellogg became famous were such illuminating titles as *Constipation: How to Fight It* and *What is the Matter with the American Stomach?*

But some of the best insights into his motivations come from *Man the Masterpiece or Plain Truths Plainly Told about Boyhood, Youth and Manhood,* written at the Battle Creek Sanatarium in 1885 and published in a London edition in 1890. In it Kellogg rails against the deterioration of the human race and urges his followers to eat a cereal-based diet. 'The growing want of the times is for real men of moral worth ... The human race is growing weaker physically,' he wrote. In fact 'the most hideous monsters of vice' were 'waging an unceasing war upon the purity and morals of the race'. Meat eating had led to carnivorous appetites, when the Bible made clear that man in his primitive innocence subsisted solely on the 'fruits of the soil'. Kellogg went on that he could allow a little meat in connection with fruits and grains, a not unreasonable nutritional prescription and one that might do a deal for saving the planet today, but he added that those wanting to avoid unspeakable 'sexual sins' should pay great attention to the diet. From his experience as doctor-owner of the Battle Creek Sanatarium, he could vouchsafe that the vice of 'self-abuse or masturbation ... has become almost universal', at least among young boys in the US. The peasantry of Europe, thanks perhaps to the greater simplicity of its habits in diet, had succumbed to the 'horrible vice' somewhat less, he noted.

To a person struggling to repress evil desires, simplicity in the diet is of the greatest consequence, he went on. 'The diet should consist of fruits, grains, vegetables and milk. Overeating should be carefully avoided as it produces a plethoric condition ... causing congestion of the genitals. Ices, confectionery, and pastries of all kinds should be sedulously avoided ...'

Kellogg was generous with further practical advice. If all these precautions failed and parents should discover a small boy was addicted to the practice of self abuse, they should administer proper punishments. In young children the application of a blister, so as to render the parts tender, often worked, he advised. If that and prayer failed to work, parents could use the following method: 'Draw the prepuce down beyond the glans, passing a silver wire through the skin on either side, and twist the ends together ... the pain produced is not great and is in most cases an advantage rather than an objection ...'

As well as prescribing daily cold water baths, exercise drills, and unorthodox medical interventions, creating health-giving foods for patients was a major preoccupation. Kellogg, his wife and his younger brother William Keith experimented in the Sanatarium kitchen to produce an easily digested form of cereal. They came up with their own highly profitable Granula, but were promptly sued by Jackson, the original maker of Granula, and had to change the name to Granola. Victorian prudery and religion may have been at the root of processed cereal development, but parables about camels and eyes of needles did not discourage any of these evangelicals from seeing the commercial advantage and using the law to protect their business interests.

Around this time an entrepreneur called Henry Perky had also invented a way of passing steamed wheat through rollers, one grooved and one smooth, to form strands that could be pressed into biscuits to make the first shredded wheat. JH Kellogg experimented further with his team in the San kitchen working on the idea of using rollers and eventually they found a way of rolling cooked wheat to make flakes which could then be baked. By 1896 the first wheat or Granose flakes were being sold commercially. They were followed by an adaptation when the Kelloggs worked out how to use cheap American corn instead of wheat to make the first cornflakes, although initially they had problems keeping them crisp and preventing them from going rancid. This great leap forward is of a piece with other major developments in the industrialization of our diets: it is usually the combination of technological advances and the right economic conditions that lead to radical changes in what we eat.

It was a chronically dyspeptic businessman and former patient of Kellogg's at the Sanatarium who unleashed the power of marketing on breakfast. Charles Post set up the rival La Vita Inn in Battle Creek and developed his own versions of precooked cereals. He distributed them with such encouraging tracts as *The Road to Wellville*. 'The sunshine that makes a business plant grow is advertising,' he declared. He placed ads for his cereals in papers with paid-for testimonials from apparently genuine happy eaters. He also cheerfully invented diseases which his products could cure. His Grape Nuts were miraculously not only 'brain food' but could also cure consumption and malaria, and were even, despite their enamel-cracking hardness, said to be an antidote to loose teeth.

By 1903 Post was making over a million dollars a year and Battle Creek had turned into a cereal Klondike. For four years cereal companies were opening at the rate of one a month. At one point there were over 100 cereal factories operating in the town to satisfy the new craze, many making fabulously exaggerated claims about the health benefits of their products. This symbiotic relationship between sales, health claims and the promotion of packaged breakfast cereals has continued ever since. Nor was it a coincidence that this particular Klondike sprang up in the American Mid-West, whose vast tracts of virgin land had been recently opened up by settlers and turned over to the agricultural production that powered US development.

John Harvey Kellogg was more interested in his crusade against sexual sins and bad eating than maximizing profit, but his brother William, who had worked for John at the Sanatarium for years, felt differently. The Kelloggs had tried unsuccessfully to protect their flaking process with patents. When WK saw how much others were making from the new foods, he launched his own advertising campaign, giving away free samples and putting ads in newspapers.

The road to nutritional corruption opened up early. The Kellogg brothers argued over whether to make the cereals more palatable by adding sugar – the addition was anathema to John who saw sugar as an adulterant and a scourge, but William reckoned it was needed to stop the products tasting like 'horse-food'. WK won.

Global expansion followed quickly. Britain saw its first cornflakes in 1924 when the company set up offices in London and used unemployed men and boy scouts to act as a sales force for the imported cereal which was shipped in from Canada. By 1936 UK sales topped £1 million, and Kellogg's was ready to open its first British manufacturing plant in Manchester in 1938. But then the war got in the way, and between 1943 and 1947 production of cornflakes and rice krispies ceased as the factory was forced to make do with turning home-grown wheat into rationed wheat flakes. It wasn't until the American Marshall Plan provided aid to rebuild Europe after the war that the rise of processed cereal could begin again.

The technology used to make industrial quantities of breakfast cereal today is essentially the same as that developed from the kitchen experiments of those fundamentalist healers, although new ways have been found to add the sugar, salt and flavourings.

Cornflakes are generally made by breaking corn kernels into smaller grits which are then steam cooked in batches of up to a tonne under pressure of about 20lbs per square inch. The nutritious germ with its essential fats is first removed because, as the Kellogg brothers discovered all that time ago, it goes rancid over time and gets in the way of long shelf life. Flavourings, vitamins to replace those lost in processing and sugar may be added at this stage. It then takes four hours and vast amounts of energy to drive the steam out of the cooked grits before they can be rolled by giant rollers into flakes. The flakes go to be toasted at very high temperatures, up to 300 degrees Celsius for five to six seconds, before being dried for packing. Other flaked cereals are made in a similar way. Frosted versions have a sugar/corn syrup mixture sprayed on later in the process. Vitamins may also be sprayed on to the finished product. Economy versions of cornflakes are made from 'finings', the fine dust left after corn milling, which is turned into pellets and shaped into flakes by indents in the rollers. The giveaway sign that finings have been used rather than more expensive grits is flakes that are uniform in size and shape.

Steamed wheat biscuits such as shredded wheats are made with wholewheat grains which are pressure cooked with water. They are then passed between rollers which squeeze them into strands and build them up into layers. The layers are cut into squares and baked till dry. Weetabix-type cereals are similarly steam cooked wholegrains with salt and sugar, rolled very thinly and then pressed into biscuits. These processes begin the breakdown of the raw starches in the cereals so even though they are wholegrains they are absorbed more quickly in the body – and they typically have glycemic index scores of around 75, close to the GIs in the 70s or low 80s of cornflakes, Bran Flakes, Special K and Rice Krispies, compared with 45/55 for minimally processed grains such as porridge or mueslis without sugar. (Glucose has a GI of 100 and is what these indexes measure other foods against. They indicate how fast different foods are converted to glucose and absorbed into the bloodstream.)

Puffed cereals were first invented by Alexander Anderson at his laboratory in Chicago at the turn of the twentieth century and were developed by him for the market under the aegis of another company selling itself on the back of religious associations, the Quaker Oats company. Anderson began with rice heated in a sealed test tube which exploded. Several detonations later, he and his engineer adapted a breach loading recoiling cannon to mass produce puffed or exploded grains. You cannot help but admire the ingenuity of the chemical engineering but, as so often with industrial food research, wish the science had been applied to a better cause. Today's adaptations of the technology are giant sealed cylinders that heat the grains to high temperatures. When they are unsealed the steam pressure in each grain causes it to expand, and they are dried before they collapse. As with corn, rice has its nutritious essential oils removed during milling to make long-life processed cereals.

Cereal shapes meanwhile are made from flours that have been finely milled. They are mixed with water and heated, then extruded through small holes so that they can expand into their final shape. The heating and mechanical working of the cereals breaks down the cell structure of the starch so they tend to have high GI values – in fact very highly milled starches can be worse than sugar in terms of glycemic index, and as bad in terms of dental health. Vitamins which are destroyed in the heat process are added back into the flour mixtures along with sugar, salt and flavourings or once again sprayed on to the finished product. Wholegrain cereal shapes can be made from wholegrain milled down to a powder or from recombined fractions of flour milled down to white.

Worries about the nutritional value of such highly processed grains surfaced early. Post's company was one of the first to begin the heavy duty presweetening of cereals with sugar coating in the late 1940s. The sales were enviable. The Kellogg company however held back, according to interviews with former employees in *Cerealizing America*, the highly entertaining account of cereal history by Scott Bruce and Bill Crawford. The charitable Kellogg Foundation which had been set up by then to promote children's health and education was a major shareholder and was concerned that flogging sugar-coatings to the young might not be compatible with its purpose.

Many of the health benefits claimed for breakfast cereals depended on fortification rather than micronutrients from the raw ingredients, most of which were either destroyed by the process or stripped away before it. The earliest fortification was with vitamin D, the so-called sunshine vitamin, and acted as a marketing tool. It was the war years and governments' need to maintain the nutritional status of populations subject to food shortages that saw a more general fortification with a range of vitamins and minerals. Heat-sensitive B vitamins, vitamin C and iron and calcium were added. Today a new wave of fortification is coming, and once again its principal purpose is marketing. Inulin, a form of fibre from plants, known to the food industry until recently as a cheap bulking agent thanks to its ability to retain water and mimic the mouthfeel of fats, is now added as a 'prebiotic'. They have coined this word for it because it resists digestion in the upper gastrointestinal tract and reaches the large intestine almost intact where it is fermented by bacteria, encouraging the production of friendly microflora, which the industry markets too, as probiotics. The inulin, in other words, does what the fibre naturally occurring in whole-grains would do if it hadn't been stripped out by over process-ing. It has the added advantage to manufacturers of lowering the GI of the cereals that processing raised in the first place. But you can charge more for fibre you put back in than for a wholegrain and its fibre that you have left alone.

Companies are also looking at adding omega-3 fatty acids such as DHA. (Where my cat food goes, breakfast cereals follow.) There are technical difficulties with this. Since the DHA tends to come from fish, it makes things taste fishy, and its flavour has to be masked with other additives. In addition, the long chain molecules in DHA can be damaged by the high temperature, high pressure processes. Specialist ingredients firms that supply the food industry are working on ways of taking a dairy protein and carbohydrate to form what they call a slurry with tuna oil that is then spray dried to encapsulate the DHA. The process both protects the DHA and locks in the fishy taste until the encapsulated material reaches the lower gut. If all that sounds more like pill technology than food technology, that's because essentially it is.

All the technology at their disposal has not helped the manufacturers deal with one serious problem however. Industrial cereal processing produces acrylamide. Acrylamide is a chemical compound that has been known to cause cancer in animals for many years and was classified as a probable human carcinogen in 1994. It was thought for a long time that our main exposure to it came from tobacco smoke, or the workplace, and to a very small extent from drinking water as a result of chemical treatment. The World Health Organization sets very strict limits on levels allowed in drinking water which are just one microgram per litre, or one part per billion. Then in 2002 Swedish researchers unexpectedly found high levels of acrylamide in Swedish construction workers whose blood they were checking for occupational exposure to the compound. They could find no obvious source of the compound at work, and the men did not smoke. They started testing foods to see if they might be the source and found high levels of acrylamide in certain types of food where no one had realized they were present before. Acrylamide in food turns out to be formed mostly in starchy products heated to high temperatures during processing. Ordinary crisps contained levels that were 500 times the levels permitted by WHO in drinking water. Breakfast cereals, industrial breads, snack potato products and chips were the main source of acrylamide in the diet, with crisps and chips having the highest levels. One single crisp could take you up to the maximum level set for drinking water. The findings caused alarm around the world and food safety authorities in several countries commissioned urgent research on their own foods. The UK Food Standards Agency quickly confirmed the Swedish results, highlighting significant levels of acrylamide in supermarket chips, leading brands of crisps, crispbreads and breakfast cereals.

The FSA advice to consumers was blandly reassuring – no need to change their diet, the industry would be working to reduce the formation of acrylamide. It gave the impression that not burning your toast or over-chipping your chips at home were the main things to worry about. But as intense research continued, a rather different picture became clear. A large proportion of acrylamide intake comes from industrially prepared food. 'Acrylamide contribution from home-cooked food is in general relatively small,' the latest research from a huge project commissioned by the EU now says. If we burn our toast, not surprisingly most of us don't eat it but start again.

The EU project also found that when bread is properly fermented over time with yeast, little acrylamide is formed; the problem arises when bread is made in fast industrial processes, as sadly most of it is today. Sour dough breads are better than factory breads too. Intensive farming plays its part. Cereals grown in poor soils low in sulphur are more likely to have higher levels of the amino acid that is linked to acrylamide formation. Using lower temperatures for cooking products such as crisps can help but that slows down production and costs money. When it comes to acrylamide in breakfast cereals and cereal products, the levels found were not as high as in crisps, but the industry has struggled to come up with solutions. The European food and drink industry association, the CIAA, has compiled a toolbox on acrylamide for manufacturers, and from it you get a sense of the huge effort that is going into industrial pilots to see how acrylamide levels could be reduced. But there are no easy answers, and sometimes the toolbox makes clear that the ways of lowering acrylamide are just incompatible with making these types of products. 'The Maillard reaction [the browning process] which leads to the production of acrylamide also produces the colours and flavours which give baked cereal products their essential characteristics . . . research has shown that there are as yet no practical options without adverse impact on the sensory and organoleptic properties.' The industry magazine *Food Manufacture* wrote nervously in 2006 of consumers currently appearing to be 'oblivious to the danger' but warning that acrylamide could be 'the next food scare round the corner'. Since then further independent research in Holland has confirmed a link between acrylamide intake from food and cancer. Those eating 40 micrograms of acrylamide a day were twice as likely to get cancer of the ovary or womb as those who had low intakes. That's equivalent to half a pack of biscuits, a portion of chips or a single pack of crisps. The FSA's original tests suggested a serving of breakfast cereal could contribute about nine micrograms. And still the official advice concentrates on making sure you don't overcook food at home.

That processed cereals had become little more than sugary junk with milk and vitamin pills added, was an accusation made as long ago as the 1970s. A US congressional hearing into breakfast cereal in 1970 was told by an adviser to President Nixon on nutrition, Robert Choate, that the majority of breakfast cereals 'fatten but do little to prevent malnutrition'. Choate was outraged at the aggressive targeting of children in breakfast cereal advertising. He analysed sixty well-known cereal brands for nutritional quality and concluded that two thirds of them offered 'empty calories, a term thus far applied to alcohol and sugar'. Rats fed a diet of ground-up cereal boxes with sugar, milk and raisins were healthier than rats fed the cereals themselves, he testified to senators.

Battle Creek today is a small backwater in Michigan three hours' drive from Chicago. There is not much sign now of the cereal gold rush that changed the British palate, and the flake factories working day and night have mostly gone. But the legacy lives on. In their place alongside Kellogg airport and the Kellogg Foundation is Kellogg's Cereal City. Built in the shape of an old American grain store in post-modern nostalgic architectural style, it is a museum testament to the power of marketing that so maddened Choate. Here you can order a multi-coloured Fruit Loop sundae and take a tour of the collection of early cereal boxes or hear and see the first radio and television programmes that advertised them. Walking through the collection I too was struck by how much our breakfast today is the child of advertising. Trading on our insecurity about health, manipulating our emotions and selling to us through health professionals has always been part of the great puff.

The antique cardboard boxes on show underline how from the first breakfast cereals sold not just a meal but a way of life: Power, Vim, Vigor, Korn Kinks and Climax cereals are among the early brand names, though the latter was not named for another of JH Kellogg's obsessions but rather after the nearby town called Climax. One of my favourite sections of the museum was the cabinet of boxes and pamphlets recording the original health claims that anticipate today's persuasive messages. 'Keeps the blood cool!' 'Makes red blood redder!' There were the cereals that echoed today's claims for pre-biotics: 'Will correct stomach troubles!' or indeed the claims on my cat food: 'The most scientific food in the world!' John Harvey Kellogg's mechanical vibrating horse and saddle is a prize exhibit, displayed alongside early photographs of naked patients mounting it to have their innards shaken in the hope of 'stimulating colonic activity'. A pail to collect the results is always placed alarmingly on hand.

Wandering further along, I caught crackly soundtracks from some of the first radio programmes in the 1920s that record the sponsorship deals that helped both the new medium and the cereal empire grow. 'Kellogg's announces another thrilling new adventure . . .' The actors in the radio plays moved seamlessly in the breaks into little speeches extolling the virtues of cereal before reverting to character for the second half of the show.

Getting children hooked, making them associate breakfast cereal with fun and entertainment, blurring the lines between advertising and programmes, exploiting new media – today it is the internet and viral marketing – was one of the main aims of competing manufacturers from the early days, as the museum displays show, and a crucial part in conquering the British breakfast. Kellogg's sponsored a children's programme called *The Singing Lady*. In 1931 the artist Vernon Grant heard the programme and was inspired to draw the Kellogg's Rice Krispie ad characters Snap, Crackle and Pop. His cartoon characters were used in ad campaigns that catapulted Rice Krispie sales up into the league of the more established cornflakes brands. Walt Disney was powerfully influenced by Grant's work. And when the Great Depression hit America in the 1930s following the crash of the stock market, WK Kellogg doubled his ad spend.

In 1939 Charles Post meanwhile introduced his own characters, a trio of bears, to sell his new Sugar Crisps. (The original three bears were of course happy with plain porridge.) Kellogg's responded with Tony the Tiger and Katy the Kangaroo, although Katy retired after a year. Post also bought a licence from Disney to use his Mickey Mouse character on his cereal boxes.

The museum records how giveaway toys were being used by then too, to attract children's loyalty and to encourage early pester power and repeat purchases. But gratification in those days took longer than today. Radio ads for the toys told children to allow '6–8 weeks for delivery'. The giveaways were only actually made once the marketing men had been able to see how much demand there was for them.

Cereal advertising likewise helped shape early television, the medium architect Frank Lloyd Wright dubbed at the time 'chewing gum for the eyes'. A chance meeting on a train in 1949 between the then chairman of Kellogg's and an advertising man called Leo Burnett led to a working relationship that both transformed the cereal market and made the mould for TV ads. Burnett used 'motivational research' to work out how to appeal to women and children with different kinds of packaging. Subliminal marketing was born. With his help Kellogg's broadcast the first colour TV programmes and commercials for children. The result was that by the mid 1950s the company had captured nearly half the rapidly expanding US processed cereal market and was in a prime position to build its empire in Europe using the same methods.

The UK market for those cereal boxes was worth over £1.27 billion in 2005. It too has been created and maintained by advertising. It is characterized by health claims, now as then. Along with other highly processed foods such as fizzy drinks, and fast food brands, breakfast cereals are among the most highly marketed products.

Kellogg's has consistently been the largest advertiser of its cereals in this country, spending roughly £50 million a year in recent years, about twice what its rival Cereal Partners spends. Cereal Partners is a joint venture with Nestlé which markets that company's breakfast cereals in Britain and manufactures cereals for leading supermarkets' own label brands. The respective investments are duly reflected in the companies' market shares. We buy what we have been persuaded to buy. Kellogg's manufactures seven of the top-selling cereal brands – Cornflakes, Crunchy Nut, Coco Pops, Special K, Fruit 'n Fibre, All Bran and Bran Flakes. Nestlé has the second largest market share. The market is highly concentrated in the hands of a few manufacturers, as in so many other sectors of our food system.

Without advertising we might never know we needed processed cereal and revert to porridge or bread instead. Or as Kellogg's European president Tim Mobsby put it to MPs conducting an inquiry into obesity in 2004, 'if we were not to have that capability [of TV advertising] there is a probability that the consumption of cereals would actually drop . . . that is not necessarily a positive step forward.'

The following spring I was one of a handful of reporters flown in a private jet by Kellogg's to its Old Trafford cornflakes factory, as part of its campaign to protect its portfolio and its ability to market it, particularly to children. The ostensible reason for the trip was that Kellogg's was launching a new acquisition in the UK, Kashi, a brand of mixed-grain puffed cereal free of all additives, invented by and now acquired from a small Californian company. But criticism of the food industry for selling obeso-genic products high in fat, salt and sugar had reached a crescendo in the UK and the breakfast cereal manufacturers were the subject of unwelcome attention. Before touring the factory with its vast steel pressure cookers, miles of pipes carrying vitamins and flavourings and stainless steel rollers and high temperature toasting ovens, we were ushered past the giant Tony the Tiger cut-out in the entrance lobby and up into the strategic planning department for a presentation on nutrition policy and labelling.

Here the company nutritionist explained how Kellogg's had decided to take a lead in promoting a new kind of labelling to help 'mum' make 'healthier choices'. (For some reason, mothers as targets of marketing are nearly always reduced to the singular form and stripped of any definite or indefinite article that might credit them with brains or individuality.) Rather than the traffic light labelling the government's food standards agency was researching, Kellogg's and other leading food manufacturers had decided to go live with a system of labels based on guideline daily amounts. These would avoid identifying foods as good or bad with red, amber and green and instead give figures for how much fat, salt and sugar a portion of the product contained as a proportion of a guideline amount, calculated by the industry, which you should eat a day of those nutrients. Needless to say the industry's guideline daily amounts were more generous than official targets, particularly on sugars. The FSA had already rejected this scheme as too complicated to be helpful but Kellogg's told us that it had 'lent them one of our researchers so we've been in on the consultation process and we've been able to get the GDAs into the final FSA testing'.

In response to pressure from the FSA, the Association of Cereal Food Manufacturers had already reduced salt by a quarter in five years, she went on. Cornflakes were even tastier than before because you could taste the corn more now. So why was there so much salt in the first place, we asked. The managing director of Kellogg's Europe Tony Palmer confessed that 'if we'd known you could take out 25 per cent of the salt and make cornflakes taste even better, we would have done it earlier. But it's also about the interaction with the sugar – as you take the salt out, you've got to reduce the sugar because it starts to taste sweeter.' But isn't the target to reduce sugar consumption too? Why not just cut down on salt and sugar, we wondered. Well, sugar helps keep the crispness and is part of the bulk, so that would be difficult, we were told. Mr Palmer's eyebrows started working furiously as he answered: 'And the risk is, if you take the salt out you might be better off eating the cardboard carton for taste,' he said.

The public relations team moved us rapidly on from this unfortunate echo of Senator Choate's 1970s' accusation of nutritional bankruptcy to a presentation on the Kashi Way. 'We hold the spirit of health in all we do,' one of them explained, echoing this time the quasi-religious marketing babble of the founding cereal makers. Since this was a puffed cereal, what levels of acrylamide did it contain? I wondered. No one was sure, but they'd come back to me . . . They never did. Perhaps they thought I had lost interest.

Although I was aware that breakfast cereal manufacturers were among the top marketers of processed foods in the UK, it was only when the broadcasting regulator Ofcom tried to draw up new rules to restrict TV advertising to children of junk foods, that I saw quite how dependent consumption was on us being manipulated by the manufacturers' messages. Kellogg's led a ferocious campaign of lobbying to stop the restrictions. As well as educating journalists with trips such as mine to the cornflakes factory, it lobbied MPs, ministers and regulators.

One of its public relations agencies Hill and Knowlton boasted on its website how it had managed to change government and Whitehall thinking on Kellogg's behalf. 'A series of meetings with Number 10, the Department of Health, the Food Standards Agency, the Health Select committee, one-to-one briefings with key individuals and an event for parliamentarians' had enabled them to disseminate Kellogg's messages, with the result that 'the campaign resulted in a significant shift in attitudes among core government stakeholders,' they claimed.

The industry is adamant that its products are a healthy way to start the day, and has recruited Professor Tom Sanders, head of the nutrition department at King's College London, to defend 'breakfast cereals served with semi-skimmed milk' as 'low energy meals that provide about one fifth of the micronutrients of children'. However, a survey published by the independent consumer watchdog *Which?* called 'Cereal Reoffenders' took a rather different view. When it analysed 275 big-name breakfast cereals from leading manufacturers on sale in UK supermarkets in 2006 it found that 75 per cent of them had high levels of sugar, while almost a fifth had high levels of salt, according to criteria drawn up by the Food Standards Agency for its traffic-light nutritional labels. Nearly 90 per cent of those targeted at children were high in sugar, 13 per cent were high in salt, and 10 per cent were high in saturated fat. Several cereals making claims to be good for you got a red light too. All Bran was high in salt; Special K got a red for sugar and salt. Some high fibre bran cereals were giving you more salt per serving than a bag of crisps. (Some of these may have since been reformulated to reduce salt and sugar.)

It was when I saw details of the proposals from Ofcom on restricting marketing of junk foods to children that I understood why the lobbying had been so determined. Ofcom had carried out an informal audit of what would be banned from advertising on TV to children if it said that nothing the FSA defined as high in fat, salt and/or sugar should be allowed on before the 9 p.m. watershed. What became clear was that breakfast cereals, although heavily marketed as healthy, would be the category to take the largest hit by a long way. About £70 million of TV ads a year from cereal manufacturers would be banned because they were promoting what the experts defined as unhealthy. The sector spent a total of £84 million on ads that year. In other words, the vast majority of its marketing effort would be wiped out. It had everything to lose, because, as the House of Commons had been told, without marketing to manipulate our desires, we might not eat processed cereals at all.

Back at the Battle Creek Museum you can see how Kellogg's would view that. Before exiting the exhibition into the shop where tourists were entering into the spirit by sporting strings of Fruit Loops as headbands, I passed a section on 'global expansion'. Here was the company's very different vision for the future. The scale of the ambition was startling. Ninety per cent of the world's breakfast cereal is consumed in just a handful of countries, I read. 'The company has rededicated itself to reaching 1.5 billion new cereal customers around the world in the next decade ... and bringing about a fundamental change in eating habits.' As well as advertising in new markets, it has been sponsoring school nutrition programmes and health symposia for professionals – perhaps for health visitors such as mine. This activity is part of a 'massive program of nutrition education directed at improving the world's eating habits with accelerated expansion into countries where ready-to-eat cereal is unknown', it proclaimed.

Improving the world's eating habits has the attraction, as the nineteenth-century evangelicals and American entrepreneurs discovered, of being what economic analysts call a 'high margin-to-cost business'. The raw materials of breakfast cereals, commodity grains, are cheap (or at least were cheap until biofuels recently entered the equation). It is true that the cost of energy used in production is considerable – it takes 7,000 kilo-calories of fuel energy to process a typical medium sized box of breakfast cereal that provides only 1,100 kilocalories of food energy – and the price of energy and the fossil fuels from which it is derived has been rising inexorably.

But one of the biggest costs is not the value of the ingredients, nor the cost of production, but the marketing, which, as you might expect from all the activity described above, is typically 20 to 25 per cent of the sales value, according to analysts JPMorgan. It is worth remembering that next time you buy breakfast cereal. About a quarter of your money is going not on the food but on the manufacturer's cost of persuading you to buy it. That still leaves room for gross profit margins on processed cereals that are 40 to 45 per cent, with operating margins around the very healthy 17 per cent mark.

Start selling this kind of processed diet to new consumers in the booming economies of China and India and your profits, and those of the country that has dominated grain exports and trading, the US, will soar. This is what the food industry calls adding value. The added value is not nutritional value of course; quite the opposite. The added value is shareholder value, and as a very rough rule of thumb I reckon on nutritional value being stripped away in inverse proportion to the share-holder value added.

The farmers producing these cheap raw commodities for processing will not, on their own, grow rich. In fact figures from the US Department of Agriculture show that the average American corn farmer lost about $230 for each acre of corn planted over the five years to 2005. Nearly three quarters of the market value of US corn exports was being covered how-ever by payments in the form of various subsidies from the US government. The figure for rice was even higher with 99 per cent of the value of US rice exports being paid by the American taxpayer in some years, according to analysis by Oxfam.

US agricultural subsidies totalled $165 billion in the eleven years 1995 to 2005. Just five crops accounted for 90 per cent of the money – corn, rice, wheat, soya beans and cotton. That handful of ingredients I keep finding in everything. If you want to understand why all these commodities, cotton aside, make it not only in to the cat food but in to most other processed foods you eat, this is where you have to start. (Sugar, dairy products and tobacco have been heavily subsidized by Western governments too but most fresh fruit and vegetable production have received minimal support.) Agricultural commodities have been kept cheap for the transnational food corporations by government policy.

Corn was the largest recipient of US subsidies, taking $51 billion of taxpayers' money between 1995 and 2005. At the farming level, just 10 per cent of farm companies, most of them large corporations, or family companies with outside investors, rather than small farms where family owners work the land themselves, collected nearly three quarters of the payments.

Until 2001 the American public was not even allowed to know where all its money went, much less all those of us round the world who end up eating these things as a result of their economic interventions. Ken Cook, president of an American public interest watchdog, the Environmental Working Group, was at the forefront of a long campaign to get the subsidy data published. It took Freedom of Information filings and court cases and years of laborious detective work to expose the system. But now the information is out in the open, he says it is clear that the benefit has been to the big processors that use the commodities, the export companies that trade in them and corporate farms rather than to small family farms. The extent to which the US system of subsidies has distorted global trade and determined what we eat has emerged. (In Europe, achieving transparency about agricultural subsidies and where our tax goes has taken even longer, but when examined, the effect has been the same: the large processors of concentrated fats and sugars for the food industry and a small number of large

26

landowners have been the real beneficiaries – see Chapter 3: Milk and Chapter 5: Sugar.)

Cook explained it to me shortly after my visit to Battle Creek. 'The producers who get the subsidies are big operations that have gotten bigger because there is no practical limit on the money they can get through the subsidy programmes, so they just keep expanding. They have actually been the agent of the demise of smaller family farms because when a parcel of land comes up for rent, the big guys can pay whatever, knowing they'll collect the subsidy. Land prices have shot up – it's like having a rental apartment in the basement only it's Uncle Sam paying the rent, so there's no risk. We grow far more than we need for domestic purposes. So we depend on exports to market the rest. This is the framework for debating farm subsidies: the context is not one of saving the family farm or rural America or feeding the world – that's a myth. The context is globalization – we have a profound crop export dependency,' he said. And in 2002 the US farm bill authorized $176 billion to American farmers over the next ten years, making sure the cheques would keep coming.

Encouraged by such subsidies, US farming companies have overproduced on such a scale that American agricultural surplus has regularly accounted for nearly half of global corn production and more than two thirds of global corn exports in recent years. Subsidies have allowed American companies to export grain at less than cost of production, making it impossible for other countries to compete.

Corn and other hard grains have in other words long been part of an economic policy designed to promote the export of US agricultural surpluses while bringing the money from added-value markets back home. In this they mirror patterns of trade established between previous empires and their colonies (see Chapter 5: Sugar).

The current pattern of this 'export dependency', to use Cook's jargon, was set after the Second World War. The US came out of the war with its agricultural base intact but the farming lands of its European allies and of defeated Germany had been devastated. So too had the agriculture of Asia. Before the war Western Europe had depended on Eastern Europe's food surpluses, but these were now non-existent and in any case would from then on be shut off behind the Iron Curtain. With millions of people desperately hungry and living in bombed out cities, the US took on the role of feeding the world and announced its Marshall Plan to help rebuild shattered Western European economies with financial aid.

The Marshall Plan was inspired by a humanitarian desire to end the misery of acute food shortages. But it also clearly had political and economic ends. By sending financial aid to Western Europe with which it could buy food, the US nipped nascent communist stirrings in the bud – adequate food supplies in Western Europe provided a marked and attractive contrast to the austerity that persisted in communist-controlled Eastern Europe. Reluctant US farmers in the Mid-West were won over by the argument that their long term prosperity depended on Europe buying their exports. The Marshall Plan also had another crucial role: it ensured that removing tariff barriers that might hinder US access to foreign markets was made part of the new terms of trade with the non-communist world. Of the $13 billion in financial aid paid under the Marshall Plan between 1947 and 1952, over $3 billion was spent by European countries on imports of US food, animal feed and fertilizer. The US government offered its own farmers financial incentives to grow more to deliver surplus, which they did on a grand scale, with the result that between 1945 and 1949 the US supplied half of the world's total wheat trade, setting a pattern for grain trading for the decades to come.

The Marshall Plan played a key role in this way in internationalizing the distribution of food and part of its legacy is the food system today. The American exports it delivered created whole new patterns of consumption and drove the development of markets for the processed products of US surplus – for it wasn't just grain but soya too that poured in.

Once Western Europe had recovered sufficiently to be less reliant on transatlantic food imports, the US moved on to new ways of using its agricultural surplus. In 1954 it passed the Agricultural Trade and Development Act, known later as Public Law 480. Title 1 of Public Law 480 allows friendly developing countries to buy US agricultural products at a huge discount with generously long repayment terms. Enacting it, President Eisenhower said its aim was to 'lay the basis for a permanent expansion of our exports of agricultural products with lasting benefits to ourselves and peoples of other lands'. When President Kennedy recast the programme as 'Food for Peace' a decade or so later he articulated its purpose as: 'Food is strength, and food is peace, and food is freedom, and food is a helping to people around the world whose good will and friendship we want.' People whose friendship we want are not always the most savoury but geopolitics has other priorities. In the early days, most food aid was given to governments judged to be facing a communist threat, including military dictatorships in Latin America. By 2003 the largest recipients of food aid under PL 480 title 1 were Indonesia, Jordan, the Philippines and Uzbekistan – a roll call of countries notable for their strategic importance to the US as much as for topping any league of poorest, hungriest, or democratically inclined nations.

US food aid is still used to encourage countries to 'expand free enterprise' in their agricultural sectors, that is to open up their markets to foreign imports. And where US food aid flows, Western-style diets have a habit of following.

Since the 1970s, the other main instruments in promoting imports of US and EU surplus to poorer countries have been the international financial institutions, dominated by the US. Their structural adjustment programmes have made opening up agricultural markets a condition of loans to indebted developing countries (see Chapter 6: Fish and Tomatoes).

While the US food aid system undoubtedly plays a useful role in some humanitarian crises, Oxfam argues that it often serves US economic and foreign policy interests more than those of the poor countries it purports to help. Food aid and subsidized exports of US grain tend to flood markets and depress prices in the poorer countries that receive them. They often have the effect of undermining the local agriculture. Once the food aid is cut back, it tends to get replaced not by newly invigorated local agriculture, but by commercial imports run by US-based transnational corporations, and urban populations tend to adopt the diets of the West. The commodity traders that get the contracts for US food aid also have a big say in what it consists of under emergency programmes. Soya oil, dry milk powder, corn and rice tend to be sent in strong US surplus years, though when global prices are high on the markets, the food aid tends to dry up. So the answer to my children's question, can you send broccoli to the starving, is definitely no, the starving must have the same handful of surplus commodities that form the basis for the processed foods we and our pets eat.

The Canadian government articulated what impact this US export dependency has on rich countries today as well as poor ones when it threatened to take legal action against the US at the World Trade Organization in 2007. Its legal case was that Canada, a major producer of corn itself, had nevertheless ended up being a net importer of US corn because US subsidies had depressed prices, causing 'serious prejudice' to its farmers. Even as prices declined between 2003 and 2006, US production increased significantly, showing that production was immune to market signals. There is little of the free market here.

It can be hard to grasp how any of this makes economic sense. If the American taxpayer has to pay for nearly three quarters of the value of US corn exports, for them to be dumped, or even given away as food aid, what's the point?

Agribusiness welfare is the point. US agricultural subsidies were introduced in the 1930s, when the combination of drought and intensive farming practices had led to the dustbowl that brought agriculture to the brink of disaster, and the Great Depression had led to the collapse of its urban markets. They were meant to rescue American farmers but have done little to protect most of them or rural employment. What they have done is give US-based transnational food and trading companies a dominant position in the world. As subsidies encouraged overproduction, and the government ended up covering the cost of surpluses, a drive for exports followed, and the big corporations reaped the benefit. In a few cases EU subsidies have achieved the same for European transnationals, generally those that established their power bases pre-war when Europe was still the centre of the grain trades and before the US had built its post-war hegemony (see Chapter 3: Dairy and Chapter 5: Sugar).

Manufacturers and retailers of added-value processed foods from ready meals to fast food takeaways have been supplied with cheap ingredients. Behind them, largely invisible to the general public but controlling a great part of international food supply and major beneficiaries of this welfare, are the behemoth trading and primary processing companies mostly, but not exclusively, US based.

This idea of subsidy as agribusiness welfare is not new. Campaigners in the 1970s such as Susan George and Frances Moore Lappé, authors respectively of the seminal bestsellers *How the Other Half Dies* and *Diet for a Small Planet*, expounded it back then, when grain shortages and price spikes put the subject high on the political agenda. But we have forgotten it. Moore Lappé founded a think tank called Food First and its former co-director Peter Rosset explained the system simply: 'The US exports corn and wheat at prices below the cost of production. The US agricultural system has been designed to give American grain-trading giants like Cargill and Archer Daniels Midland the edge in capturing the domestic market of other countries. These companies penetrate Third World markets with a one–two punch. First the companies work closely with the US government representatives and negotiators at institutions like the World Trade Organization, World Bank and IMF to force Third World countries to open their markets to agricultural exports. Once their markets have been forced open, these companies must still be able to out-compete local farmers. To do that, they need an abundant low-cost supply of commodities, and indeed they are able to get grain so cheaply that nobody else has any chance at all of being able to compete, because the second punch is delivered like clockwork every six years by a new farm bill designed to depress US farm prices to, and in many cases below, the cost of production.'

Cargill, the largest privately owned corporation in the world in most years, was said in testimony to the US senate in 1999 to control 45 per cent of global grain trade, including 42 per cent of US corn exports, a third of all soya bean exports and about 20 per cent of wheat exports. It is also the world's largest crusher of oilseeds such as soya and rapeseed. Since it is a private company that does not publish accounts, more recent and accurate market share figures are hard to find, and it declines to comment on its market shares, but it has if anything consolidated its position since then, though its areas of concentration shift (see Chapter 8: Soya). Its revenues in 2007 were $88 billion. Most of us eat its products in some form every day, yet many people have never heard of it. Nor had I before I started writing about the politics of food, but since then it has been hard not to stumble across its operations in every country whenever I visit a food factory, industrial farm, or fast food or supermarket supplier.

Archer Daniels Midland (ADM), another US-based grain trading corporation, controls about 30 per cent of global grain trade. It is one of the world's largest processors of soya beans, corn, wheat and cocoa, and also has a huge portfolio of interests from making sweeteners and food processing ingredients to energy and animal feed production. Its global sales in 2006/7 were $44 billion. Almost half of them came from making animal feeds, vegetable oils, and emulsifiers from oilseeds such as soya.

Two other grain and oilseed giants are part of this trading nexus that dominates food supply. Bunge, which expanded through the late nineteenth century as a grain trader in South America, is now a transnational with headquarters in the US. It is the world's largest exporter of soya beans (see Chapter 8: Soya), and a major corn and oil processor. The Louis Dreyfus group, a French family-owned private company, has vast grain, sugar and energy trading interests around the world, and now focusses on financial aspects of commodity trading (see Chapter 5: Sugar). In the US it has joint grain ventures with ADM and Cargill.

These four global companies make their money not just from agricultural commodity trading. They play the markets, have vastly complicated corporate structures to enable them to shift transactions and profits from subsidiary to subsidiary, while also trading futures and derivatives; they control refining and crushing plants, and turn those cheap subsidized commodities into a myriad other ingredients from starches to syrups to fats to animal feed. Cargill in the UK alone has divisions dealing with financial services, oilseed crushing, oil and fat refining and hardening, grain and oilseed trading, poultry, cocoa processing, production and sales of glucose syrups and powders and of sweeteners and starches, of animal feed, flavouring and texturizing ingredients manufacturing, transportation and logistics, and energy trading. It is twice the size of its nearest competitor ADM.

The modern supermarket is a vital part of this equation too. The trading and processing giants take the raw materials and divide them into parts to be turned into higher value processed foods, but bringing them to us and selling us the illusion of choice requires the ever-expanding floor space of the giant retailer. Buy oats for porridge and a packet of sugar to sprinkle on it, and you only need a corner shop; make toast from good wholemeal bread well made, and you need to search for a traditional baker; but be persuaded to choose from fifty different kinds of breakfast cereal processed from the same few ingredients into endless superficially different forms and you need a hypermarket. The evolution of the modern food system has depended on the supermarket. But in many ways the powers behind the throne are these giant trading corporations with no public face.

Breakfast cereals are just one of the most visible incarnations of this empire that specializes in adding value to cheap commodities through processing. They are not even the half of it, however. Over 30 per cent of the world's grain goes to feed animals. The surest way to add shareholder value to cheap subsidized commodity crops is to use them as animal feed, turning the carbohydrates and proteins in corn and soya into higher-value proteins in the form of meat and milk; it is in persuading the world to move up the food chain and controlling it. When you buy a steak or a chicken breast or a prime piece of pork from a supermarket, you have been moved up this food chain. Needless to say, the same US-based transnational trading companies have led and dominated this step up the consumption ladder. The supermarkets with their integrated slaughtering and packing factories have enabled them to draw us in. Between them, in the space of a few decades they have transformed our attitudes to meat and other foods. They have created a system of extraordinary reach. We are indeed subjects of empire, an American economic and cultural one.

Like most empires it is a power which can be said to bring some benefits, but which carries considerable destructive force. It is paradoxically also one of startling fragility.

2. Meat and Vegetables

I was having a sort of survivalist panic attack. I was in a car on the way to mid Wales. It was a very full car – five good-sized adults all competing for the same air – and just a little smelly from an agricultural damp that clung to the farm vehicle's interior. We had had no lunch, and a particular statistic was making me feel anxious: it takes three quarters of a gallon of oil to produce a pound of beef steak. We had been discussing peak oil and how the future would look without the source of energy that we now rely on in every part of our daily lives. We had been arguing over how soon there would be a clash over resources between growing crops for fuel and crops for food. The fragility of our food system had just sunk in. But my mind kept wandering back to the steak. I have a weakness for steak, especially flash-fried in slivers with garlic and ginger and soy sauce, and tossed into a large salad as a treat. A steak habit was looking distinctly suspect.

We were all driving to a public meeting in Lampeter, a small community in the middle of nowhere, which was planning to put itself on the map by turning itself into a Transition Town. The government might dither over climate change, economists and geologists might squabble over when exactly the oil would run out, but the people of Lampeter had decided not to wait; whether it was five, ten or the optimist's thirty years till oil production hit a peak and went into rapid and irreversible decline, they were joining a new movement now. They were going to plan their own energy descent.

As a measure of our earnest intent, we had taken the train from London, but that left the last leg of the journey to the

Welsh interior to the only practical mode of transport for those not having a few days to spare, the car.

As we bowled up and down the hills towards the Brecons, the banks and ditches speeding by the window seemed to drum out the same message. Daffodils, daisies, dandelions, violets and primroses were flowering all at once in unseasonable profusion, their natural rhythms confused by the record spring temperatures of a warming planet. We were late, and lunch now seemed doomed. It was not quite clear where our next meal would come from.

Rob Hopkins, the tall, lean co-ordinator of the Transition Town movement, was folded in next to me on the back seat, explaining why we needed to mobilize for a new war effort. The world divides into early toppers and late toppers and Rob is an early topper. The early toppers, many of them prominent geologists who used to work at the heart of the oil industry, think we have either reached the point of peak oil already or will do in the next five to ten years. New discoveries of oil were at their maximum forty years ago and world reserves are currently being depleted three times as fast as new reserves are being discovered, as global demand for energy soars. In other words we have very little time, if any, to plan for a post-oil economy.

The late toppers, who include most governments and oil companies, think we have longer, perhaps till some point in the 2030s, although our then environment minister David Miliband had recently said we should start preparing for a post-oil economy that would come in the next fifteen to twenty years. 'I trust the independent people who have no vested interests but are all oil industry insiders,' Rob was telling me. 'But it doesn't really matter who's right, because either way you need time to prepare and we've either got almost none or very little. This is the first generation that is running out of one energy source before identifying another. It's one of the most dramatic shifts humanity has had to face.'

It wasn't as though I hadn't heard of or written about peak oil before. But the speed of change was startling. I had imagined supplies would tail off, prices rising steadily, leading to more and more economic volatility but also driving research for alternatives. Now the graphs suggested a different scenario. Once you hit peak oil, production drops, not in a manageable curve that you can descend gently, but in a steep swoop, as though you are falling off a mountain.

There was a definite sense of global awakening that spring of 2007. The Intergovernmental Panel on Climate Change had just published its new, sombre assessment of the inevitability of global warming and its consequences. The apocalyptic prospects of climate change had for years seemed too vast for most people to contemplate, but now finally they were hitting home. The Australians, having refused to sign up to the Kyoto Protocol to control greenhouse gas emissions, were having national second thoughts as they faced the reality of the worst drought on record. Their then prime minister John Howard had just announced that the government was close to switching off irrigation to great swathes of their agricultural land. Nearly half the country's farming – most of its fruit, wine and rice production – was under immediate threat as they faced the choice of using what little water was left either to keep supplying the cities or to water the crops. The US, having been in almost complete denial about the coming energy crisis and climate change had suddenly started piling into biofuels. Having given us half a century in which they shaped the nature of global food consumption with the disposal of their agricultural surplus, the Americans were doing a sudden about turn. With the price of crude oil constantly breaking new records, they wanted their surplus back to keep their cars on the road. The US, having created its dependency and taken care of nearly 70 per cent of international grain trade, was slamming into reverse. Its government had started pouring subsidies into production of ethanol from corn. Grain prices were soaring. A new economic order was emerging, but we were left with the legacy of the old, with diets created out of that excess.

What's more, the calculations didn't stack up. Biofuels looked increasingly like a quick way to exacerbate climate change rather than slow it. Anyway, even if all the corn produced in the US was turned into liquid fuel it would only meet 20 per cent of American demand. To grow enough biofuel crops in the UK to keep all our cars and lorries running would require four and a half times the amount of arable land we actually have. You can import biofuels of course, but cutting down rainforest to produce them in tropical countries can release more carbon than the fossil fuels you are trying to replace.

Besides, if the world keeps hurtling off in that direction, the really urgent question would even more quickly become, as my stomach kept reminding me, where is the food for humans going to come from? Should land be used for growing food for us, for animal feed or for fuel? When Cuba suddenly hit the end of oil – thanks to the collapse of its source of cheap energy, the Soviet Union – and was unable to bring alternative fossil fuels in from elsewhere because of US embargoes, the Cuban national body weight fell by one fifth in two years. There wasn't enough to eat. About a fifth of its population are now engaged in growing food, using intense permaculture to coax the maximum out of every urban and rural space.

In the driving seat of our increasingly doomy car heading for Wales was Patrick Holden, director of the organic farmers' organization the Soil Association, and himself a dairy farmer near Lampeter. He could foresee the complete breakdown of civil order as the effects of peak oil and climate change hit Britain. At least in the last war there was still an agricultural ring around London, he pointed out grimly, but now all that had gone. Hungry Londoners would be marching down the motorway fighting over food. A civilization is never more than a few missed meals away from anarchy. Like Noah before the flood,

Patrick was preparing for the transition already, laying pipes under his fields for geothermal heat exchange to warm his house, planning his own electricity-generating wind turbine. He grows carrots and produces his own beef and milk, and was about to get into cheese making. His farm, on the top of a Welsh hill of glacial shale, is climatically and geologically challenged, but he has built up the fertility of its soil over years by crop rotations and does not use energy guzzling synthetic fertilizer. He was unlikely to go hungry or cold. But he was worried about his contribution to the fuel crisis and climate change once his food had left his farm – last season his carrots had been driven all over the country into national centralized supermarket supply systems. He was determined to get back to selling them nearer his farm. 'One planet' agriculture has to be organic at the very least but it also has to be local, he reckoned.

The problem for most of the rest of us, as Rob insisted, is that since 1945, conventional farming has evolved not as a way of making best use of finite resources, but into a system for turning oil into food. Almost all of our food requires the use of oil in its production. According to the US Department of Agriculture, modern food consumes roughly ten calories of fossil fuel energy for every calorie of food energy produced. In persuading us to move up the food chain, the industry has consumed a vast amount of crude.

Just where all the oil goes has been chronicled by the Green MEP Caroline Lucas and co-authors Andy Jones and Colin Hines in their report, 'Fuelling a Food Crisis'.

Twenty-one per cent of the UK's total energy use is accounted for by its food supply. Synthetic fertilizers, hydrocarbon-fuelled farm machinery that has replaced manual labour, plastics made from oil, and pesticides made from its toxic by-products, have all helped improve global yields dramatically but they have also meant that today's industrialized farming uses fifty times as much energy as traditional agriculture.

And that's just on the farm. The plastics needed for packing food that is now transported long distances, the juggernauts that provide warehousing on our motorways, the just-in-time delivery systems that add food miles, the centralized distribution systems of our supermarkets that move food round and round the country, the aviation fuel that flies in fresh food from around the world, and the out-of-town stores that require us to drive our cars to do our shopping, all burn large quantities of fuel. Each British household consumes 130kg of packaging from oil-derived plastics a year; two thirds of that packaging is used for food.

More and more of the food we eat is also heavily processed before we consume it. Food manufacturing is highly energy intensive. High temperature ovens, rapid cooling chambers, bottling plants, they all use lots of energy. Remember the medium sized box of breakfast cereal that contains 1,100 calories but uses 7,000 calories of fuel energy to make? You can make the same sorts of calculations for frozen vegetables or canned fruit or heavily packaged ready meals.

Without a steady, cheap supply of fossil fuels, in other words, our food would look very different.

Synthetic fertilizer alone accounts for a third of the energy consumed by agriculture. Fertilizer prices have nearly doubled in the last three years as oil and gas prices have risen. But without it, today's industrial farming would be impossible. Its reductionist chemistry has ruled our agriculture for more than half a century.

The price of fertilizer does not sound like a promising subject of study, but just as you need to get to grips with the tedious minutiae of lorries and distribution centres to understand how supermarkets have taken control of our food shopping, so understanding the small white pellets today's farmers spread on their land helps explain the post-oil dilemma.

A brilliant nineteenth-century German chemist, Justus von Liebig, was the first to show that you could take any substance and by combusting it reduce it to its chemical components. He analysed the chemical constituents of the soil, which previously had been thought of as some mysterious and indefinable life form. If you knew what chemical constituents plants took out of the soil when they grew, he reasoned, you could simply put them back after each crop. Successful agriculture would be a matter of chemical replenishment rather than husbanding of complex living ecosystems. This idea paved the way for the invention of chemical fertilizers. Much of science has moved on from this reductionist approach, but intensive agriculture has stuck with it.

As well as carbon, oxygen and hydrogen, which they get from air and water, plants need nitrogen to grow.

By the mid nineteenth century, the decline of the natural fertility of the soil was already a major concern. Both Europe and America had started depending on imports of natural nitrogenous fertilizers. Guano imperialism had emerged: the US seized nearly 100 islands and rocks around the world between 1856 and 1903 to secure its supplies of that particular natural fertilizer.

Nitrates were shipped in from Chile, as guano ran out. Even the great political thinkers applied their minds to the problem. In 1867 Karl Marx wrote about the wider social and political implications of soil fertility in *Das Kapital*. 'Capitalist production . . . disturbs the metabolic interaction between man and the earth. It prevents the return to the soil of its constituent elements consumed by man in the form of food and clothing. All progress in capitalist agriculture is a progress in the art, not only of robbing the workers, but of robbing the soil.'

Then Fritz Haber, another brilliant German chemist working at the beginning of the twentieth century, devised a way of taking nitrogen from the atmosphere and combining it with hydrogen to produce ammonia. The process involved heating the two gases under pressure to extreme temperatures in the presence of a nickel catalyst to make them react. His discovery meant that nitrogen products such as fertilizer and explosives

41

which had previously been dependent on natural deposits of nitrates could instead be synthesized in industrial quantities. Carl Bosch helped scale up the process for the powerful German chemical company BASF. The main aim had been to help the German war effort by providing the material for making munitions but the Haber–Bosch process became the basis for the modern nitrogen fertilizer production which transformed agriculture.

Before artificial fertilizer, farmers had had to take care of soil fertility by rotating crops, planting legumes and clover whose roots have the ability to fix atmospheric nitrogen in the soil, to feed nitrogen-greedy crops such as wheat and corn later, or nitrogen had to come from animal manure spread on the land. But with the Haber–Bosch process they were liberated from such constraints and once the war effort of two world conflicts was over, the green revolution could take off. The nitrates, no longer needed for explosives, were surplus to spread on the land. Instead of mixed farming, farmers could adopt monocultures.

Today the nitrogen in fertilizer comes from the limitless supply in the atmosphere, but the hydrogen to turn it into that fertilizer comes from prodigious quantities of hydrocarbon fuels, from oil and gas. World fertilizer use has shot up since the 1950s, moving from very little to 70 million tonnes in 1970 and then nearly doubling between 1970 and 2000 to just less than 140 million tonnes. The global fertilizer market is dominated by Cargill, ADM and Bunge. Cargill, for example, owns two thirds of the company that is the world's largest producer of fertilizer ingredients, with major factories in North America, South America, and China. Global grain production has nearly tripled in the same past half century thanks to nitrogen fertilizers, but nitrous oxide – a greenhouse gas more than 250 times more potent than carbon dioxide – has also soared, thanks to fertilizer use.

There is a chart farmers can use to calculate the cost/benefit equation of adding synthetic fertilizer. As you apply your chemical food to the soil, the crops' yields go up and the extra money you make covers the cost of the inputs. As oil prices continue to rise and gas prices go with them, the point on the curve at which the costs outweigh any financial benefit moves back nearer and nearer to the beginning. As synthetic fertilizer gets more and more expensive, grain crops get more expensive, animal feed gets more expensive and so on down the chain. Food from post-oil agriculture will indeed look very different.

The report 'Fuelling a Food Crisis' calculated at the end of 2006 what would happen to food prices if the price of energy doubles or quadruples over the next decade as some analysts have projected. If you take into account the fossil fuels used in fertilizer, storage, transport, packaging and production, a doubling of energy prices would take the cost of producing a burger from its current level of 42p to 90p. A quadrupling of energy prices sends it up to £1.62. That means that a burger that you can buy for about 80p in a fast food outlet now would have to cost £2 or more. Meanwhile, the cost of putting a factory chicken on the table, assuming it is not being sold as a loss leader by a supermarket, would go up from about £4 to about £9. Suddenly the whole basis of cheap, fast, processed food and supermarket logistics starts to fall apart. When the report was written crude oil was about $75 a barrel. By January 2008 it had already broken the $100 barrier.

Until recently we have been protected from fuel price rises by the stranglehold supermarkets have on the market. They have prevented manufacturers and suppliers from passing them on. Between 2002 and 2005 the price of oil increased over 250 per cent and costs of farm inputs rose between 50 and 150 per cent, but food inflation was kept relatively low. That's not to say the effect was not felt. Squeezed between the retail giants and energy hikes, several food manufacturers posted profit warnings. The number of insolvencies in the food manu-facturing sector rose.

By spring 2007, however, the lid had blown off. Food price inflation globally was heading for its largest annual increase in thirty years. The UK's consumer price index showed annual food inflation of 6 per cent, its highest in almost six years and well above the rest of inflation. In China, food costs were increasing twice as quickly as other kinds of prices, up 7 per cent. There had been riots in Mexico as tens of thousands of poor Mexicans protested at a 400 per cent rise in the price of the corn flour they use as their staple in tortillas. Italians had been out on the streets protesting at the price of pasta. The French had been marching about bread prices. Rapid rises in food prices and civil unrest are historic partners. Many experts predict a period of further steep food inflation and the political turbulence that will bring.

Back in our car, as we pushed on towards Lampeter, there was still no obvious source of lunch, but Rob was reassuring us that each human produces enough nitrogen in their own urine to fertilize all the food he or she needs. So, if we all made compost and remembered to pee on it, perhaps we could mitigate the impact of fertilizer prices, climate change and inflation, I tried. Sadly no: EU regulations snuffed out this thought at birth; they have stopped the use of human waste in agriculture.

The only answer seemed to be serious emergency planning. We decided to ring ahead and ask one of the meeting organizers to buy us some sandwiches. Happy to oblige, the message came back down the mobile, the options were chicken, egg or beef . . . a choice that raised all my survivalist anxieties again, because, between the twin emerging crises of peak oil and climate change and the old imperative of feeding a growing global population, what's obvious is that we should be eating lower on the food chain not higher. One planet agriculture means more vegetables, grains and pulses for direct human consumption, not more meat and animal protein. Unfortunately, eating lower down the food chain would require putting a whole industry into reverse, a bit of a challenge when you are squashed in a car rattling along on today's infrastructure.

All of this was beginning to sound like familiar territory, not just to Patrick who had first come to Wales in the 1970s to set up a commune, but also to the third occupant of the back seat of the car, Rosie Boycott. Rosie is a former national newspaper editor turned part-time small organic farmer, but her career had started famously with setting up the feminist magazine *Spare Rib*. As well as knitting patterns, the magazine had published a regular commune column which meant Rosie driving off for weekends in a blue Hillman to visit a series of self-sufficient hippies. She remembered the brown rice and construction-grade wholemeal bread being rather hard on the digestive system. The worry then had been Malthusian: how to feed the people of a planet that was adding 70 million mouths to its population every year and in particular how to make sure there was enough protein to go round. Books such as *Diet for a Small Planet* were arguing passionately for a more vegetarian diet. Now the most urgent preoccupations, greenhouse gas emissions and energy shocks, have to be added to that worry, but the corollary of all three is the same. Meat is a luxury.

Much of the last fifty years has been spent persuading us in the West of the opposite: that meat can be cheap, that we need the complete protein that animals rather than plants can give us. Intensive agriculture and factory processing have given us apparently limitless cheap supplies – they have revolutionized livestock production but not without unforeseen and profound consequences.

The livestock revolution – the separation of animals from the land and the industrialization of livestock production – began in rich countries about seventy years ago, but really took off from the 1950s. It required cheap energy to power it, and fertilizer-grown sources of concentrated protein and carbo-hydrate to feed it.

Before cheap energy and fertilizer and the surplus that

45

fertilizer was able to produce, farmers had been constrained in their production by how much their land could support. In fact from the earliest agriculture until fifty or sixty years ago, livestock farming had remained relatively unchanged, as John Webster, Professor of Veterinary Science at Bristol University, explains in *Limping towards Eden*. Sheep and goats for meat were left to forage for themselves, grazing on grass and scrub the farmer and family could not eat themselves, and making use of poorer land. Chickens and pigs were fed waste and acted as scavengers of food that would otherwise not be used. They were allowed to range free so that they could find their own food, which had the added advantage that they spread their own manure. Cows grazed on grass, the green sward which humans couldn't digest, so turning it into food they could. Since cows provide milk it was worth farmers growing some food just for them. They could also provide power by acting as draught animals. Male calves would be fattened for a while and then killed to be eaten. This age-old system was sustainable but did not produce much more than subsistence for most farmers.

With the arrival of cheap power early in the last century, it became possible to move animals into intensive housing. Now food, fertilizer, machinery and power could be brought in.

The mass production of cheap drugs post war, particularly antibiotics, was the other essential ingredient in the livestock revolution. You can only keep large numbers of animals in close confinement if you have the means to control the disease that inevitably accompanies the practice. (In fact even cheap drugs have been unable to control the disease this kind of farming spreads, as successive outbreaks in recent years of foot and mouth, avian flu, swine fever and previously barely known illnesses such as blue tongue have proved.)

A farmer could now produce as much animal produce as his access to capital would allow. Farmers no longer needed to grow their own grass or forage, they could import animal feed in the form of grains and oilseeds instead. The Americans were offering it cheap. European governments, through their Common Agricultural Policy, were about to subsidize their grain and oilseed crops to help provide the raw materials too.

This animal version of the industrial revolution has made it possible for the populations of developed countries to consume meat in a completely new way. Global meat production quintupled in the second half of the twentieth century. We now get through an average of 84kg of meat per person per year in the UK. The Americans scoff a third as much as that again. And now the Chinese are moving the same way – their meat consumption has risen exponentially, from 4kg per person per year forty years ago to 54kg now.

The livestock revolution has turned cheap commodity crops into higher value proteins. Not surprisingly, the big grain trading corporations dominate not just grain but the global animal feed and meat markets too. Up to three quarters of the animal feed production in Europe was estimated to be controlled by Cargill, ADM and Bunge and their subsidiaries in 2001. All three have major expansion programmes to produce feed in China, as well as feed operations in many other countries. The leading animal feed company in the UK has emerged from a former subsidiary of another transnational, Unilever.

Cargill and ADM have major global chicken, turkey and pork producing interests too. Cargill's subsidiary Sun Valley produces half of the all the chicken products used by McDonald's across Europe and is a leading supplier of chicken to UK supermarkets. It processes about a million chickens a week from its factories in Europe and the UK.

Breaking the connection between animals and the land also meant that meat could be sourced from anywhere in the world. Brazil is now the world's largest exporter of beef; and a major exporter of poultry; less than twenty years ago the vast majority of its beef was for its own consumption. The UK has become its fourth largest customer, and Brazilian beef and poultry makes its way into supermarket ready meals and catering. Factory farms in Thailand are also the source of much of the cheap chicken that we consume in processed foods and takeaways. Cargill is the largest poultry processor in Thailand.

The livestock revolution is seen most dramatically perhaps in poultry and pig production; there are now twice as many chickens on earth as humans at any one time – nearly 15.5 billion of them – and nearly 1 billion pigs. Where once eating these meats would be an occasional luxury, today it is an everyday event. Consumption of dairy products, eggs and seafood have also increased dramatically. (It's not just the animals that get fed corn and soya surplus – fish in fish farms do too.) Now nearly a third of all grain grown in the world goes to feed livestock, and 90 per cent of the world's soya beans end up as animal feed.

Developing countries are starting to follow the patterns of livestock farming in the West. As their populations urbanize, they too want to move up the food chain and adopt Western diets.

Britain was the first country to become mostly urban, being the first to undergo its industrial revolution and the first to displace its peasant agriculture with more mechanized farming. This is why Britain has indeed been more susceptible to colonization by processed foods than others. The US, as early urbanizers, were more susceptible too, and this is why patterns of diet-related disease, cardiovascular disease, cancers and obesity, emerged earlier and more clearly here than in other countries.

The trouble is if all of China, India and other poorer countries start eating the way we do, we'll need at least three planets to do it.

An equation written by the Indian environmental activist Vandana Shiva succinctly explains why. She estimates that the livestock of Europe require an area of vegetation that is seven times the size of the EU to keep them in feed. Several developing countries that have undergone the livestock revolution have become dependent on imported grain. Twenty years ago Egypt use to be self sufficient in grain but now imports 8 million tonnes a year and livestock account for over a third of its total grain consumption. (Its dependence was built up with the help of US food aid, of which it was for many years one of the largest recipients.) China was a net exporter of grain until ten years ago, but is now the second largest importer in the world. China was also once the leading producer of soya beans in the world but it is now an importer of them too, buying them mostly from the US.

Intensively reared animals are an inefficient way of producing calories, however. They use many more food calories than they produce in the form of meat because they waste most of the energy and protein value of their feed in digestion and bodily maintenance.

There are arguments about the figures, but if you take US Department of Agriculture calculations, it takes 16kg of grain to produce just 1kg of beef. That steak I was fantasizing about doesn't just guzzle crude oil, but raw commodities too.

If you look at it purely in terms of meeting people's protein needs, factory animals aren't very efficient at converting what they eat either. Farm an acre of decent land and you can produce only 20lbs of beef protein from it, but give the same acre over to producing wheat, and you'll get 138lb of protein. If you are worrying about feeding the world and growing enough protein to go round, mass meat production makes little sense.

There's no question that meat can provide invaluable micronutrients – minerals such as iron and some vitamins such as B12 that are hard to come by except from animal products. Eating a little can be good for you. And livestock can of course be grazed on land that is not suitable for grain crops or in a rotation that fertilizes the land. But the problem is we have come to see meat as a primary source of food and calories, and most of the meat we eat has been produced with the extravagant use of grains, rather than being reared extensively on grass. If everyone moves up the food chain like this, there just won't be enough land to feed all the animals and people, never mind having room for biofuels.

This sort of intensive production also changes the composition of the meat. Factory animals, fed high-energy cereal-based and high protein feeds and kept confined suffer the same fate as we do when we eat fast food and fail to take exercise. They become obese. Professor Michael Crawford, head of the Institute of Brain Chemistry and Human Nutrition at London Metropolitan University, showed me the work he and his researchers have done in his laboratory testing supermarket meat and comparing it with records from thirty-five years ago. A chicken in 1970 contained 8.6g of fat per 100g, but today contains nearly 23g of fat per 100g. Over that same period the amount of protein in chicken fell by more than 30 per cent. Most of us buying white meat do so thinking it's lean. Chicken became so popular precisely because we were all encouraged as part of a drive to prevent heart disease to switch from red meats high in saturated fat to white meat and pork that was supposed to be healthier. But now the white meat is fatty too. Whereas foraging chickens in the past would have eaten a mix of grains and wild seeds full of a wide range of nutrients, now their diets are based on the same limited number of ingredients as ours. The amount of omega-3 essential fatty acids in their flesh has changed as a result. They contain less than one sixth of the long chain omega-3 fatty acid DHA they had just a few decades ago. 'There are miserable amounts of DHA in modern birds and for the first time since records began in the 1870s, the fat in a chicken outweighs its protein. The same decline can be seen in battery eggs when compared with those from farmyard chickens that are free to forage; the omega-3 levels are greatly depleted,' Professor Crawford explained. The same trend can be seen in beef production. 'The beef industry has been encouraged by subsidies which require carcasses to have a specific composition, to produce animals that are 30 per cent fat, and provide six times as many calories from hard saturated fats as calories from protein. The fat used to go to tallow for candles, now we are eating the tallow in the flesh,' he told me.

If you do eat meat, there are plenty of health reasons for eating a little that has been well reared rather than a lot that has been intensively produced. Cutting down on meat significantly reduces the risk of cancer. The World Cancer Research Fund brought together a team of renowned experts in a huge project to examine the links between diet and cancer. Having reviewed all the science, they reported that cancer, so far from being the inevitable consequence of ageing, is in large part a preventable disease, with diet playing a crucial role. Urban and industrialized societies have diets high in meat, milk, hardened fats, processed starches, salt and sugars, and as a result have more cancers of the colorectum and hormone-related cancers such as breast, ovarian and prostate cancer than non-industrialized societies. But by changing our diets we could reduce cancers by a third, the experts found. The same changes that reduce our risk of cancer reduce our risk of heart disease and stroke.

The expert panel found strong evidence that red meat and processed meat consumption causes bowel cancer. Eating lots of meat is also linked to cancer of the oesophagus, lung, stomach, and prostate. They recommended that we avoid processed meats as far as possible and limit our intake of cooked red meat to less than 500g or just over a pound a week. Instead, if you want to prevent cancer you should eat plenty of relatively unrefined grains and pulses with each meal along with a wide variety of fruits and vegetables. Most adults in the UK eat more protein than they need – though what we are said to need is a moveable feast, with the US government recommending considerably higher intakes than the British. A couple of slices of wholemeal bread, a helping of lentils, a cheese sandwich and the odd nut will get the average woman up to her requirement for the day of 36 to 45g. You don't have to eat meat for iron – dark green leafy vegetables are good sources and you can increase absorption by eating iron-rich vegetables with good sources of vitamin C.

The environmental arguments for changing our patterns of meat consumption and eating meat sparingly and occasionally rather than daily are compelling. The UN's Food and Agriculture Organization produced a report in 2006 about livestock's 'long shadow'. It makes uncomfortable reading. Livestock production now contributes to the world's most pressing environmental problems, including global warming, land degradation, air and water pollution and loss of bio-diversity, it says.

Livestock are responsible for a bigger share of all greenhouse gas emissions than the whole of global transport. They account for nearly a fifth of the world's total emissions. Researchers at the University of Chicago translated what that means in terms of action we could all take. They looked at the carbon dioxide emissions alone from meat production and found that the average burger consumer emits the equivalent of 1.5 tonnes more CO_2 every year than the average vegan. That's as much as the difference between using a conventional car rather than a green hybrid over the course of a year. If you want to do your bit to slow down climate change by cutting your own CO_2 emissions, you can do as much by cutting down on meat as by trading in your vehicle.

Cows produce prodigious quantities of methane too, a far more potent global warming gas than carbon dioxide. Despite popular prejudice that they fart too much, in fact most of the methane gas comes from their burping. Just as with humans, what their diet consists of makes a difference to the volume of gas generated. A more digestible diet with clover and the right sort of grass reduces the amount of gas produced in their stomachs, but currently farmed ruminants account for up to a quarter of man-made methane emissions across the world.

Somehow ordering high protein sandwiches for our lunch to eat in the car as we burned petrol on the way to Lampeter did not feel quite right, but we were desperate.

The gathering, when we finally got there, was the biggest public meeting anyone could remember. The town has two smallish supermarkets, but has hung on to all its independent shops too – there are butchers and bakers and sewing shops and solicitors and insurance brokers still on the high street. The electrical shop, itself a rarity these days, actually mends things as well as selling them new. West Wales generally has a long tradition of alternative living, but the scale of this event was different. More than 450 people filed into the arts hall in a place where the total population is just 4,000. Inside the hall, the clock was stuck an hour behind time, and a book stall was offering a variety of useful titles, from *The New Complete Book of Self Sufficiency* to *Composting, a household guide. Slow* and *Heat* sat alongside tomes called *The Diamond in Your Pocket, Discovering Your True Radiance* and *The Lilypad List: 7 Steps to the Simple Life.*

Rob gave them his talk about The Petroleum Interval, the period that in the great expanse of history will turn out to have been very brief, a mere interval during which we have had the benefit of an extraordinarily energy dense fuel. A tank of petrol is the energy equivalent of four years of human labour but it's running out. Since 2004 world production has stalled despite rapidly rising demand. We have to start moving to a post-petroleum world. You didn't have to believe him; you could take it from the Hirsch report written for the US government's Department of Energy.

'The world has never faced a problem like this. Without massive mitigation more than a decade before the fact, the problem will be pervasive and will not be temporary. Previous energy transitions were gradual and evolutionary. Oil peaking will be abrupt and revolutionary. As peaking is approached, liquid fuel prices and price volatility will increase dramatically, and without timely mitigation, the economic, social and political costs will be unprecedented . . .' We may well face 'demand destruction', in other words deep recession and shortages.

I noticed that by now the people of Lampeter, from ageing hippies with long grey beards, ponytails and combs in their back pockets to young activists from the local school, were shifting uneasily in their plastic seats (made with oil), and drawing anxiously on their water bottles (made with oil) if not reaching for their medicines (made with oil). Rob told them they were likely to experience a range of common symptoms that, in his experience, accompany initial peak oil awareness.

One might be an irrational grasping at unfeasible solutions. At hydrogen for example. No good: running the UK's cars on hydrogen would need sixty-seven Sizewell B nuclear power stations or a wind farm bigger than the whole of the south west region of England. Or biofuels. No again; it would take over 25 million hectares of arable land to run the UK's vehicles on biofuels and the UK only has 5.7 million hectares. Imports? There are more than 800 million malnourished people in the world, he said sternly.

Other symptoms might include (a) exuberant optimism – I could see how that might feel: they'll have to change the world now, I told you so! It's the end of suburbia, hooray! The sheer waste and expense of the supermarket's oil–dependent distribution systems will make them uncompetitive, double hooray! Or (b) nihilism – what if no one changes, there's nothing to be done. Or (c) survivalism – in which case that new complete self sufficiency handbook would come in handy, presumably.

After Rob, the *Guardian* columnist and environmentalist George Monbiot, who lives near Lampeter, tried to cheer them up. Unlike Rob, he had become persuaded that the end of oil was not nigh, only nigh-ish. We may have another ten to thirty years. We would not run out of energy exactly because we still have lots of coal. The problem with that was that if we switched back to fuels from coal that increase our emissions, climate change would undo us even faster than peak oil. The politicians might be tempted, but they must be resisted.

Four hours into planning their energy descent, the people of Lampeter moved into the dining hall next door to fortify themselves for the struggle ahead. They collected steaming bowls of cawl for supper and sat at refectory tables with pencil and paper to plan becoming a Transition Town. Cawl would be the meal of the future. A traditional Welsh peasant dish – root vegetables, herbs from the wild or the kitchen patch, a little meat from a cheap cut of a local animal, slow cooked in a broth in one pot that you keep adding to – the recipe had been recorded by another Lampeter local, the cookery writer Elisabeth Luard in her encyclopaedic volume on European peasant cookery. I remembered being given the book when it first came out in 1986; it is wonderful.

Its descriptions of the rich tradition of simple peasant food seemed particularly useful now. 'The fundamental issue of peasant existence is survival. The earth must be husbanded, coaxed, and cared for, it cannot be exploited or it will take swift revenge . . . the old peasant kitchen habits of frugality were part of that husbandry . . . peasant communities had no organized trade . . . fuel in particular was precious. It needed energy to collect and was often in short supply . . . beans-and-bones dishes are classic and staple peasant food in all Mediterranean countries . . . the whole household gathered at mealtimes and ate from a communal bowl . . . there were wooden boards for portions of bread . . .'

This is the antithesis of supermarket factory meat, in which only a small range of prime cuts are sold, and a large part of the industrially processed animal is treated as waste or shipped around the world to other markets. Around the refectory tables in the Lampeter hall, sipping their broth and chewing their coarse bread, the townspeople were thinking of the things they'd like to happen – a ban on advertising that encourages excess consumption, turning the local supermarket into a giant allotment, reopening the railway line that had been closed. Then they thought of the things they might actually be able to do: install a community wind turbine, encourage low-energy buildings, swap skills, grow more food. In Transition Totnes, Rob's current home town, they are planting hundreds of nut trees because acre for acre they produce as much carbohydrate food as grain and act as carbon sinks at the same time. Local businesses are being audited to show them which parts of their operations become unprofitable as the price of oil rises; a process that often provides an abrupt wake up call. Someone in Lampeter suggested that a local landowner could give the town an acre for a community vegetable garden. Someone else remembered a playing field that would serve the purpose, if the council agreed. The man from the council stood up and welcomed the ideas. He talked of unitary plans and community development plans and somehow, like the weather forecast that you know you want to hear but fail to absorb, somewhere between his sustainable development targets and waving arms, we were lost. Nevertheless on a show of 450 hands, Lampeter decided emphatically that it would meet again to plan the next stage in its energy descent. And then its people spilled out on a clear spring night into the car park and, just this one last time, drove home.

I rejoined my companions from our car journey, and we drove on to Patrick's farm nearby. There, I am ashamed to say, we ate supper all over again – a huge dish of lasagne made with beef from his own organic cattle and unpasteurized milk from his own herd. (Patrick, like most dairy farmers I have met, favours unpasteurized milk for his own consumption because heat-treating kills some of the nutrients in fresh milk, and in particular destroys lactase, the enzyme that is naturally present and that we need to digest lactose. Some experts believe this may be an important factor in the rise of milk allergies in modern times.) Our second supper was served with a vast bowl of delicious fresh salad grown under plastic by the organic nursery just outside Lampeter.

Was this how it would be: those with access to resources or those with enough money would buy their way out of trouble; the rest might go hungry or eat cawl? I suppressed these uncomfortable thoughts and tucked into the feast.

The organic salad was mysteriously free of all the blemishes and slug holes that accompany anything I manage to grow myself and I asked the grower, Anne Evans, who had come with us from the Lampeter gathering, how on earth she managed it. She had been a leading supplier of organic leaves to the super-markets, but was now bringing most of her sales back to her own area. It was partly that farming with low environmental impact only to send food off into energy-intense centralized supermarket distribution systems seemed insupportable, but the decision had also been forced on her by supermarket eco-nomics. Her partner, Peter Segger, had been the pioneer in bringing organic food to the mainstream through the 1990s. He had invested several million pounds building a pack house near Lampeter to meet supermarket requirements. But Waitrose had decided to rationalize its supply in the early 2000s and wanted a smaller number of 'category managers' to organize suppliers all around the country. Its organic vegetable contract was awarded to a company in the east of England and Peter's company became a casualty. There was no longer anywhere local to pack her produce. Not even being an award-winning grower, nor Peter being the man who had practically invented supermarket organics, had been enough to save them. The secret of the leaves though, Anne said, was in the compost, and in labour. Instead of the fossil-fuel-hungry synthetic fertilizers that stimulate a fast but sappy growth of leaves, leaving cell walls thin and the plants themselves vulnerable to disease and pests, Anne produced her own organic compost from mixed vege-table waste and animal manure. Yields might be lower but what was produced was stronger and intensely flavoured. Night-time forays with a torch also helped deal with slugs and snails, together with biological controls. Organic farming has a habit of keeping more people employed on the land than intensive agriculture, as well as husbanding resources more sustainably.

I heard another vision for the food system that night too, as Patrick told me of his struggle to ensure that the carrots he grew were sold locally rather than trucked around the country and back, undoing all the good he achieved by low-carbon farming. He wanted a kind of production that aimed at nutritional quality over quantity, at substance before cosmetic appearance, at fuel economy rather than waste. It was a vision tempered like Anne and Peter's by harsh experience of the structural failures of the current system. Patrick had been growing carrots organically for over twenty years, supplying the leading supermarkets for many of those years, until the price they were prepared to pay fell below his cost of production. He had decided at that point to market his vegetables as local carrots to be sold mostly in Wales packed in bags that told the story of his family farm. Sainsbury's agreed to sell them in its stores in the region. They were more expensive but people seemed prepared to pay more for something they trusted that was local and sustainably produced. It had all come to grief the season before though, when Sainsbury's decided to drop not just Patrick but Prince Charles and his royal Highgrove roots too. Their crops had been rejected by the supermarket's quality control system. Patrick had been told that his carrots would no longer be accepted because they were rotting after packing, leaving him, without notice, with a third of his crop unsold. To add insult to injury he had been fined £3,380 plus VAT through his account manager for sending goods they decided to reject to the supermarket depot. Sainsbury's said the vegetables were just not up to scratch when harvested. Patrick believed rather that he and Prince Charles had become victims of the supermarket's industrial processes. These processes involved tonnes of carbon emissions, thanks to imposed food miles and giant washing machines designed, according to the machine maker's website, to wash and polish carrots so that 'when displayed on the supermarket shelf, even weeks after washing, they still look like wet, fresh carrots'.

Sainsbury's had been making 'buying local' a key part of its marketing to eco-conscious consumers. But Patrick said they were in fact unintentionally making it impossible for the kind of small family farms their customers imagined were behind their organic labels to supply them. Over the course of the next few weeks we discussed his dilemma. 'Supermarkets are preaching localism but it's just tokenism, their systems are still going in the opposite direction towards fewer companies being category managers and towards greater centralization and industrialization.' Originally Patrick's carrots had been packed at the pack house owned by Peter nearby or in a pack house in Leominster in Herefordshire just across the border before being returned, mostly to stores around his farm. The Highgrove carrots were also sent to Leominster. But when Peter's company closed down, Patrick and Prince Charles' farm had to send their carrots to a Sainsbury's superpacker in East Anglia, in Patrick's case trucking them 230 miles. The two farms had tried to combine loads to reduce costs and emissions. But the superpacker in Peterborough was not geared to dealing with small consignments. Patrick's carrots had to be tipped into larger containers for the washing supermarkets require, damaging up to 15 per cent of the crop, he said.

The Wyma Vege-Polisher boasts on its website that as well as making carrots look wet and fresh, it can improve the look and yield of not just carrots but potatoes and other roots. It removes the surface membrane and polishes carrots to 'a deep glow'. Potatoes can have their skins 'lightened up' and skin fungi or sprouting caused by storage removed.

After grading for cosmetic standards, however, Patrick and Prince Charles' Highgrove carrots were suffering further losses, with up to half the crop being graded out and going to waste, according to Patrick. The pack house wasn't keeping the carrots as long as the Wyma website boasted it might but it was holding batches for days until the right volumes had accumulated for packing. That and the effect of washing meant they were prone to rot. And then Patrick was told they were no longer needed. He believed he had been delisted, although Sainsbury's later told us that neither he nor Prince Charles had been delisted, which the supermarket defined as meaning they would be unable to supply again. Sainsbury's said that it had actually deranged Prince Charles and Patrick. It took a while for the supermarket jargon to sink in and for me to realize a hyphen might be needed. De-ranging means you might be allowed back next season. Patrick decided to tell me the story because he said 'everyone who has supplied a supermarket own-label will have a similar story to mine, but most daren't tell it. This isn't confined to one supermarket. Sainsbury's have in fact been more supportive of organic farming than some others.' A climate of fear still pervades farmers' dealings with the all-powerful retailers. He knew his day job as director of the organic farmers' association gave him special influence and felt he should speak out because the system was undoing the hard work organic farmers put in to reducing their contribution to climate change. 'My crop, which was grown for low environmental impact, ended up acquiring a greater carbon footprint than conventional carrots grown on an industrial scale because it was being trucked across the country. I don't think there was anything wrong with my carrots – an organic box scheme took them in the end and its customers were very happy with them. The current supermarket practice is still driving towards greater centralization, which is completely at odds with Britain's food security and long-term public interest. What we need is a complete reversal of the thirty-year process that has dismantled the lattice work of small, local supply chains,' he said.

Sainsbury's was adamant that it had gone to great lengths

to accommodate what it called Patrick's preferred way of supplying his carrots, but that its overriding priority had to be the quality of food it sold to its customers, and that he had not measured up. It said it would work with him and Prince Charles' farm to find a solution for the following season. Such high profile producers must have been embarrassing to lose. In the end Patrick, thanks to a determined stand, did manage to bring his carrots back home, and Tesco, Waitrose and Sainsbury's agreed to make special arrangements to use a small new pack house in Wales which supplies local stores.

But as we finished our meal that night in Patrick's farmhouse kitchen, a nagging thought returned. I had after all just eaten not one but two suppers. Perhaps if lunch had not been in such doubt, the guilty pleasure would have been less. But our double-dinner gaggle of society suggested a future that was troublingly far from the prospects raised earlier by brief moments of exuberant optimism or by the valiant attempts of local producers to make a shift to truly sustainable agriculture. As the effects of peak oil, pressure on land and water resources, and climate change converged, it obviously was going to be all about access, and money. As ever, the international markets had seen it all coming, I realized, even if governments and the rest of us had not.

The price of raw agricultural commodities – of the animal feed that keeps the livestock revolution in business, of the base ingredients of thousands of packaged foods such as breakfast cereals, of the produce that farmers in Britain sell to make a living – is set in Chicago. It is here that the world's oldest futures and options exchange, the Chicago Board of Trade, was established in 1848. I had visited it in its present 1930 skyscraper home the previous spring after my trip to Kellogg city at Battle Creek. The signs of the coming fight for resources were already visible.

The 650-ft building, topped by a faceless statue of the goddess of cereals Ceres, is toweringly imposing from the street, while the lavish art deco scrolls, black and white marble, and white brass piping inside give it the air of an early palace of entertainment. Outside, before the financial day begins, teams of traders pump themselves up on chain-smoked fags and outsize McDonald's coffees. The coloured blazers they use to make themselves easily identifiable on the trading floor have been reduced to bright jackets with string-vest backs against the heat generated by a day's speculation; they keep on their toes in sneakers.

Spectators can watch the agricultural floor from a small raised platform which spares you the crush of the open outcry system when the market bell rings the off but does nothing to insulate you from the noise of its speculative frenzy. From a series of pits, traders yelled at one another and waved their arms in violent gesticulation – palms out to signal sell, palms in to signal buy. There were the scalpers who buy and sell within seconds, the floor brokers hedging for corporate accounts, the locals speculating on their own accounts, and thousands of runners rushing back orders to the market recorders. On a June morning in 2006 it was the day to discover the price for corn to be delivered in December that year; 2006 had been a record summer for corn and other agricultural futures contracts – people were already wondering where it was all going to come from, what with India and China importing more to feed intensive livestock production, and the US pushing corn for ethanol production. Soya was up dramatically on the news that China had bought a 22,000-tonne cargo of soya oil. The bellow from this incarnation of raw market capitalism was overwhelming.

The futures and options markets evolved to help farmers and traders manage the risk of price fluctuations from spikes and troughs in supply and demand caused by poor or bumper harvests. Chicago became the home of the markets because it was in a key position geographically as the railroads were expanding between the Mid-West farmers in the newly opened-up agricultural areas and the older American settlements on the east coast with their large urban populations of consumers. Through the markets buyers and sellers of grain could hedge their bets by buying futures against changes in price and transfer the risk to speculators happy to take it.

Since you don't have to have the commodity in your hands to trade in futures in it, there is plenty of room for speculation. In fact, the growth in speculative trading in grains and other agricultural commodities post-war has been exponential. Just as global trade in financial derivatives is nearly double the size of the total real global economy, so speculative trade in food is far greater than the volume of food actually grown. The amount of soya traded in futures, for example, is more than thirty times greater than the amount of soya produced. All this activity makes the futures markets highly volatile and can lead to great fluctuations in price – precisely what the hedgers and farmers were trying to protect themselves against in the first place. And as the commodity world becomes more globalized, more and more farmers around the world are exposed to the risk of sharp price changes. With a global market, processors, manufacturers and supermarkets can in theory source their materials from anywhere in the world as long as they have the fuel to move them. Meat and dairy farmers are at the mercy of speculative pressures on the other side of the world. Those who play the market cleverly can do very well out of it. The transnational grain giants have vast financial trading operations and great expertise in financial instruments. Even so they too sometimes complain that the volatility of the markets is no way to do business in the supply of such an essential of life as food. But for farmers who have imperfect information, and who have to plan and plant ahead, it can mean being squeezed out of existence. Since land lost to farming often cannot easily be restored, governments have long intervened to mediate between farmers and the workings of the markets. Stabilizing prices was one of the things early subsidies in Europe were meant to do but they have not. Instead, by rewarding overproduction and providing surplus for dumping they have contributed to undermining farm incomes and commodity speculation.

The leading market analysts watching the Chicago Board of Trade could see which way the tide was running even back then in 2006. Dan Basse, president of one of the most respected commodity analyst companies AgResource, was shouting an explanation to me over the roar coming from the agricultural pits. As the people in South East Asia get more disposable income they all want to eat like the Americans. World demand for corn and other grains has been rising, but global corn stocks are exceptionally tight. Since 1999 global corn demand has in fact outstripped global production in all but one year and world reserve stocks of grain have been reduced to just fifty-seven days of consumption, the lowest in thirty-four years, and well below what most agencies consider advisable. The last time reserves were this low, grain prices doubled.

The shortfall was partly because the Chinese and Indians wanted so much grain to feed animals for milk and meat. But the amount of grain being used to produce ethanol for cars was also exploding. A quarter of the 2007 American corn harvest was expected to go to ethanol. The ethanol revolution, a revolution on a par with the livestock revolution, was already underway, according to Dan.

President Bush, in a speech in 2005 at a Virginia biodiesel refinery, had encouraged America to produce biofuels. 'By developing biodiesel, you're making this country less dependent on foreign sources of oil . . . our dependence on foreign oil is like a foreign tax on the American dream.' Investors in the US had been piling into building ethanol distilleries, reacting to high oil prices, responding to big subsidies announced by Bush, and to the fact that they could get twice the price for ethanol as the cost of production. Once the new distilleries were on stream by 2008, demand for grain would go even higher, just as

China would be increasing corn imports for its animals and its growing population. 'They used to have two years' supply in hand, but not any more, they got out of storage. It's the same picture with soy, though the picture is not quite as dramatic because Brazil and Argentina have been able to produce near record amounts, having cleared virgin territory to plant more,' Dan persevered over the noise.

The soaring prices hadn't changed what farmers were making much; the rise on the markets just meant the price at which subsidies kick in had been passed for those producing grain, so their money was coming from the market rather than the government. For those buying corn to feed to animals the rises were crippling. The US government subsidy for ethanol was now going to the blenders, not the farmers. Here were the usual suspects, capturing the value of the market. Cargill and ADM are two of the largest ethanol producers. Global edible oil stocks were nearly at a record low too. Dan had already absorbed what our car-ful of campaigners on the way to Lampeter discussed a year later. 'We'll be quickly into a food versus fuel debate, a food fight between the livestock producer and the ethanol industry. There'll be a shortage of vegetable seed oil in eighteen months; we'll need expanded acreage in Brazil and Eastern Europe and the Black Sea . . .'

Even if the stimulus of steep price rises led farmers to plant more, Dan was sure the speed of this change meant there wasn't going to be enough. 'Someone will still end up being squeezed.' The price of food would go up, and although rich Americans and Europeans might be able to weather that, what about the rest of the world?

As I walked out past the traders' favourite McDonald's coffee stop, the exuberant optimism Rob later identified briefly came over me. Could this mean the end of the fast food burger? All those junk food uses of corn – the high fructose corn syrup, the water absorbing dextrins, the constipating modified starches – all those applications had arisen out of American surplus.

Perhaps real ingredients would become worth using again. Perhaps the obesity crisis would be solved in one abrupt stroke.

But it wouldn't be like that of course. Poor countries would not be able to afford the grain we and our cars and our high margin-to-cost way of eating would demand. We would be in competition for that grain with them and the poorest, who just wanted to eat it straight to survive, would lose out.

On the Friday afternoon before Christmas that year, the Department for Environment, Food and Rural Affairs slipped out a report on food security and the UK. Food security is the jargon for whether a country or household can feed itself. There was some concern, the report said, because the UK's self-sufficiency in food had been in noticeable decline in the last decade. In other words we now grow far less of the food we need than we used to. Climate change, international energy concerns, geopolitical tensions and international terrorism meant a growing sense of the potential for disruption to domestic food supplies . . . but, the authors concluded, market mechanisms are very efficient at bringing supply in line with demand. The UK's best policy was international trade, and pursuing growth in areas in which it has comparative advantage, rather than growing more or pretending it could ever be self-sufficient in food – so long, that is, as it had energy security. That seemed a rather large caveat to such a complacent conclusion.

The Ministry of Defence does its own thinking ahead. The Development Concepts and Doctrine Centre is a directorate within it which looks at strategic trends over the next thirty years. Its interpretation of trends was rather less than reassuring.

'During the next thirty years every aspect of human life will change at an unprecedented rate. Three areas of change will touch the lives of everyone on the planet: climate change, globalization and global inequality. Climate change [means] land for habitation will be reduced and patterns of agriculture and fertility will change . . . There will be increasing demand for natural resources, particularly food, water and fossil fuels. Growing competition for diminishing oil will lead to significant rises in energy prices ... By 2037 two thirds of the world population will live in areas of water stress. Environmental degradation and intensification of agriculture and pace of urbanization may reduce fertility and access to arable land. Food and water insecurity will drive mass migrations in the worst areas but will also be possible in more affluent regions because of distribution problems, specialized agriculture and aggressive food pricing ... Some regions will be unable to grow current food staples. A succession of poor harvests may cause a major price spike, resulting in significant economic and political turbulence as well as humanitarian crises of significant proportion and frequency.'

Reading all this, it would seem prudent, to say the least, to make sure that Britain's farmers, particularly those who work the land sustainably, survive. Sadly, the current structure of the food system, while taking good care of a handful of powerful food traders, processors and supermarkets, is forcing farmers down a path that is ever less sustainable. Squeezed between the vagaries of the commodity markets and the power of oligopolies, British farmers are being driven off the land.

3. Milk

Milk has a peculiar hold on the British psyche. A pint of the pure fresh white stuff is what we have been programmed to think our children must have if they are to grow up with strong bones and teeth. It is in fact one of a handful of foods considered so essential that they make it into strategic thinking exercises. When the country ran short of petrol during the fuel strike, milk was one of the things we panic-bought. Now when government researchers look at the security of British food they usually check the resilience of milk supply.

If we imagine how that milk is made, most of us think of cows grazing on green and pleasant pastures, chewing the cud to make food out of the grass we cannot eat ourselves. They are part of our mental picture of the British landscape. We tend not to think of milk production as part of the recent global livestock revolution, that seismic shift in agriculture that has grown out of transnational grain trading, even though large-scale consumption of milk among adults is relatively new, growing from the late nineteenth century in Britain alongside new technologies such as refrigeration and pasteurization. Nor do we think of milk as a product of today's global commodity markets and its speculative pressures, of retailer oligopoly and distorting subsidies.

Yet that is what it has become, and as a result British dairy farming is in crisis. There were 35,000 dairy farmers in the UK ten years ago, now that number has almost halved. An average of three dairy farmers pack up each day. The exodus from the industry is still accelerating. A further 3,000 dairy farmers told the Milk Development Council in a survey in spring 2007 that they planned to leave in the next two years.

The power structures that have emerged in the food system are driving the dairy farmers who cling on away from environmentally sustainable outdoor grazing. Instead they are moving towards intensive feeding of cows kept indoors for longer and longer periods. European subsidies started the push towards intensification and overproduction. Now imported grains and concentrated feeds have increasingly taken the place of grass and pasture, as dairymen desperately try to extract ever higher yields from their cows to stay in business. Meanwhile the money to be made from dairy products has been captured by transnational food manufacturers making highly processed goods and by supermarkets. Both the cows and we are being moved up the food chain, while the traditional farmers are pushed out of it all together.

Kemble Farms, a large dairy farming business in the Cotswolds, is one of the most efficient milk operations in the country, yet even it was struggling to make money when I visited in 2007. I knew small farmers were already suffering to the point of despair, with suicide rates rising, but now it seemed even big farm companies that had done everything the policy makers said they should to modernize and compete in a global market couldn't make the economics work. I couldn't make sense of it, and hoped Kemble's large landowners might explain.

I was met at the station, which is now a London long-distance commuter stop, by David Ball, the farm manager who had joined the estate straight from agricultural college thirty years before. As he drove me to the farm, he reminisced about the old days – 'fifteen to twenty of us employed on the land back then, and we're down from a dozen people to three just in the last fifteen years'.

The estate, 2,300 acres of rich agricultural land near the source of the Thames, is owned by the Phillips family, with the third and fourth generation through the female line now farming here. The family also farm a further 1,000 acres taken on under contract from two neighbours. Both of those neighbouring families had themselves been farming for generations but their holdings of 700 and 300 acres had proved too small in the last five years to remain viable. They had been forced to give up.

In the Kemble farm office built of honey-coloured Cotswold stone, we looked back through leather-bound ledgers containing several decades of family history and recording the farm sales: as late as the 1940s the produce was being counted in fifteen lambs here, a few dozen eggs there.

Today Kemble's cows, Holstein Friesians bred for productivity, give so much milk they are emptied three times a day. Yields are typically 9,000 litres per cow per year, not the highest known since some farms have now broken the 10,000 litre barrier, but already way above average and spectacular compared with just a decade or so ago when average yields were nearer 5,000 litres per cow; thirty years earlier average yields were 3,500 per cow. Kemble is such a model of efficiency in fact that the Chinese Minister of Agriculture from Hunan province came here to learn how this kind of modern dairy business could be imported to meet exploding demand for milk products in his country.

The herd size, usually around 700 cows, puts Kemble Farms into the super-efficient league too. The average number of cows on a dairy farm in the UK now is 100, in 1994 it was seventy-nine; immediately post-war a dozen or so cows on a mixed farm was not unusual.

The family business had invested £2 million in an aircraft-hangar-sized shed, where the cows can be kept indoors for nearly half of the year and fed the concentrated feed they need to maintain such levels of production, to achieve economies of scale and cut labour costs. It was still not enough for today's milk markets.

Decades of intervention from Brussels had certainly delivered a weight of bureaucracy if nothing else. Each cow here now had a passport, and David had not only to register the number of cows, but log each field individually and submit a list of what was growing in it to DEFRA for subsidy payments and quotas. 'It all goes into a huge computer with French software that doesn't work, so that they can monitor payments. What it's meant for us is that ten to fifteen years ago I was a farmer, a skilled practical farmer, now I'm a record keeper. Every time I go out to a field to make a decision I have to stop and think, hang on, am I contravening any one of a dozen rules?' David explained, as we hosed down our boots. With the repeated outbreaks of foot and mouth that have accompanied our modern way of keeping and moving animals around, biosecurity lapses can cost dear, and any newcomer represents a potential hazard. I wanted to see their milking in their state-of-the-art milking parlour, so we climbed in to his smart pick-up truck and drove to it – efficiencies of scale meant it would take too long to walk.

When I arrived, the huge shed was eerily calm, as if operated by some unseen guiding hand. Cow 777 was just passing from the herd in the holding yard, nudged by an automated gate into the hi-tech rapid-exit batch milking system. As she did so, a signal from the transponder clipped to her foreleg was read by the estate's computer. It identified her and logged her in while she filed unquestioningly down the approach lane to the milking machines. By entering the empty berth at the end of the line, she opened the bar for the cow behind her and so the herring-bone rows of stalls filled up without the need for human intervention. In the pit below, just three Eastern European workers moved quietly up the lines, attaching milking teats to thirty-six sets of udders at a time. As the machine's vacuum began to suck, 777's milked flowed down the pipes and through an underground meter that measured and recorded her output, while information from the pedometer also attached to her foreleg was analysed by the latest software to calculate how far she had moved inside the adjoining cowshed since her last milking. When she comes into season she walks more than usual and the computer will mark her down for her next artificial insemination. If she has not walked as much as usual she might have an udder infection or the lameness to which cows bred for intensive dairy production are prone, and the computer would filter her out for possible antibiotic treatment. As 777's udders emptied and the milk stopped pumping, sensors in the machine detected the interruption to the flow and water was forced automatically back up the pipes to clean both cow and equipment. Then the teats popped off by themselves, leaving 777 to exit back down the funnel area into the shed next door.

David explained why they had rationalized and intensified, as I surveyed the hangar, with its rows and rows of cows stretching as far as I could see. 'We used to have three separate sheds and 500 cows. But in 1999 we moved them all into one unit. We could see that with deregulation of the milk market and opening up in Europe, the price of milk per litre was going to come down and we'd become unprofitable. The fact that people in the UK like to drink fresh milk unlike on the Continent and that liquid milk is too expensive to cart around from country to country gave us confidence, we knew there'd continue to be local demand. So we thought so long as we were efficient we should be able to make a profit. We were right, the price did drop, from 25p per litre to about 18p, and we are in no position to influence it.'

Kemble Farms' costs, for fuel, fertilizers, water and animal feed, had gone up 8 per cent in the previous twelve months. The value of the cows themselves had gone up as the Chinese and Russians had been buying up stock to build their national herds. But the price Kemble was paid for its milk by Dairy Crest, the company that processed and packed it for Sainsbury's, had fallen by 8 per cent over the same period.

'Fuel costs have increased 92 per cent in the last three years, chilling milk is energy intensive. The cost of our deliveries has gone up. At least we produce our own forage and some of our concentrated feed is our own wheat, but some is also made from the by-products of human food production. We take the high-protein meal from soya once the oil has been extracted, and the by-products from the sugar industry for high-energy carbohydrate. Feed has gone up 17 per cent in the last year alone. Fertilizer uses huge amounts of gas for its production – that's up 30 per cent in three years. But the price for our milk has gone down over the last year by 1.3p a litre. If you go back a year we were profitable, despite huge investment, thanks to economies of scale and improved efficiency but now we are selling milk below the cost of production.'

Like much of the rest of the British dairy industry, despite its industrial scale and despite being clearly so well run, Kemble found itself looking at an economic black hole. 'We either pack up or intensify further,' David said ruefully. 'We've already increased our output 15 per cent in the last year. We could keep more cows and get a further 25 per cent. We're aiming for 10,000 litres per cow in the next few months.'

But all this clearly felt wrong; it was going against the grain for someone like David. Kemble Farms has high standards of animal welfare and is audited by the RSPCA Freedom Foods. At the moment the cows here manage an average of four lactations before they have to be culled. In many intensive factory farming systems, they only manage two or three before becoming so worn out they are unproductive. 'We would be driving everything, the animals, the plant, to the maximum. In a factory we are used to the idea of 24/7, but with animals and land there are other considerations. We resist treating cows like machines. From the consumer point of view dairy means cows in nice pasture but we're being driven away from that, to intensify production from these animals until we follow the pig and poultry world. It may be nice and cheap and supermarkets say that's what people want, but do they?'

★

The price we pay for fresh milk in the shops has risen roughly 20 per cent since 2002, going up by 9p. The supermarkets' margin on fresh milk has increased more than five-fold in the last decade.

During that decade the share of the price we pay in the shops for milk that went to the processors, the companies that collect, pasteurize and bottle milk, stayed about the same, but the farmers' share kept going down. It actually fell by more than 6p a litre.

'Look,' Colin Rank, one of the family that owns Kemble Farms, said to me as he showed me a graph mapping how the split between the different parts of the dairy chain had changed. 'You can see the division of the spoils: in the 1990s the retail margins were very small. You can see the point at which the supermarkets flex their muscle and their share of the price goes up. The price to processors goes down a little shortly after, and it's followed by a fall in the price to the farmer. There's no risk for the supermarket, they take the cash in the morning from the customer and only have to pay out ten days later. That's what a controlled market looks like.'

Just three processors now dominate supplies of fresh milk to the big supermarkets, which in turn account for nearly two thirds of sales to the public. Arla has an estimated 43 per cent of the market. Formed from a merger of Danish and Swedish milk cooperatives that dominated sales in those countries, it took over Express Dairies in the UK in 2003 to become Britain's largest supplier of milk and dairy products. Robert Wiseman has 35 per cent and Dairy Crest 22 per cent of the fresh milk market.

The supermarkets, Tesco, Asda, Sainsbury's, Waitrose and M&S, have each reduced the number of suppliers they use to just one or two companies, all of them drawing almost entirely from these three dominant processors. A series of takeovers and mergers in the last couple of years will see the processing sector become even more concentrated as it seeks to stand up to retail power. The pattern seen in breakfast cereals is repeated in the dairy sector and indeed in almost every other food processing and manufacturing sector.

Such concentration of market power carries its dangers, as Adam Smith, the eighteenth-century political economist and hero to today's free marketeers, warned as long ago as 1776. 'People of the same trade seldom meet together, even for merriment and diversion, but the conversation ends in a conspiracy against the public, or in some contrivance to raise prices,' he wrote in *The Wealth of Nations*.

In theory, this super-efficient large-scale system of food production gives us competitively priced goods, but the British authorities decided recently that the dairy industry had been guilty of just the sort of conspiracy Adam Smith warned that concentrated markets tended towards. The Office of Fair Trading accused the major dairy groups and supermarkets of colluding to fix the price of milk, butter and cheese between 2002 and 2003. It agreed fines with them of £116 million at the end of 2007 following provisional findings from a three-year investigation. Sainsbury's, Asda, Safeway, Dairy Crest and Robert Wiseman all admitted to anti-competitive practices and to colluding to raise the price of milk in the shops. Arla escaped fines having been granted immunity in return for providing information to the inquiry. Tesco denied the OFT's allegations however and decided to fight the rulings. Morrisons subsequently initiated legal action against the OFT for libel. The cases were continuing.

The supermarkets and processors said in their defence that they had put prices to shoppers up because they wanted to help farmers by giving them a fairer price at a time when they were under severe pressure after the foot and mouth outbreak, but the farmers' unions said farmers had seen little long-term benefit.

In dealing with this concentrated buying power, the farmers have been left with almost no leverage. The Milk Marketing

Boards, first set up in 1933 to make sure all farmers, small and large, received a decent price for their milk, used to hold a monopoly on the collection and selling of farmers' milk. Dairy Crest had originally been formed as the processing arm of the MMB. But in 1994 the MMB was broken up and the market deregulated as part of the sweep, driven by world trade talks, to make agricultural markets freer and in theory more responsive to consumer demand. The selling monopoly at farm level was broken but buying monopolies among supermarkets and processors in milk were left to emerge untroubled by the competition regulators. The family at Kemble Farms had no particular nostalgia for the Milk Marketing Board monopoly, nor any problem with free markets, it's just they knew they weren't in one.

'The processors have regional monopolies,' Rank explained. 'We used to have an arrangement with a local dairy – our volumes matched his requirements. He supplied small local outlets and hotels. The milk from our farm would be found in the Kemble shop. It was low on food miles and because it was a short supply chain there was more money in it for us and for him. Then Dairy Crest bought him out and closed him down. Processors have been taking out operators like that around the country. We were left with no choice about where we sold our milk. Wiseman don't source milk from this area. Arla don't have a plant near here either. We had a meeting with Dairy Crest when they took on our contract and discussed our price. But within a month they had dropped it by 1p. We couldn't do anything. When the processor sits down with the supermarket to do a deal he doesn't think, 'this is going to hurt my margins'. He thinks, 'whatever price I end up agreeing with the supermarket to win the contract, I'll be all right because I can tell the producer what that price will be.'

The result has been a huge rise in supermarket profits from fresh milk but the decimation of British dairy farming. This is so far from being what consumers want that even the supermarkets decided in 2007 that the squeeze on such a key group of producers was damaging their image. The Women's Institute, a radical and redoubtable organization from its inception, had waged a highly successful campaign to save dairy farmers. Thousands of WI members could see the damage to the social fabric in rural areas that the crisis was causing. Although not generally known for philanthropic largesse, the supermarkets agreed to increase the price they paid for milk so that farmers could get a little more. Tesco, which sells about a quarter of all the country's fresh milk, promised that it would create a group of 850 Tesco dairy farmers who would be given a slightly higher price. It followed moves by other supermarkets to support farmers who become dedicated suppliers by paying them a premium which takes into account their rising costs. Like being green, being nice enough to farmers for them to survive had suddenly acquired a competitive edge. The move would, however, mean farmers becoming even more dependent on retailers to whom they would be contracted.

With the dominant player making a move, the processors could follow. Kemble Farms learned shortly after my visit that it too would get a rise of 1p per litre. That would only move it from loss to break even on milk, David said. It would still leave them receiving less for their milk than they did two years before. The irony for Colin Rank was that his cows were drinking water from a Cotswold spring that he could bottle and sell for 80p a litre, several times the price he could get for his milk. 'We're giving it to cows and devaluing it by turning it into milk. Like all dairy farmers we could pack up tomorrow and do something better with our capital but we do it because we have an emotional investment in the land and the animals. And we know there's a market for our products if only the market worked.'

Few thought the belated gesture from supermarkets would save the dairy industry in its current structure. 'It's very difficult to see how a herd of less than 100 cows can remain competitive,' the government's head of sustainable farming Sir Don Curry told me.

Just what that prediction would mean struck me on a bright spring day not long after as I walked Hergest Ridge with my children. As we climbed up to it, the sky larks ascending before us, we drank in the sweeping views of high rolling hills all around, across from Herefordshire's highest point over to the sharp outline of Hay bluff, and down to Radnorshire in Wales. Lines of shadowy trees not quite in bloom marked the contours. The white blossom of blackthorn ran along the hedges and fields of green brightened to gold where the sunlight struck. The bleating of spring lambs searching for their ewes filled the air and down below cows turned out to pasture grazed the fresh grass. Dotted in the folds of the landscape were the clusters of barns and yards that made up dozens of small farms.

This corner of England has been my green lung for years. A place to snatch visits to friends away from the smoke of London, the nearest bit of country to the metropolis that still feels truly rural now that most of southern England has been dissected by motorways and ring roads. It is a landscape both wild and shaped by its farming, its patterns of livestock holding evolved over time to make best use of the land, some of it marginal. If predictions about the effect of climate change on food security come true these will be just the sort of farms we need – producers who make use of Britain's grazing land with low environmental impact.

I had come hoping to see Richard Joyce, a dairy farmer who campaigns to save such small farms in his area. But the first day I rang, he and his wife Cynthia couldn't even think how they could fit me in. The fall in the price of milk had made times hard and to save costs they had cut down on hired labour and taken on more of the work themselves. It was a day when they would be without help with their Jersey herd, which would mean getting up with the alarm at 5.30 a.m. and work-ing through with only a couple of short breaks to the end of milking at 8.45 p.m. Then they'd be in for tea and out again until 11 p.m., bedding down the cows on to straw or getting them out in the field again. They wouldn't have fifteen minutes to call their own.

When I did catch up with him later in the week, Richard looked worn down with tiredness. A sixty-three-year-old Herefordshire farmer's son, he bought his own farm in the Welsh borders forty-five years ago. It was just thirty-two acres then and it had been his life's work to build it up to the seventy acres the family now farm with a herd of eighty pedigree Jersey cows and 300 or so sheep that graze just below Offa's Dyke. We walked up the track from his down-at-heel farmhouse towards the Dyke, the banks full of celandine and daffodils, a rare stand of larches below just coming into leaf, while he tried to articulate the changes he'd seen, but he frequently left sentences hanging, as though the thoughts were too depressing to finish. 'I feel as though we're back to the 1930s, we've come a complete cycle with farmers in desperate straits. By golly, a tremendous number have gone from round here . . .

'We have fifty-three different species of bird on these seventy acres. We leave the fields up here as flower meadow. You can see how mixed the sward is – we let it up for mowing most years, and the butterflies that come out of it, well I can hardly bear to cut it . . . But this is a very run down farm you're looking at, I'm afraid; we haven't done these gates yet, you struggle to get to the maintenance and . . .' As with many other small dairy farmers, investment in repairs or new equipment has had to wait.

Thanks to the madness of EU subsidy regimes that first encouraged overproduction, and then tried to restrict it with the use of quotas, Richard had debts to the bank. From 1984 dairy farmers in the EU could only produce milk if they had a quota, and that quota set limits on their production. A secondary market in buying and selling quotas quickly developed, with speculators who had nothing to do with farming trading in them. Manchester United Football Club even owned milk quota at one point. If you wanted to expand your dairy herd, you had to buy extra quota, often at considerable expense. Now the quota system is being reformed under changes once more designed to make farming more responsive to the market. Subsidy payments to farmers have also been changed recently, so that they no longer depend on how much a farmer produces but on how many acres he or she farms and are linked to new targets such as environmental stewardship. Everyone agrees reform is necessary, but the changes will be particularly tough for small farmers. 'Milk quota went up in price so steeply. Now it's almost worthless. They are talking about getting rid of it, but it was bought with such pain, such pain,' Richard explained.

'My subsidy payments will be cut by two thirds because the new single farm payments are based on your hectarage not what you produce — the big landowning institutions and farmers will be raking in the money and the small farmers will lose out terribly.'

Richard receives a premium for his milk since his Jerseys produce the highest quality, but even so he said he was just getting the cost of production for it. 'But that's only if you don't include paying ourselves.'

In a typical year, Richard calculated, he writes more than 100 cheques for around £1,000 a piece to different local firms. A web of small family farms like his have supported a whole rural economy. We reached an ancient dew pond with crystal clear waters at the top of the farm hill. From here we could see right across the Wye Valley. Richard counted off the neighbours one by one. 'One up there, disappeared and split up, the farm buildings all converted to posh cottages; another over that way he's gone into selling machinery because he couldn't make a go of it any more. In Almeley there'd be fifteen to twenty of them dairying a few years ago, now at most two are in milk.' We fell silent for a while, Richard's thoughts apparently lost to the distance. 'I don't know, it seems desperately sad to me,' he said finally.

We turned back down to the brook and dingle where wild anemones grow, and on to see the cows come in for milking. Charlie, a local man who works part-time, was forking hay into troughs for the pedigree animals, talking to his beauties. Some of them are in their tenth lactation; milked less intensively than supposedly more efficient farms, the animals tend to remain productive for far longer. 'They've all got names,' Richard told me. 'That one's Confetti, she was born on a family wedding day. That one there, Patience, well, who knows why I ever called her Patience, she's the most impatient cow you've ever seen, always rattling the door in the parlour.' He sighed and said anxiously he didn't want to sound like a moaning farmer.

'We're so fortunate having our feet on the soil here. You are dealing with life itself. It's such a stabilizing environment, for children and for society all around. In a small town people have a connection to the land and a chance to get out and enjoy it. What pulls us down is the encroaching years. My wife and I are working over ninety hours a week; it's just not sustainable for even a young person.

'But you know, someone going out of dairy isn't just a businessman saying I'm selling up now. It's the farm you or your father or possibly your grandfather had roots in. It's endless rows between spouses over the breakfast table. It's schools closing in the countryside because the children aren't there anymore. There's more than they ever dream invested in farms like this.'

The crisis was not unanticipated. Sir Don Curry told me it was clear to him that when the Milk Marketing Board was broken up many British farmers would be left unable to compete. Their power was being fragmented just at the point the global milk market was consolidating. The processors have been battling to win market share and contracts with super-markets so they have been undercutting each other, knowing they can pass on the low price to the farmers who have nowhere else to go.

It's not just the supermarkets though. Only half of the milk British farmers produce is sold as fresh milk. The other half goes into manufacturing, which can use milk of lower standard, or imported dried powder or butter fat. Many types of yoghurt for example are made not from fresh milk but from recon-stituted milk powder. So our farmers have to compete on the global commodity markets, where prices have been weak, (although again the use of grain for ethanol has affected feed prices and is changing the picture). On the milk commodity markets a few transnational giants exert huge buying power. These commodity prices have set the base price for fresh British milk on the farm.

One of the main reasons commodity prices have been so low until recently is that rich countries have used subsidies to depress the price of their exports, just as with corn and rice in the US (see Chapter 1: Cereals). Across all OECD (Organization for Economic Co-operation and Development) countries in the year 2000, subsidies accounted for the equiva-lent of nearly half of the value of milk. In the EU, export refunds for milk and milk products, worth about €1.4 billion in 2004, were paid to processors and exporters rather than dairy farmers. The pattern in European dairy production mirrors that of the US with its corn surplus and its export dependency, although the motivation for creating surplus in Europe was originally quite different.

The Second World War and its terrible privations made European governments determined to make sure that we never faced such shortages again. Most were already supporting their dairy farmers with various interventions and had taken over control of production during the fighting. After the war, governments wanted farmers to maximize home-grown supplies and paid them subsidies to increase production. They offered them maintained prices, and protected them with tariffs and restrictions on imports. With rationing still a recent memory, The European Commission introduced its agricultural subsidies with the Common Agricultural Policy a couple of years after the Treaty of Rome was signed in 1957. The aim was to make food plentiful and affordable, make sure farmers were paid, and increase productivity while providing some insulation from the volatility of speculative markets. But by the 1980s despite several changes to the system, this subsidized production was generating huge surpluses and enormous waste, and a public outcry as milk lakes and butter mountains built up. Much of the surplus was dumped at prices below the cost of production on world markets, so quotas aimed at cutting production were brought in.

Just as in America, agricultural subsidies have done little in the long term to save small farmers. But there is plenty of evidence that they have provided corporate welfare and contributed to the emergence of dominant dairy giants.

The global market in dairy processing for manufacturing, as with fresh milk sales, has become highly concentrated as transnational companies have consolidated their power in the last decade. The turnover of the top twenty global dairy corporations increased by 60 per cent between 1992 and 2000.

Nestlé is the largest in the market by far, with a dairy turnover of €14.3 billion in 2006. Two French giants Danone and Lactalis, and US-based Dean Foods and Dairy Farmers of America, account for another €29 billion between them. Also in the top ten are Kraft Foods, Unilever, Arla, and the huge New Zealand and Dutch dairy cooperatives Fonterra and Friesland Foods. New Zealand's cooperative Fonterra is unusual in not receiving subsidies and managing to control about 30 per cent of global dairy exports.

Since subsidies were clearly doing so little to save our

farmers, I set out a couple of years ago to analyse who exactly was getting the money from the Common Agricultural Policy. Until 2004 the names of those receiving CAP payments had been, outrageously, kept secret. The *Guardian* and colleagues there, Rob Evans and David Hencke, had been part of a campaign led by Jack Thurston of the Foreign Policy Centre to force disclosure under new Freedom of Information legislation. Since it was our taxpayers' money we thought we had a right to know and expected to find rich landowners, barley barons and the aristocracy topping the list of those getting handouts. Just as campaigners had found in the US, it proved as painful a process as drawing teeth. Eventually the government's Rural Payments Agency which administers the subsidy payments in the UK released a list of top recipients but declined to say why the companies on it qualified for support, arguing that the information was commercially confidential. Together with a researcher I started ploughing through the list, trying to work out why for myself. At the same time other groups of journalists and campaigners in Europe were using FoI legislation to establish where payments were going in their countries.

The CAP budget in 2004 was €43.6 billion, nearly half the total EU budget. While the bulk of it was indeed made up of direct aid divided between millions of farmers (€30 billion), most of that money went to a very small percentage of the largest farmers, and nearly €14 billion went on other CAP schemes such as export refunds to large companies and BSE payments to large-scale renderers and abattoirs who had been contracted to clear up the consequences of intensive production and its recurring outbreaks of disease.

The largest individual payments in the UK were going to transnational food companies and not farmers. Millions of pounds were being paid to the manufacturers of bulk dairy fats and sugars to produce the sort of processed foods that health experts were telling us to cut down on.

The largest recipients in the UK included companies such as

Tate & Lyle, Nestlé, Cadbury, Kraft and exporters of processed dairy products. The top payment in the UK for 2003/4 was made to Tate & Lyle and its subsidiaries, which took more than £227 million over two years from CAP. Nestlé received £11.3 million in UK payments in 2003/4 but that was only a fraction of its total handout, which had also been received in other countries such as Holland and Belgium.

Meadow Foods received the second largest individual UK payment that year, £25.9 million. It is a leading manufacturer of dairy ingredients for food manufacture in the UK, Europe and the US, supplying more than 100,000 tonnes of ingredients a year from concentrated fat for ice cream, spreads, and chocolate making to milk proteins for coffee whiteners, low fat spreads, sausages and yoghurts, and whey proteins for sports drinks, processed meats, soups and confectionery, as well as label glue and leather finishes.

Philpott Dairy products, the export arm of Dairy Crest Ingredients, received £14.8 million. It supplies bulk fats, cheeses, dairy powder and concentrates to processed food manufacturers. Fayrefield Foods Ireland received £14.4 million and Dale Farm Ingredients £11.3 million from the RPA. They too both supply bulk dairy products to manufacturing.

New information coming out from campaigns in Holland, Denmark and Belgium showed the same pattern. The largest individual payments were being made to transnationals and manufacturers of bulk ingredients for processed foods or drinks. The largest recipients of Danish CAP payments included Arla, the bulk milk processor; Danisco, one of the world's largest producers of food ingredients for manufacturing and of sugar – its products include probiotic bacteria cultures for dairy products, emulsifiers, and enzymes for pork and poultry feed to get 'more meat from wheat'; Danish Crown, the giant processed meats company; and Novozymes, which makes enzymes for the food industry. In Holland the largest payment went to Friesland, the dairy processor. Other huge cheques were written for Mars and Nestlé, brewers Heineken and Grolsch, tobacco giant Philip Morris, and, bizarrely, Shell and KLM among others. KLM, I was told, received its payment for restructuring the countryside – in this case by pouring Tarmac over it to make a new airport runway. The French and the Germans, who have a habit of being most intransigent on CAP reform, refused to release information about where their share of subsidy money had gone. Jack Thurston, who was a former special adviser to the UK Ministry of Agriculture and fellow of the German Marshall Fund of the United States, was not surprised that there had been such resistance to publishing the figures in France. Most of it, he was certain, would be going to agribusiness there too and he had been told by officials that it would not be conducive to public order if French farmers and consumers found out.

Most of the transnational companies were getting the CAP money as export refunds. The rationale was that CAP maintained artificially high prices to EU farmers through tariffs and production quotas. So when transnationals exported dairy fats or sugars they were entitled to refunds on the difference between the EU price and the lower world market price. It turned out you could even get an export refund for flying the little cartons of milk served in individual portions on airplanes up into international airspace. The companies say that the money they received has been passed back to farmers in the form of higher prices, including some in Africa, the Caribbean and the Pacific who have had preferential access to the EU markets. This would be news to the struggling dairy farmers in the UK I had spoken to.

Campaign groups such as Oxfam instead argue that the CAP has given a handful of oligopoly transnationals fixed prices and guaranteed markets while encouraging excess production. Surpluses have been dumped on international markets at subsidized rates and have thus kept world prices artificially low, further benefiting the transnationals at the expense of the farmers. Describing the now reformed EU sugar regime, an Oxfam report said: 'Stripped to its essentials, the regime is a system of corporate welfare . . . [it] sanctions what is effectively a cartel.' The same applies in the dairy sector, and with grains and cereals.

Just who did best out of these farm subsidies seemed to be no surprise to anyone except the consumers who were actually paying for them. 'Yes, it's the processors that have benefited from CAP,' the National Farmers' Union's policy director Martin Hawarth told me. 'If you look at who receives the payments, it all comes down to manufacturing ingredients. These are the things that are in nearly all processed products around the world. Subsidies have provided them as cheap raw materials and the money's gone on the bottom line for manufacturers and processors, not farmers.'

Faced with such distorted global markets, farmers today can do little except intensify. They increase the size of their herds to spread fixed costs, and they increase yields by feeding their animals the lowest cost high energy, high protein diet they can buy, which is often made up of imported feed ingredients, increasingly supplied by the few large transnationals, such as US-based Cargill, ADM and their subsidiaries. The small farmers go out of business. This is a global phenomenon – you could hear the same sad story that I heard in Herefordshire from milk farmers in countries rich and poor alike, from the US to Brazil, from France to Pakistan, from Italy to China.

Much of dairy cow feed in the UK now depends on imported corn and soya derivatives, largely bought from the US and Argentina, where genetically modified crops are the norm, and from Brazil where GM crops are now being widely planted following their legalization in 2005. The British public has been clear in its opposition to GM crops, but that has not extended to an understanding of where the food for their cows comes from.

Hundreds of thousands of tonnes of corn gluten – that

by-product of the starch, sweetener and alcohol processing industries – was imported to the UK from the US for feed in 2005. Together with imported soya, it made up about a fifth of the animal feed used by British farmers.

Farmers could use clover-rich grass, mixed with cereals and legumes grown less intensively in this country, which would decrease nitrate pollution since these crops fix nitrogen in the soil, and help as climate change bites since they have deep roots which make them better in drought. But yields would go down and they can't afford it.

The drive for ever greater yields has even led to companies advertising 'zero grazing' for dairy herds. In this system the bother of cows going out is eliminated altogether. They can be kept indoors, consuming 'their maximum intake in the shortest possible time, so they spend less time and energy walking around and more time lying down ... this greatly improves yields and therefore profit!' as one website boasts.

None of this is much fun for the cow. High yielding dairy cows have to produce milk for ten months of the year and produce a calf each year to come into milk. A cow producing milk to suckle its own calf makes about ten litres of milk a day. Intensively fed cows can be expected to produce over seventy litres a day. They have to eat a huge amount to keep up the supply of milk. They are, as John Webster, professor at the University of Bristol's leading veterinary department explains, 'the apotheosis of the overworked mother'. They have been so overbred for high yields that their mammary glands' capacity to produce milk exceeds their ability to digest enough nutrients to keep up. If a high-yielding Holstein cow is fed concentrated feeds and silage from heavily fertilized grass her feelings 'may be defined as simultaneously hungry, tired, full up and feeling sick ... Cows need time to stand and stare, that is rest. Very high yielding cows have practically no spare time at all; they are operating at the limits of their physiology.'

Webster has done extensive practical work with the industry and is a leading authority on animal health and welfare. His research has shown that half of these intensively kept cows go lame in any one year, and 20 per cent in a herd are likely to be lame at any one time. They go lame partly because they have to stand on concrete for so long, partly because their udders are too heavy between their hind legs, and partly because the cubicles they are in make it hard to lie down. They are also predisposed to mastitis – a painful infection of the udder, which requires the frequent use of antibiotics – and to infertility. It is common to have to cull them after two or three lactations because their fitness just breaks down.

This dash for yields has created a further problem. To come into milk a dairy cow must produce a calf each year. The female ones can go into the herd, but half of the calves will be male. They used to be reared for beef. But a dairy cow that has been genetically selected for high yields of milk produces calves that are not much good for beef. They have a lousy bone to muscle ratio. In the past these low value male calves could be exported to the Continent to be fed up as white veal for slaughter at six months or less. That involved long stressful journeys and keeping the calves in crates, conditions that most people in this country found unacceptable. Mortality in veal rearing was typically around 20 per cent. In any case the trade was brought to an end by restrictions on the export of live animals following BSE, although it has recently resumed on a small scale. The result is that British male calves are now worthless and most are shot at birth. The intensive dairy industry has become a system that produces animals as waste.

The simple answer would be to use breeds of cow that are better suited to both milk and beef production. But dairy farmers would lose yield if they did, and they can't afford that.

Quite apart from these serious considerations about animal welfare, waste, and the state of the countryside, intensively produced milk appears to be nutritionally depleted. You are what you eat, perhaps not surprisingly, is turning out to apply as much to cows as to humans. David Thomas, a chiropractor and nutritionist who prescribes and sells mineral supplements, has trawled through government tables on the chemical composition of foods published in 1940 and again in 2002. Using the official bible of those tables, McCance and Widdowson's *The Composition of Foods*, he found that the iron content of milk had dropped by more than 60 per cent in the sixty years. Milk appears to have lost 2 per cent of its calcium and 21 per cent of its magnesium too. Most cheeses showed a similar fall in iron, magnesium and calcium levels.

The food and farming industry argues that the testing methods have changed, making it difficult to make such historic comparisons, and the government's Food Standards Agency agrees that differences over time could be due to changing analytical methods or other factors. But other experts point out that in fact minerals have been easy to detect and measure since the nineteenth century and such huge differences are hard to explain away. Thomas attributes the change to intensive farming and industrial production. Today's agriculture does not allow the soil to enrich itself but depends on chemical fertilizers that don't replace the wide variety of nutrients plants and animals need. Moreover cows are not grazing the land half the time but like us eating things they never used to eat. The diversity of the food chain has been shrunk. While Thomas's work has been questioned by the industry as the work of an amateur with a vested interest in selling pills, it's harder to dismiss other studies that have found a marked difference in levels of the omega-3 essential fatty acids in milk produced by different farming methods.

The largest of these, a three-year study by researchers at the Universities of Glasgow and Liverpool published in the *Journal of Dairy Science* in 2006, found that on average a pint of organic milk contained 68 per cent more omega-3 fatty acids than conventional milk. Omega-3 fatty acids are called essential because they cannot be produced in the body and must be eaten. Diets that depend on processed foods tend to be short of them. They have been linked to reduced risk of heart disease, and some forms of cancer, and are also vital to normal brain functioning.

In the study, omega-3 levels went up significantly in milk in the months when cows were able to eat outside, feeding on fresh grass. Clover, which is high in omega-3 fatty acids, was also found to make cow's milk that was higher in them. Organic farmers generally use more clover and grass forages than intensive dairy producers who depend on concentrates. Imported corn and soya are the fast food of cattle diets, and only produce fast-food-quality milk and meat.

The breed of cow and how hard she was milked made a difference too. The lowest levels of omega-3 were in milk from Holsteins and Holstein Friesians bred to be high yielding on conventional farms. Traditional breeds such as Jersey cows gave more omega-3.

The industry sees the answer to its prayers, not in going back to producing better quality raw milk less intensively, nor in working more sustainably in the face of climate change, nor in trying to make sure the profits are fairly shared, but in moving up the food chain, and in trying to break into those high margin-to-cost, highly processed foods.

At crisis conferences of the dairy world I have attended recently, the talk is of the need to 'add value', of adding that shareholder value in other words that is flavouring and packaging and marketing. They discuss 'dairy peptides for blood-pressure-lowering cheese applications' and 'probiotic yoghurt drink beverage marketing'. They see their salvation in going the way of the American cereal pioneers and dreaming up expensive new products we never even knew we needed.

A whole new category of highly processed foods has

emerged in the last five years, variously called 'techno foods', or 'nutraceuticals' to acknowledge the blurring of lines between hi-tech food production and the drug industry, or 'functional foods'. The latter phrase raises the uncomfortable question of whether the rest of our industrialized diets have in fact become dysfunctional, but is nevertheless the one preferred by the food industry. These functional foods are supposed to confer specific health benefits.

Nestlé, Unilever, Danone and Kraft have invested heavily in these so-called functional foods. The global market was worth $9.9 billion in 2003 and is predicted to keep growing by 16 per cent a year. The dairy industry is quite right in arguing this is one of the parts of the chain to be in rather than primary farm production if you want to make money. Nestlé's head of nutrition summed up the trend in 2003 telling *The Economist* that his company was 'moving from an agrifood business to an R&D-driven nutrition, health and wellness company'. We are back on *The Road to Wellville*.

The pioneer in functional dairy foods was Yakult, a yoghurt drink made by the Japanese company of the same name. It burst on the European market in the 1990s as a fermented milk drink with an added strain of healthy bacterium, Lactobacillus casei Shirota. The strain had been isolated by Yakult's Dr Minoru Shirota in the 1930s and marketed as good for the digestion. It was sold in pharmaceutical form from 1975.

Then it was launched in the UK in 1996 in heavily sweetened form in what look like little toy milk bottles. The utilitarian design of its packaging gave it an aura of healthy purpose. The miniaturization of its packaging was as attractive to children as doll's house furniture. Sales took off, helped considerably by £40 million-worth of marketing in the UK alone. French multinational Danone was quick to follow with Actimel, which now outsells Yakult. Danone subsequently formed a strategic alliance with Yakult, and now owns 20 per cent of its shares.

These yoghurt drinks describe themselves as 'probiotics'.

Who first coined the word which simply comes from the Greek 'for life' is not clear. In the 1950s veterinary reports talked of pig feed with probiotic-added bacteria to help the animals gain weight faster. Needless to say the notion that probiotics help you gain weight is not one that has been fixed upon in more recent marketing efforts. The current use of the word aims at something quite different and seems to have come into vogue in the 1990s.

The live cultures found in plain yoghurt have been said for years to boost beneficial gut microflora, particularly after illness. However, in industrial processing cheap yoghurt, often made from reconstituted skimmed milk, is pumped by high-speed machinery along miles of pipes, which tends to kill the live microorgansims in the culture. Today's probiotic foods claim to act by restoring the balance of microflora in the digestive tract with the addition of millions of specialized bacteria. Many of the dairy-based functional foods contain lactobacillus and bifidobacterium bacteria, which are naturally present in the gut and aid digestion. The theory is that eating extra good bacteria top them up and keep bad bacteria at bay.

A dinky bottle of Actimel that costs over 35p a pop, contains 100g of drink made, according to the ingredients list on a strawberry version bought in 2007, from small quantities of yoghurt, skimmed milk, liquid sugar, strawberry, dextrose (i.e. more sugar), stabilizer (in this case the thickening agent, modified tapioca starch), flavourings, sodium citrate, and cultures of the bacterium L. casei Imunitass®. But thanks to the L. casei Imunitass® bacteria, this little serving of drink 'helps to strengthen your natural defences' according to Danone's website. Danone's Activia meanwhile with its patented bifidus 'digestivum' bacteria is 'clinically proven to help improve digestive transit'. Eat your heart out, John Harvey Kellogg. The cod Latin of these patents suggests rigorous scientific classification but is not without the flexibility required of the modern market. Actimel's Imunitass is sold as Defensis in France where consumers' preoccupation with their health finds subtly different expression and because Danone does not have the rights to the name Imunitass in all countries. Danone told me in 2006 that its probiotics had been developed after over ten years of clinical research, and that it had conducted over twenty-five scientific studies on the Defensis bacteria.

Thanks to a detailed submission by Danone's advertising agency to the industry's advertising effectiveness awards in 2006, we have an inside view of just how the marketeers managed to manipulate us.

In 1999, that submission explains, Danone had set its sights on the UK market for yoghurt and 'Actimel was chosen as lead foot soldier', with the aim of getting us 'drinking Actimel every day'.

But persuading us we needed to have a daily dose of this sort of functional food was not plain sailing. Nestlé launched its own probiotic drink LC1 Go but withdrew it when it failed to take off despite huge marketing. Actimel spent millions on a TV advertising launch in Britain in 2001, but by 2002 it was clear that the British public was not convinced. 'Forty per cent of Actimel's advertising audience [held] a highly sceptical view as to its benefit ... Like competitors before us, we had over-estimated the UK market's desire for little drinks containing live cultures and failed to crack the communications code that would unlock widespread demand for good bacteria.'

Undeterred, the company and its ad agency set out to find a solution. Consumer research showed that if they could claim in TV advertising that Actimel's L. casei Imunitass worked 'to balance the body's intestinal flora thereby strengthening the body's natural defences' they could get people trying it. Unfortunately the ad industry's self-regulating body wasn't impressed either. 'The Broadcast Advertising Clearance Centre did not accept Danone's scientific evidence supporting its natural defences claim,' the submission admits. It was back to the drawing board, or to 'a strategic hothouse' in summer 2002, it goes on to explain. They were determined to find a 'strong emotive brand benefit' to justify their high price and get the mass market buying it as often as possible.

Yet more research showed how they could lead consumers down a certain thought process to get them to buy. They worked out that 'immune system' was the catch-all phrase to sum up the body's natural defences to disease. So the logic was as follows: Actimel contains friendly live bacteria called L.c. Imunitass therefore L.c. Imunitass is involved with the immune system; a strong immune system means feeling healthy. 'The feeling healthy hot button was pressed when represented as freedom from fatigue and resistance to catching coughs and cold . . . feeling good.'

Over the next two to three years Danone spent nearly £22 million advertising Actimel in the UK. The ads used subliminal clues such as bad weather and people with coughs and colds to infer its 'strengthen natural defences' and 'helps your immune system' messages and supercharged women running around after drinking Actimel for two weeks to imply that it gave you energy. Sales rose 426 per cent. The brand is now worth £111.5 million a year in the UK, four times what it was when they started. And, staggeringly, probiotic drinks are now regularly drunk in nearly 60 per cent of all British households.

Actimel sells at about £2.70 per kilogram. If it were packaged in boring one-litre cartons you'd be able to compare it to plain milk or other yoghurt drinks and would probably baulk at the price. But cleverly packaged in a daily dose bottle that conceals the premium being charged, it looks appealing. The profit margins on this low-cost high-price little yoghurt drink are, according to the agency, about 40 per cent. It reckons that Danone will have made over £36 million profit as a result; getting back £1.67 for every £1 it spent on advertising. The figures for the company are, as the submission says, 'fantastic'.

If consumers are happy to rush to contribute to this new Klondike, why should anyone worry? Well, one problem is that probiotic foods claiming to be good for you can be high in other unhealthy ingredients. When I first looked at their labels, Actimel's 14 per cent sugar was matched by Yakult's 18 per cent. The independent consumer watchdog *Which?* looked at a range of probiotic products in 2006 and found two thirds were high in sugar. These products were claiming to help digestive health but depended on the refined carbohydrates that feed bad gut flora and that have often created the problem in the first place. The best and cheapest way to encourage a range of beneficial bacteria in the gut flora is to eat complex carbohydrates high in fibre. (I asked Yakult why they used so much sugar, and was told that the bacteria were so sour, without sweetening the products would simply be 'unpalatable'.) Some probiotics are now lower in sugar. Actimel strawberry was down to 11.4 per cent sugars in 2007. Yakult was 17.2 per cent sugars, and light versions are now available, in which some of the sweetness comes instead from the artificial sweeteners aspartame and acesulfame K. Artificial sweeteners are however controversial additives (see Chapter 5: Sugar).

The other problem is that there is still no independent assessment by our regulators of whether probiotic products do what they claim. The independent *Drug and Therapeutics Bulletin* said when it reviewed the scientific literature in 2004 and 2005 that the evidence as to whether probiotics actually work was patchy in relation to the gut and unreliable in terms of improving general well-being or helping with allergies. The evidence was strongest for helping with diarrhoea caused by antibiotics or with flare-ups of inflammatory bowel disease. People suffering from these problems might find them useful, but of course what the food industry needs is for as many of us as possible to believe we need to eat them as often as possible, to take them as though they were a daily dose of medicine.

As the market skyrocketed, the UK government's regulator, the Food Standards Agency, belatedly thought it had better do something. It commissioned a technical report, published in 2005, to find out whether the bacteria probiotics were making claims for could actually survive digestion to reach the gut and, if they did, whether they could theoretically have an effect on gut flora. The brands tested are named in separate appendices so with some detective work it is possible to match the results on strains in the lab to the bacteria in the big brands and understand their discouraging findings.

In laboratory tests the FSA researchers found that large numbers of probiotic products did not even contain the bacteria they claimed on their labels. The major manufacturers' products, including Actimel and Yakult, did at least contain what they said. The bacteria in these withstood the first stages of digestion but didn't do so well further on. L.casei Imunitass – the Actimel bug – displayed 'poor survival' in simulated digestion in the lower intestine. The Yakult bug Shirota did better, surviving in measurable levels. But overall the additions of these probiotics did not affect the number of total bacteria in the gut and the supposedly healthy Lactobacillus bacteria, the good ones you are paying all that money to get into your digestive system where they are supposed to strengthen your defences, those bacteria remained 'subdominant' in laboratory conditions in a ten-day experimental period. The FSA said it had commissioned the research with a view to checking the probiotics were safe rather than whether they worked, and that since other foods eaten at the same time, and what they were digested with, would make a big difference, further research would be needed 'to achieve a comprehensive overview of the efficacy of probiotics in humans'. It has not however commissioned any. When I asked what advice it would give to consumers who wanted to know whether it was worth buying probiotic products, it simply said: 'The Food Standards Agency does not issue advice regarding the consumption of legally marketed food products such as probiotics. Manufacturers need to assure themselves of the safety of these products to comply with food law. The Agency is aware that there are a number of assertions made regarding the health benefits of probiotics by companies who market these products; however the Agency has not commissioned or evaluated any research in this area.' Nearly ten years after the market for these new foods was created, the regulators are only just catching up with them.

Proposals to prevent food companies selling products with health claims unless they have first proved them, and unless the products are healthy enough overall to merit carrying a health claim, that is are not too high in sugars, fat or salt, were approved by the European Parliament in 2007, despite the food industry lobbying hard to stop them. Member states have been asked to submit lists of health claims on food products to the European Food Safety Authority with dossiers of scientific evidence to be assessed. The UK FSA has submitted about 2,000 health claims from manufacturers. The Germans are believed to have put in over 4,000. Faced with such a barrage, it is perhaps no surprise that it will be 2010 before a list of claims that have been approved is finalized. And it will be 2022 before rules to prevent products high in sugars, salt or fat making health claims are fully enforced.

I asked the companies in 2006 how they could justify their claims. Yakult, which markets its products as 'self-defence for your gut' where the 'majority of your immune system is located', said it had its own independent research to support them, and the fact that its bacteria survived digestion. It pointed out that Yakult is categorized as 'a food for specified health use' by the Ministry of Health in Japan. 'To achieve this status foods must be rigorously and independently examined to verify that consumption of the product can have a beneficial effect,' it said. Danone, which sells its probiotics with the claim 'helps strengthen natural defences', said it too had done extensive research on the value of its probiotics and that various further studies were underway to show that its added bacteria survived. 'Many beneficial effects for probiotics·in general have either been demonstrated or investigated by the scientific community as a whole,' it said. The company told me that in November

2005 it had begun a four-year partnership with the Pasteur Institute, where 250 of the institute's scientists are developing the company's dairy products, researching more about the benefits of existing probiotics and identifying new ones. Danone also said that its research shows Actimel has a measurable effect and that when taken regularly on a daily basis, it can have positive benefits for healthy people, for example by helping to lessen the effects of minor ailments like coughs, colds and infections. Since then it has indeed added to its body of substantial research showing the efficacy of its probiotics. It conceded however that the 'results reported by individual Actimel users can be as individual as their gut flora profile and overall diet and other lifestyle factors'.

You can see why the dairy farmers would like a slice of this lucrative action. But this is not what we need to be healthy or for our food system to be sustainable. We do not need specialized hi-tech additives to put right what industrial processing destroyed in our diets in the first place. There is no silver bullet food ingredient that will make us feel healthy and well. What we need is a fairer distribution of the profits made from our purchases. We need our money to reward those growing and producing simple good foods, not those who deconstruct ingredients and then in a never-ending cycle of innovation resell them to us with vast quantities of packaging and marketing.

Some are predicting that at the current rate of attrition among British cow herds, we will have to import fresh milk in five years. It's not just sentiment to say that we need farmers like Richard Joyce in Herefordshire or David Ball in the Cotswolds to survive without having to intensify. If rapid climate change leads to food shortages, rising grain and animal feed prices, and clashes over resources, it may not be long before we wonder how we ever managed to squander such a valuable heritage as our dairy farmers and their cheap fresh milk only to replace it with an imported, invented, highly processed, marketeer's conjuring trick.

4. Pigs

Henry Cumberlidge is The Complete Pig Man. He comes to our local farmers' market on Sundays with a small selection of pork cuts from the keeper's cottage in Buckinghamshire where he lives at the bucolic address of Featherbed Lane, Holmer Green. His rare-breed Oxford Sandy and Black pigs are reared entirely outdoors in family groups in the woodland behind his cottage where they are fed without the use of GM soya feeds or fishmeal, or antibiotics, probiotics or any other growth promoters. (Ask a stock man what probiotics are for and they will tell you without hesitation that they are for speeding up fattening.) It takes twice as long to get them to slaughter weight as it does to fatten the pigs bred for intensive farming that retain more water in their flesh. When Henry's hogs are ready, they go to a local abattoir, where the difference between the two types of pig is obvious: the one hairy and magnificently substantial all over, the other built like a body-builder with disproportionately pumped up back legs, tiny ears, no tail, and no hair.

Henry butchers and processes the meat from his pigs on his smallholding himself. His aim is to use every last bit of these fine animals so that nothing goes to waste. His inspiration comes from decades-old recipe books found in charity shops. So as well as ham from the hind legs and bacon from the back and belly, he makes pâtés and terrines that use the offal and the shoulder, he breads pigs' trotters and boils brawn, using the heads to make stock. He raises hot water crust pork pies filled with the jelly. His bacon is made with a traditional curing mixture of sea salt, brown sugar and spices, and when I first bought from him it was without the saltpetre or potassium nitrates that the World Cancer Research Fund report on diet and cancer advises us so strongly to avoid because they are converted to carcinogenic nitrites during digestion. They are added in most industrially made pork products as preservatives but their real value is that they make cheap meat look pink. Jane Grigson, the culinary goddess of charcuterie, is firm: potassium nitrate 'has no value whatsoever as a preservative' since salt does the job anyway, but it does give meat that would otherwise be a murky greyish brown an 'attractive rosy appearance'; it should only be used in tiny quantities, if at all. With today's refrigeration and a rapid turnover, Henry finds nitrates are not necessary. You have to get to market early before he runs out if you want to be sure of buying Henry's bacon or pâté which are both delicious. Bacon made this way is indeed brown-ish rather than the fresh flesh colour that nitrates and saltpetre achieve, and not all his customers like the appearance, but after a while perky pink bacon seems as odd to the eye as tartrazine-yellow supposedly smoked haddock.

There is a very special quality to the fat of these pigs. The finest pig fat I've ever tasted was on an air-dried ham from Spain. The ham, sold by Spanish food specialists Brindisa, came from pigs that had only eaten acorns and what they could forage in woods. It was so meltingly soft it had a texture closer to olive oil that has crystallized in a fridge than to lard. The pigs' diet was so fine in fact that they were producing unsaturated instead of saturated fat. At about £1 a slice it was sadly not an experience I have ever been able to repeat. Henry's pig fat though comes a very honourable and affordable second. It is quite unlike the stringy wet flab of intensively fed factory meat. But most of our pork is not like this. More than three quarters of it is now bought through supermarkets and the livestock revolution and intensive pig production have given us a quite different kind of meat from just a handful of cuts.

Most pig farmers in Britain are in crisis as deep as dairy farmers; the number of pig herds has halved and the amount of pork and bacon we import has doubled in a decade. The big transnational pork processing companies and the supermarket giants have found a way to add their value to it, however. Once again the value added is not nutritional but shareholder value. The gains have been privatized and the social and environmental costs externalized. For the globalized pig industry is one of the most polluting kinds of factory farming today, and it is taxpayers who tend to pick up the bill, while around the world large-scale factory slaughtering, processing and packing of meat has depended on workers paid rock bottom wages, many of them migrants. The social cost has been the death of the real job; the added value in this case has come from the cheapness of the labour.

The workers protesting outside the Tulip meat factory in Thetford in 2007 were among those at the sharp end of this system. They were about to join the dole queue as the company closed the plant and relocated production to another factory in Cornwall. They would be joining a growing army of ordinary people who pay the price for our new system of acquiring food just-in-time, 24/7, from anywhere round the world at the lowest cost. For them and their towns and communities this system is proving anything but cheap.

Tulip UK is part of the transnational Danish Crown group, one of the largest producers in the world. Like other sectors of the food business, the pig slaughtering and processing industry is highly concentrated. About two thirds of British pork, bacon and ham comes from just two companies, Tulip and Grampian. Grampian is dominant in poultry too.

Tulip's Thetford site turned pork, most of it imported from Denmark, into cuts of bacon or joints for most of the big supermarkets. Tesco Finest and Tesco Value, Sainsbury's Taste the Difference, M&S Butcher's Choice, Asda – most of the brands had been packed there.

Danish Crown and its subsidiaries, which include Tulip and

Danepak, received EU subsidies totalling €84 million between 2000 and 2005, making them the third largest beneficiaries of the Common Agricultural Policy in Denmark. As well as being highly profitable, they pride themselves on the welfare standards for their animals, the family farmers who supply them, and their staff.

But the Thetford closure would leave most of these Norfolk employees out of work with little redundancy compensation, according to the unions; many of them were in any case migrants employed through agencies who were entitled to nothing. Up to 700 people who worked there regularly would have to look for jobs elsewhere.

I had first come to Thetford, a small market town in Norfolk that was the birthplace of the eighteenth-century champion of the rights of man Tom Paine, in 2003. Back then I had spent some weeks interviewing migrant workers for my book *Not on the Label* about the appalling conditions in which many of them were employed – not at the Tulip factory, but through gangmasters in food factories and pack houses in the surrounding area that supplied the leading supermarkets and fast food chains. Most of them had been Portuguese, or Brazilians masquerading as Portuguese on fake identity documents, living in overcrowded accommodation, and being ripped off by gangmasters. They had been sucked into East Anglia by the hundreds of low-paid, unskilled, production line and agricultural jobs that the supermarket system of just-in-time ordering had created.

Half of new jobs created since 1997 when Labour came to power turn out to have gone to migrant workers, and the majority have been jobs like this – not real employment with security and a pension for old age, but precarious casual work that has depended on migration.

These are jobs that require complete flexibility: twelve- to sixteen-hour shifts packing potatoes or pears or cutting chicken one day, perhaps no work the next, late nights, weekends, whatever labour the volume of orders demands as it goes up and down at short notice. The buying power of the supermarkets has enabled them to make sure that any financial risk associated with fluctuation in demand is carried, not by them, but by their suppliers, who get no guaranteed income for estimated orders that may shrink by half or more in the space of a few hours, and yet get fined if they cannot fulfil orders that suddenly double.

The only way for suppliers to cope with such variations is to pass the risk on down the line, to a workforce that they can turn on and off at a moment's notice and move around the country to wherever it suits them to produce. These are not the sort of jobs that fit with any kind of settled family life, and migrants have filled many of them, either because they are desperate enough to take them or because they are prepared to put up with the conditions for a short period of time to save money for a better life when they go back home. Already back then on my first visit people had worried about serious tensions in the town.

A year later, there had been hours of violent rioting outside the Portuguese-run Red Lion pub in the main square where I had met several of the foreign workers. At first, the riot had been reported as an outbreak of football hooliganism that had followed England's defeat by Portugal in the European cup, but in fact the attack had been a racist one. A mob of over 200 local youths had surrounded the pub and hurled missiles from paving slabs to bricks and bottles at its windows while shouting racist abuse. About forty Portuguese workers and their families had desperately barricaded themselves inside for over two hours while police, who were unable to bring the crowd under control, waited for reinforcements. Eight were injured that night, and ten young men were later jailed for the attack.

People in the town I spoke to had been shocked, though not particularly surprised by this manifestation of racial hatred. Thetford had a population of about 21,000 according to the last census, but local councillors' estimates put it at about 28,000 to 29,000. Large numbers of Portuguese workers had arrived in the surrounding area in the space of a few years; the numbers, like all migration statistics, were disputed but one study had put the number of Portuguese in Thetford and nearby Swaffham at about 6,000 in 2003, with an uncertain but substantial number of migrants from Eastern Europe and China, many of whom were undocumented. Since the accession of Eastern European countries many more had arrived for work, mainly from Poland and Lithuania. The town itself had absorbed large numbers of migrants. That was when unemployment was low. Now the town was facing the prospect of major redundancies.

The Tulip factory had been Thetford's largest employer since Thermos had closed its production lines five years previously and relocated to China where the labour is cheaper. In the Georgian town council offices behind Tom Paine's statue, the Labour mayor Thelma Paines, who thought she might be able to claim a distant family link to the radical reformer, and the town manager Susan Glossop were proud of the work that had been done to bring the communities together since the riot. They said they didn't want Thetford to be talked about as a case study in migration but as the conversation went on they admitted they were concerned that a round of job cuts now that included new Europeans who had only recently settled in Thetford would provoke more tension; they worried that people would start asking why their taxes were going to support jobless foreigners. Unusually for a rural area, a quarter of the town is now under eighteen, and it can be a bit volatile, Thelma, a garrulous, life-long, local politician was telling me. 'In the short term it's bloody devastating,' she said. We were sitting in the old meeting room surrounded by portraits of previous mayors in their regalia, middle-aged men mostly, of middle England, and a handful of women, looking earnest in their chains of office. Thelma had come to the area herself some forty years before with her husband. She started out working at the Tulip factory site thirty years ago and had seen all the changes. The pork processed in the area used to come from locally reared pigs but now most of the raw material was imported.

All the English people in Thetford I spoke to agreed the migrants were hard working but they all also felt there were problems associated with such rapid population movements – housing was in short supply, and people from poorer parts of the EU were bringing in public health problems which they felt were straining the NHS – levels of smoking and associated illnesses among Eastern Europeans were high, and GPs were reporting a rise in the sort of mental health problems that go with bad housing and poverty of opportunity. Many of the workers I had interviewed at factories other than Tulip on my first visit had suffered repetitive strain injuries but since they were casual staff sent by gangmasters it was usually the NHS that picked up the bill while the factories themselves escaped any obligation. Schools had to teach in up to eight languages with few extra resources, and language barriers among the adults remained.

The Tulip factory itself was on an industrial estate on the outskirts of town, past housing estates sliced in two by the main A-road. Here the deprivation among the local population had been deep enough to justify EU regeneration funds.

I walked past the loading bays and lines of parked juggernauts on the sprawling site to the main factory entrance where workers had planned their protest about the redundancies at the end of their shift. As I arrived a right-wing nationalist on a bicycle was shouting abuse at the organizers. When challenged, he rode off back towards the estate, still railing against foreigners.

It wasn't the first time the factory had seen cuts. In 2003 the company had made over 170 full-time employees redundant. Agency staff had been brought in not long after, most of them migrants, whom the local workers said were on poorer terms and conditions – lower rates of pay, less overtime money, less holiday, more anti-social shift patterns. The full time employees had had no pay rise for three years and had watched as their incomes were eroded by inflation. They were convinced that the reason the company was shifting its production to Cornwall was to cut labour costs and employ more migrants on the minimum wage. Tulip said the explanation was different, that the factory was too old to be profitable; its age meant it required more energy to keep running than newer plants. It acknowledged that it used agency labour after earlier redundancies but said this was because it was very dependent on seasonal variances and needed agency workers to give it flexibility to meet customers' changing demands. But the engineers who were about to lose their jobs too didn't think that was the whole story. Why had £8 million-worth of new machinery and production lines been recently installed if that was the case, they asked. Thelma, the mayor, acknowledged that the age of the site was indeed a problem, but was wondering how the company could square moving to Cornwall with reducing its carbon footprint, when Thetford was near the ports for Denmark, and Cornwall was a long, long way west of most supermarket distribution centres and Danish pigs.

It was mid afternoon when I arrived and the 6.30 a.m. shift was just finishing. A crowd of several dozen workers was being joined by their families and children straight out of school as they collected placards from the union organizer's van. They formed an orderly line along the approach road, holding up their slogans: 'Shame on you Danish Crown!' 'Tulip workers have families too!' Then they marched the few hundred yards back down to the factory gate. Deborah had worked at Tulip for nineteen years, packing bacon and pork loin in the slicing hall for Tesco and M&S. She was earning about £6.74 an hour compared with migrants in the factory on the then minimum of £5.35. Her two sisters used to work at the factory too, but both had been made redundant in the last round. One had not worked since. What galled her was being asked to train the agency workers who had replaced them. 'This affects so many people's lives, so many husbands and wives, and cousins and children worked in the company. It's the economy round here.' At least they had been given good redundancy money; Deborah's contract had been changed recently so she wouldn't be entitled to much despite her years of service.

Danny and his wife Melissa had both joined the production lines from school, taking turns now with early and late shifts so that one of them could be at home to look after their two small girls. Both were in their thirties, and Thetford born and bred. They had put in twenty years at the factory between them.

Danny was angry, not with the migrants – they just wanted a better life for themselves and why shouldn't they, he said – but with the company. 'We're losing our jobs because they are bringing in people from other countries who are willing to take less pay. But that's bringing down our way of life. They are cheaper because they are only in their twenties and don't have children, or because they live ten or twenty to a house, but I have to pay a £100,000 mortgage.'

Andy, the organizer from the Transport & General Workers' Union, had them all in a group now near the factory offices where the management was meeting to negotiate with other union officials. He had been involved in the union's campaign to recruit workers including migrants across the meat sector to make sure agency staff were treated equally so that migrants weren't abused and permanent workers' conditions were not eroded. Now he was leading a protest chant through his megaphone to encourage the talks along: 'I don't know, but I've been told . . .' he sang out, and the workers dutifully called back an echo; then Andy picked up the beat again: 'Boss's pocket's lined with gold . . .' As if on cue, a female suit drove out of the factory gate, accelerating past the security guards and the workers in her convertible sports car with leather seats, avoiding eye contact. A couple of old bangers, driven by shift workers going home, passed after her and honked solidarity.

They all knew it was more complicated than their chant suggested. Cheryl was angry not just with the company and its bosses but with the supermarkets. She had clocked up thirty-one years at the factory taking home about £220 for a forty-hour week, and, at fifty-six, doubted she would find any other work. Her husband Denis had worked there thirty-four years. It was going to be very tough on all of them and on the town. She blamed the supermarket ordering systems in part. 'About a third of what we slice is taken out because their specification is so demanding, and the price they pay is so low. The volumes change all the time – you come to work in the morning and they want 600 boxes of a particular line, then by 11 a.m. it's gone down to 200 boxes. You get left with all that raw material. There's so much waste.' She said she'd heard that all the workers in Cornwall would be on the minimum wage, so it would be cheaper. 'They're doing it all over the country, bringing in lower paid workers, but you can't live on it, not properly. You can get over the language barrier and smile a lot but when the agency workers get made up to permanent they are on different contracts, less holiday, etc, and that doesn't foster good relations.' Her friend Dawn agreed: 'Most of the migrants are hard working and easy to get on with, but if they are prepared to take lower wages, it will cause divisions.' Some of the migrants, most of them Poles, had in fact joined the union once they heard of the threatened closure.

I asked Tulip whether the workers' view of the economics behind the decision to relocate was accurate. The company said commercial confidentiality prevented it discussing its terms with supermarkets. Nor did it answer my questions about who would be employed in Cornwall and at what rate, but it said in a statement that the issue was not about labour costs but about the age of the Thetford site itself. 'Our proposal to cease production of fresh bacon and pork products at Thetford has been made purely because, despite millions of pounds of investment over recent years, the inherent infrastructure and environmental issues at the site cannot be overcome. In terms of energy usage alone the Thetford site is almost two and a half times more expensive per kilo of product than any of our other UK sites.' It added that there was no formal union agreement in place about redundancies, a fact the union acknowledged. But the problem for social cohesion remained. Whatever the real reason for the redundancies, local workers believed it was that migrants could be used more cheaply and they resented it.

The little window on the social divide opened by the cars leaving the factory did also reveal a deeper truth, as the rest of the company's statement showed: 'Tulip operates in a very competitive marketplace that has significant overcapacity and therefore consolidation is critical if Tulip is to establish itself as the lowest cost producer.' Becoming the lowest cost producer is indeed essential for food companies to survive in a world where supermarkets enjoy buying monopolies and can always choose to source from a different country with different labour conditions if they don't like the price. Consolidation has been inevitable and shows little sign of slowing down as processors and manufacturers try to stand up to retail power here just as in the dairy sector. Whatever the reasons for the Tulip closure, there is no question that importing cheaper migrant labour to industrialized countries or playing footloose and moving to less developed countries where cheaper labour is available has been a vital way for many processors to achieve that goal of lowest cost.

Fresh meat is heavy and perishable, it is hard to import, so there will always be a market for the labour-intensive business of cutting and packing it locally. The answer has been straightforward – import, not the product, but the labour conditions of poorer countries to supply it. Both local workers and migrants have suffered in this race to the bottom.

★

For many migrants employed elsewhere in the industry, the conditions have been little better than a new slavery. When I first started writing about the plight of migrant workers in Britain's food factories and pack houses a few years ago, the general assumption was that exploitation occurred, but in isolated incidents, and was down to a few rogue gangmasters. To those on the ground it was clear however that problems were widespread and growing. We kept finding examples of egregious abuse in mainstream factories, including particularly troubling cases such as the debt-bonded labour packing fruit for a supermarket supplier's factory in Lincolnshire. The more I interviewed migrants around the country, the more common themes emerged: they were at the mercy of agencies that held power over their everyday lives, and they were nearly all physically afraid, because of their routine exposure to violence and intimidation. Much of the business was run by agencies closely linked not just to illegal labour but to other forms of crime, including people smuggling, identity fraud, drug trafficking and prostitution. But government ministers either had no idea of the scale of the problem or chose not to see it.

The numbers involved in this newly casualized, flexible workforce were kicked around like a political football, with both sides of the debate, pro- and anti-immigration, crying foul so hard it was impossible to discuss what was really going on. The anti-immigration lobby was busy conflating the distinct issues of asylum and migration for work and inflating the guesstimates, and the left persisted in a soothing rhetoric that linked any mention of migration to skills shortages rather than low-skilled labour and cost-cutting and consistently played down the numbers. Meanwhile, the public, who could see something different going on around them, got angrier.

It is now accepted that at least 500,000, and probably more, migrants are in this country illegally, many of them employed in the food and catering business. Their lack of legal status makes them particularly vulnerable. As part of my investigations for the *Guardian*, I have interviewed several former ministers and officials, who were able to talk at length about the course of these migrations once away from office or the fear of screaming newspaper headlines. Their understanding of what was going on in the food sector came extraordinarily late. The Home Office through the early years of large-scale economic migration from the late 1990s to early 2000s was so focussed on the 'bogus asylum seekers' of tabloid obsession that it hadn't really thought about the phenomenon of illegal economic migration. Illegal migration was defined in the minister's eyes as people declaring themselves to the authorities in order to claim something from them they were not entitled to, that is state benefits. It was not people working and hiding in the country undeclared, nor factories depending on them. Yet economic migration has turned out to be the more significant in terms of numbers. Other departments such as DEFRA were slow too to see what was going on in the food sector – they were distracted by farming crises such as BSE and foot and mouth, and top civil servants didn't visit processing factories.

Number Ten and the Treasury in any case remained adamant that Britain needed a 'flexible' workforce, with migrants to fill jobs British people did not want to do, if it was to be internationally competitive. The whole thrust of policy was towards 'better regulation', which meant in practice less regulation, or red tape, as business likes to call it, and certainly no additional resources to enforce employment laws that were being widely flouted.

Then the Morecambe Bay tragedy of 2004, in which twenty-three Chinese cockle pickers died, trapped by the tide on quicksands and abandoned by their gangmasters to drown, made it impossible to ignore the exploitation any more. New legislation was hastily introduced through a messy private member's bill to license gangmasters.

Government policy now was to concede the licensing

legislation but to restrict it if possible to agriculture and shellfish gathering rather than all the food pack houses and factories where the gangmaster system operated. It also wanted to hang on until the accession of twelve new countries to the EU which would provide a pool of workers from poorer European countries with the right to work in the UK. In theory labour from these countries would remove much of the problem of illegal working since processors and manufacturers would be able to employ them directly rather than depend on illegal workers brought in by gangmasters.

In practice it made no difference because cheap, dispensable, labour had become structural to the economics of food manufacturing and processing. Companies didn't want to employ people directly, because to be the lowest cost producer you have to be able to turn off your labour at no cost whenever you want. You don't want to be saddled with expensive benefits such as pensions. And subcontracting chains enable you to hide how little you are paying.

The extent to which the whole system of low-cost high-profit food was built on mass migrations and exploitation became clear to me when I was called late one night to visit a group of Poles working at a meat factory in Devon supplying Sainsbury's, in 2004.

Although they were now part of the EU and entitled to work in the UK, they were not employed directly and were not only being paid less than the local workers, but were living in terrible conditions, caught up in an underworld of irregular migration and other alleged crimes. Their story is very similar to that of many I have interviewed subsequently.

I had arranged to meet them at their house in Exeter at the end of the night shift. There were twenty of them in the house the night I visited. Ten of them were sleeping there, three or four to a small room, and ten in another house nearby. They said they had been threatened with eviction and loss of two weeks' wages if they dared to tell anyone about their conditions. They had also been told they must be very quiet and not go out in groups or the police would come, so we shook hands quickly on the doorstep and hustled in.

Within minutes the whole house was a fog of cheap cigarette smoke. They gathered their papers and we tried to decide where to begin. But they were too nervous at first. Four Iranians in a battered old car had turned up outside the house just after me. The Poles were frightened of them. And there was the Afghan upstairs. They didn't know who he was but he always arrived late at night to sleep on the floor. The Iranians outside turned out to have come to collect a parcel that had been delivered to the house from Iran a few days before. They were aggressive at first but when they realized there were English people inside too, they soon went away.

The Poles explained that they had had no idea where they were when the gangmaster's dusty black minivan first brought them to the house in the middle of the night. They had been made to wait on the patch of grass outside while the dozen or so Afghans inside were told to throw their things in black dustbin bags. The Afghans had looked frightened. They were bundled into the van and driven off, and that was the last the Poles had heard of most of them. The driver was Chinese-looking and spoke no English and in any case the Poles spoke no English either, so they couldn't ask what was going on. The Poles, new EU citizens, had been told when they were recruited back home that they would be working on supermarket salads somewhere near Southampton. There had been no mention of preparing meat for Sainsbury's in Devon. But without language, money or even the proper name of the boss of the company they seemed to have been handed over to on arrival in England, they felt helpless and trapped.

The house, in an anonymously respectable cul-de-sac in a quiet Exeter suburb that formed part of the Labour minister Ben Bradshaw's constituency, was unremarkable outside. Inside, they said they found indescribable squalor. No furniture, just mountains of rubbish, piles of syringes, soiled mattresses on the floor and a terrible smell. They had little choice but to bed down that night and go to the meat factory the next day. They spent the next three days cleaning up between shifts.

They had been recruited in Poland to come to England as soon as they were legally entitled to. Two men, Phil and Pete, from an English labour agency called IPS, had come to a hotel room in the central Polish city of Torun and interviewed workers in batches of ten, non-stop for two days. They had promised the minimum wage, good accommodation for £25 per person per week and lots of overtime. But it had gone wrong almost as soon as it started. There had been no work and no wages in their first week in Southampton. They were told they would have to pay £40 a week rent each, although they were sleeping on the floor, in the kitchen, in the sitting room, wherever they could find. There was only one bed in the house occupied by an old man they didn't know. Then suddenly they'd all been taken to Exeter in the night and left there.

Their payslips showed that £40 was being taken from each of their pay packets each week for rent although the legal maximum for those on the minimum wage was just under £25. Even a cursory glance showed that there was something seriously wrong with their national insurance numbers − several of them had the same one. They were having tax deducted at the high emergency rate although the Inland Revenue said it had not received any tax or NI payments for the Poles.

The contracts they had signed, they said without a translation and without understanding, were with a company called TGI not IPS, although IPS seemed to be running them here together with a Polish woman from a company called Supertrack. The personnel from IPS and Supertrack seemed to the Poles to be interchangeable and to operate from the same address. After deductions their payslips showed they were getting just £115 a week for forty hours, but this is not what the runners who brought their cash were actually giving them, they said. Another £15 was disappearing along the line without explanation. Most of them had not registered as required with the Home Office because the £50 it cost seemed an impossible amount when they were trying to survive and support families back home on so little. By failing to do so they had put themselves on the wrong side of the law. (It was clear from this and from other interviews I conducted that the official figures about numbers of Eastern Europeans migrating to the UK based on the registration scheme were hopelessly unreliable.)

Anna and Marek were a couple in their early forties. She was one of two women in the group sleeping on what should have been the sitting room floor. They had left their children aged 13, 11, 8 and 7 back home with Marek's mother. They didn't expect to see them for a year at least, though in the end they brought them over to settle too. But Marek had been made redundant from his job in financial services in an area of Poland where there was 23 per cent unemployment. Although he was educated it was this or face destitution, so they had come together. We looked at the photos of their children, three boys and a girl, neat as pins in old-fashioned Sunday best, posing for the camera in a living room from another era. They were angry but resigned. In the Soviet Poland of their youth, your life was either in the hands of the state or fate. You learned not to ask questions.

The younger men were more of a gang, although they barely knew each other's surnames. Mariusz spoke most and they were happy to let him, not knowing then what they would discover about him later. They showed us their payslips, explaining their confusion. They didn't know when they would get paid. A man they said was Afghan had been coming late at night with their cash, but five of them hadn't received any money that week. They didn't know who the boss was to complain to. Their payslips carried the name of yet another company, but it had no address, nothing that you could pin down.

Dave, a trade unionist from the factory, who had come back with them from their shift that night, stepped forward: 'This isn't my normal experience of being a shop steward, I'm afraid, and I have to admit I am swimming out of my depth on this but . . .' he hesitated, wavering not in his conviction but at the shock of being called upon to articulate it in the course of an otherwise untroubled English life. 'Well, all I know is we must stand firm together, as brothers, otherwise we are all powerless in the face of injustice.' I later learned that he had spent many hours acting as Good Samaritan to the Poles.

It was close to 1 a.m. three nights later when my phone rang and an urgent Polish voice said: 'Problem, problem, no house, no house.' Without a translator, it was hard to know what was going on. But next day I discovered that some of them were to be evicted first thing next morning. They had complained and would have to take the consequences. It also emerged that some of the overcrowding was due to a couple of Poles inviting friends to stay. Next morning the confusion increased when the Poles from the other house rang to say the police had come. One of them had been using the anonymous and transient world of migrant labour as a hiding place. Two violent sexual assaults had taken place in the St Thomas area of Exeter; the suspect was of Eastern European appearance and Mariusz was being questioned. He later pleaded guilty and was convicted.

By now neighbours, disturbed by all the late-night activity and resenting the squalor on their doorstep, had complained to Exeter Council's environmental health department. It had inspected and immediately written to the factory owners, Lloyd Maunder, making clear that the conditions, while not legally their responsibility, were unacceptable. My own investigations for the *Guardian* were adding to the pressure on the company. At first it said that IPS was one of the best agencies it had worked with. But after a tense meeting at the factory between the Poles, the gangmasters and the company, Lloyd Maunder informed the workers and the union that it was terminating its contract with IPS. It agreed to both employ the Poles directly at the same rate as local staff and to take responsibility for improving their housing. It also changed its labour agency.

Supertrack, IPS and TGI turned out to be part of a network of gangmasters. Supertrack Services is a substantial labour provider to several sectors, with a website that boasts, 'Only a special type of recruitment consultancy consistently generates our level of results in the dynamic world of the flexible workforce and creates the environment in which this workforce will give their best.'

The convoluted subcontracting chains involved in this case have proved to be typical of the system. Supertrack declined to comment on the allegations at the time. A previous labour provider company of one of its directors had been struck off after a Customs and Excise compulsory winding up order. It was subsequently granted a licence under the new Gangmaster Licensing Act and its website now says that the *Guardian*'s investigations contained untruths. After my investigation it was pursued by the Inland Revenue for over £3 million in unpaid tax and national insurance deducted from workers but not paid to the Revenue.

IPS and TGI were the registered names of companies run by Trevor Geddes. IPS stopped operating soon after my investigation began and its contract with Lloyd Maunder was terminated. Two of its managers set up new labour agencies. I was told I could not speak to Trevor Geddes, when I tried to contact the company. However, Peter Sanger, who said he was a consultant to him, admitted that unlawful deductions had been made from the Poles' wages and said they would be repaid. The repayment was eventually made. Peter Sanger also told me that the conditions at the house were not the legal responsibility of IPS but of the tenant Supertrack and that any payroll irregularities had been the responsibility of another company subcontracted to produce the payroll, not IPS. He denied allegations made by the Poles that they had been intimidated, saying: 'A Pole did say that I had him up against a wall with my hands around his throat threatening to kill him, but I have witnesses that it didn't happen.' He also told me that the Poles had been provided with bedding but that 'other forces were involved' in its removal.

In this case, once the problem has been highlighted, Lloyd Maunder, the meat processing company involved, employed the Poles directly. It told me its aim was to employ all staff as permanent employees, and that it had acted throughout as a diligent and caring employer, and was not party to or responsible for the shortcomings (if any) of third parties, but due to the tight labour market a small number of extra staff were sometimes brought in through employment agencies. Sainsbury's said it was very concerned by the allegations and had arranged an independent audit.

Two years down the line, with the Gangmaster Licensing Authority finally set up and beginning raids on large food factories and pack houses, things seem little better elsewhere. A coalition of unions and industry had insisted that government include pack house and food factories in the new legislation.

The GLA's first inspection, carried out in 2007, was on another company where I had previously investigated illegal labour, Bomfords, in the Vale of Evesham. Bomfords supplied more than 50 per cent of the big supermarkets' spring onions and more than a quarter of their green beans and fresh peas, as well as asparagus. Its biggest customer at the time, taking about three quarters of its produce, was Tesco, but it has supplied most of the leading high street chains. If you buy fresh vegetables at a supermarket you have almost certainly eaten food packed by Bomfords' workers.

All seven gangmasters supplying labour to Bomfords were found by the GLA to be breaking the law and had their licences revoked after the inspection. One had its licence revoked with immediate effect on the grounds that its workers were in danger and were being intimidated. They were Poles and other Eastern Europeans.

It had been common knowledge in the industry for years that Bomfords offered its gangmasters hourly rates for workers that made it all but certain that those gangmasters would be breaking the law. At a time when the minimum wage was £5.35, a gangmaster complying with the law on minimum wage, national insurance, sick and holiday pay would have to charge at the very least £6.27 per worker per hour. And that's without any allowance for the gangmaster's costs or profits. If you factored in the gangmaster's administration and overhead costs, the minimum rate would have needed to be nearly £7. But the industry's Association of Labour Providers reported that Bomfords was paying just £6.10 per hour.

The ALP had drawn the Inland Revenue's attention to how far adrift Bomford's rates were in April 2005. In the same month it had, it says, warned Tesco, as a major customer, about the rates that Bomfords was paying its gangmasters, which were not enough for them to be complying with the law, in an email which it showed me. The ALP was concerned that companies consistently paying below the indicative rate were not only 'knowingly or recklessly conniving in illegality'; they were making it impossible for gangmasters who wanted to abide by the law to compete. When I later asked them why they had not acted on this alert, Tesco told me it had no record of a specific earlier warning from the ALP. Had it received specific allegations it was sure it would have acted on them, it said. It had held a series of meetings for suppliers around that time where regulations surrounding the minimum wage and other employment law and the need to comply with them were highlighted. It had regularly audited Bomfords and had insisted on a further independent audit after the GLA operation, and had acted on any 'non-conformities' found.

After the inspection Bomfords had to employ more workers to harvest and pack its supermarket vegetables directly on significantly higher rates. A few months later it went into administration. The economics of supplying the supermarkets had stopped working for it. It owed growers, including farmers in Africa, about £18 million. Some of them were highly distressed and contacted me.

Bomfords had substantial debts: it had made two expensive acquisitions of rival supermarket suppliers. Like others facing the buying power of a handful of dominant retailers who have relentlessly kept down the price they pay to suppliers, it was consolidating to try to strengthen its position. It was building a giant new pack house where it could meet all the supermarket specifications, which involved vast capital investment – a project whose costs spiralled out of control.

One of the reasons Bomfords was able to supply vegetables more cheaply than others, and the supermarkets in turn were able to sell them more cheaply, was that it didn't pay as much for its labour as others. The business model of cheap fresh food which supermarkets have used to establish their dominance has in other words depended on illegality and exploitation.

The administrators told me that Bomfords' difficulties arose from its debts, its overspend on the new pack house and problems integrating its newly acquired businesses, but not on having to pay more for its labour. The findings of the gang-master authority's inspection were in the past as far as they were concerned. Tesco and Asda, another big customer, said the same. 'There is no suggestion that excessive wage bills or cashflow problems caused by Bomfords' customers were a contributing factor,' Tesco told me.

But the ugly questions raised by Bomfords' demise would not go away. In its history you could see a supermarket system laid bare: a system capable on the one hand of checking that every last bean and spring onion conforms to an exact size and shape, a system capable of tracking when, where and by whom they were packed, yet on the other unable to spot that every gangmaster sending workers to a major supplier was breaking the law.

The company was broken up and sold. Its main packing business was acquired by a leading rival, which also supplied Tesco. Then a few months later, the new pack house burned down one night. No one was working on shift at the time. Local firemen nevertheless entered the burning building, even though it was unsafe, because, according to a spokesman, they could not be sure that there were no migrants trapped inside. Local people believed that migrants had sometimes slept in the factory, though the company said this was not the case. Four firemen lost their lives that night as the building collapsed on top of them. A criminal investigation into the cause of the fire is still under way. The next round of GLA raids uncovered bonded labour in salad factories supplying the supermarkets.

Even where companies are complying with the law, the necessity of being lowest cost producer has led to a race to the bottom, in which the minimum wage is fast becoming the maximum wage. The Dawn Meats group is a highly profitable transnational meat processing company. Its Dawn Meats factory in Bedford has supplied red meat to many of the big supermarkets, including M&S and Asda. Management told workers at this plant in early 2007 that most of them would have to accept a pay cut of 20 per cent, reducing their hourly rate from between £6 and £8 to the legal minimum of £5.35 according to the union Unite. Over seventy highly skilled workers in the boning hall were told that would have to accept the cut, agree to be moved elsewhere, or have their contracts terminated. Some staff who had worked at the factory for over thirty years found they were losing over £150 a week. More than three quarters of the workforce were relatively newly arrived Poles. They felt they had little choice but to accept. The Dawn Group declined to comment when I asked them about this. The pattern has been repeated around the country in food factories, packing factories and distribution centres, and the main unions have reported that it is causing significant racial tension at work.

It was not until the election for the deputy leadership of the Labour party in 2007 that the impact of this sort of flexible labour market on social cohesion in Britain came out into open political debate.

Over 150 backbench MPs signed up to subsequent efforts to give equal rights to agency workers. Most were under intense pressure from a rise in the far right in their constituencies, where nationalist parties were finding it easy to exploit the fears of the traditional blue collar Labour voter. Labour's failure to argue the case for unskilled migration in a country with a rapidly ageing population and determination to talk only of the positive benefit of migration had left them exposed.

Although the varying analyses of the impact of migration on British workers appear contradictory, they in fact arise from a difference of perspective. Government tends to talk about the macroeconomic picture: fear of migrants taking British jobs is based on the assumption that there are a fixed number of jobs in the economy and that newcomers must therefore be displacing native workers. But overall employment rose between 1997 and 2007 and unemployment as measured by benefit claim fell, as demand and GDP both rose. Average wage growth was above inflation. This is why the government argues that the overall economic impact of migration has been positive.

But at a microeconomic level, migration has clearly affected particular groups of British workers. There was a sharp increase in the proportion of unemployment accounted for by those under twenty-four; 30 per cent of unemployment was in this age group; 1.2 million sixteen- to twenty-four-year-olds were neither in education, training nor work in early 2007. There was also a dramatic increase in those becoming 'economically inactive'. More than one fifth of the working-age population was economically inactive in August 2007, with older women who couldn't find work but wouldn't necessarily claim benefit or be counted in official unemployment statistics particularly affected. Those in direct competition with migrants, that is those in low or unskilled jobs, have lost out, with their wages being pushed down and their benefits seriously eroded. This was the true picture that backbench Labour MPs were picking up in their constituencies. The gain has also been real, but it has been mostly enjoyed by the owners of capital, the employers, and by the more affluent who find themselves able to afford personal services and cheap goods produced by those on low wages that used not to be within their reach.

Yet even now, the reality that the global movement of goods and capital has driven mass migrations is not fully acknowledged. Nor is the fact that dominant transnational food retailers, manufacturers and processors have created a system which is in my view dependent on exploitation – and at its worst new forms of slavery – even as their profits have risen dramatically.

For me, this is how globalization has worked: it has widened the gap between the rich and the poor. Large companies have captured the value of the food market and have benefited from lower labour costs. The affluent have been able to maintain their time-pressured lifestyles thanks to a plentiful supply of cheap food and services supplied by underpaid migrants, but they did not ask for this and many are not comfortable with it, for they pay the cost in other ways, in an increasing anxiety about the quality of that food, and in a growing unease at the decline in their wider environment – at the strain on services, at the crime associated with such wide gaps between rich and poor, at the ugliness of a growing nationalism. Meanwhile for all the talk of minimum wages and lifting people out of poverty, the poor have become poorer.

In the food sector, redundancies and wage deflation for those at the bottom of the pile achieved by various means have spread in the last couple of years, as manufacturers have been caught between the double whammy of rising energy prices and the ever-tightening squeeze of supermarket buyers. Seven hundred redundancies at Northern Foods in late 2006, nearly 100 at Heinz in spring 2007, over 800 at Burton Foods later the same year ... The consolidation Tulip said was inevitable in its pork business has been mirrored around the country, and with it the job relocations and hollowed-out communities.

The leading accountancy firm Grant Thornton has a division that specializes in restructuring distressed companies in the food and agriculture business. Its head Duncan Swift is scathing about what he sees as the failure of the competition authorities to tackle the excess power of supermarket buyers. He has seen more and more forced mergers and takeovers in the fresh food sector and has watched over a dozen food companies with turnovers of more than £20 million failing in the last five years. 'For every one of those there are two more that have become distressed and had to be restructured, thanks to supermarket ordering practices,' he told me. Grant Thornton's calculation is that 10 per cent of turnover in the UK food supply chain will change hands in the next ten years, matching what has happened in the last ten years.

The final insult is that a new form of extracting money from this structure has emerged. When a distressed food company is sold, a substantial part of its value is often said to be the very fact that it has a supermarket contract. The supermarkets are increasingly taking up to 10 per cent of the value of the sale for themselves in commission on these grounds. I was told this by a well-placed source. Professor John Bridgeman, former Director-General of Fair Trading, confirmed that he too had been told of such arrangements.

Such is the climate of fear even among large processors and manufacturers that they dare not go public about abuse of power practised by the big supermarkets. If they do they worry they will be delisted, cut out of this highly controlled market altogether. So it is through trade groups that an indication of the pain has been given. The British Brands group submission to the latest Competition Commission inquiry into supermarkets points out that two thirds of manufacturers and processors said that their gross margins had decreased in the last five years, with operating margins showing a decline of 17 per cent in two years to 2005 and the trend for profits continued downwards. Smaller branded companies were of course hit hardest.

Duncan Swift, the senior accountant's view, was this: 'What we are witnessing is the natural progression in a capitalist system. If you have dominant actors at one end of a chain, you get consolidation at the other end. You move towards strong commodity players at the top, and a few niche producers at the other end, while the middle dies.' The Thetford unemployed were joining plenty of others, and would be joined by yet more.

I bought some Thetford Danepak pork at my nearest supermarket when I got back to London. 'Only £2.49!' the little promotional sticker on the pack proclaimed. A bargain. Three Perfect Pork fresh loin steaks from the Family Farms of Denmark, it said. And there was a picture of Anders, described on the label as a typical smiling farmer within the Danish farming cooperative. 'Anders is something of a celebrity on his farm in Skandeborg – with the pigs that is. He especially loves the excitement when he treats them to fresh straw every week . . .' These pork steaks had been in the chiller cabinet with all the rest of the fresh pork, so I had failed to notice the small print which owned that they had been 'basted with added water'. In the even smaller ingredients list – I had to get my glasses to read it – it turned out that these were not what I'd thought they were. I had fallen for an illusion; they were only 90 per cent pork, the rest of their bulk being made up of water, glucose syrup, phosphates and added sodium. I'd had no idea I was buying into this. Although like most people I have become wise to the amount of water that gets added to processed meats such as cheap bacon and ham, I hadn't realized fresh meat was being treated this way too. When I later examined other fresh pork in the supermarkets more carefully, it turned out that adding water was a new trend. I cooked my Thetford pig loin in a frying pan and watched as the meat shrank and the water that had been put in oozed back out, and then turned a sticky brown that suggested chargrilled meat but was in fact added sugar, a confection, easy on the palate and apparently on the pocket, but once identified, not such a bargain and somehow hard to stomach.

The world Anna and Marek and their companions had left behind for a better life in Britain had been changing rapidly too. Poland's accession to the EU in 2004 was accompanied by the expansion in Eastern Europe of the big transnational retailers and agribusiness. When the Poles who were to be made redundant at the Tulip bacon factory in Thetford; their compatriots who were exploited and intimidated at the Bomfords pack house in Evesham; and those serving in the meat factories in the Midlands returned to their country, they would find that the system that had controlled their lives with brutal efficiency in England was being transplanted to their home land.

For most Poles, joining the EU marked the end of a long process of historical justice. It put Poland back at the heart of Europe where they felt it had always belonged. Their country's shifting borders had reflected the rise and fall of empires, Prussian, Austro-Hungarian, German and Soviet, and they wanted nothing more than to be equal among equals in a free Europe, and to experience the economic growth that would put the desperate privations of communist dictatorship permanently behind them.

But already as the celebrations took place in May 2004, the fears were beginning to creep in. Poland is one of the broadest and most fertile areas on the Continent; it has the potential to play a dominant role in European farming. Once in the EU its farmers were entitled to a share of the £30 billion-odd of Common Agricultural Policy funds that swallowed up half the union's total budget. But the terms on which Eastern and Central European countries entered meant that their farmers would get only about a quarter of the subsidies the Western European ones received. They feared that they would not be allowed to compete. Moreover, American agribusiness had already positioned itself to use Poland as a bridgehead to the lucrative EU markets, bringing with it systems that would drive intensification, rural unemployment, environmental destruction and corporate control. Transnational supermarkets such as Tesco and Carrefour had also arrived with ambitious expansion plans.

Marek Kryda was one of those fighting to make sure the true costs associated with this kind of food production were accounted for. I had met him at the European Parliament, at a series of sessions on how poorer countries might retain their sovereignty over their food. Marek had experienced the underbelly of American life as a migrant working in badly paid cleaning and security jobs in the US and was now the Polish representative of the Animal Welfare Institute, an American-funded organization that campaigns against factory farming – in one of the ironies that represents everything that is best about the US, the language and practice of protest against the American transnational corporate empire was coming from across the Atlantic too. He wanted to show me how quickly the Poland he knew was changing.

The communists had tried briefly after the war to impose on Poland the collectivization of farms that had been inflicted on the rest of the Soviet empire. But the attempt was quietly abandoned after Stalin's death, by which time this kind of agricultural production had shown itself to be cripplingly inefficient. So it was only on the former large German estates, or latifundia, which became part of recovered territory after the war, that collective state farms had operated. Over 80 per cent of Poland's cultivated land had instead reverted to private ownership, mostly in the form of small plots belonging to individual peasant families. The result is that even today a third of the population in Poland is rural, and its 2.5 million or more small farms still employ one in three people. Throughout periods of invasion, violence, and uncertainty, and eras of central planning and shortage, cultivating your own plot of land remained the surest way of keeping your family fed. City dwellers too had kept their connection with the land, and neatly tended allotments are still a feature of most urban areas. These were the sort of straits Rob Hopkins who had given the talk in Lampeter about peak oil and climate change thought we might all face again soon.

Marek and I began our tour in Poznán. In the market square, inside the ring of tram tracks, dozens of small farmers from the surrounding area come to sell their produce each day. Here I was able to count seventeen different types of apples, from the most expensive imports to far cheaper local varieties that had been kept in store and, cheapest of all, local fruit that was slightly damaged but good enough to cook. An old woman offering a few dozen eggs and unwashed carrots and beets had no need to label them free range or organic, there was no other kind of production in her village nearby. Here was a local system of food production, supplied by an agricultural ring around an urban area, a real farmers' market of the sort that Western consumers are trying so hard to recreate. If our food system is profligate with fossil fuels, this has always used them sparingly. There had never been enough money for large-scale use of synthetic fertilizers and pesticides. The farmers here were under no illusions about the glamour of such an existence; it has none. Yet, for all its hardships, it was a structure that had seen them through desperate times. They were wary of the newly arriving supermarket chains from Western Europe; these were already attracting away their more affluent customers, it was the poorest, not the middle-class and mobile, who still came here to buy their food. Bakers too had been protesting that week because they suspected some of the new supermarkets were selling bread at less than the cost of production which would be illegal but no one was enforcing the law and they worried that their businesses would be undercut. The democratic processes were still fledgling and fragile, Marek said, planning rules were lax, easily corrupted or bypassed. People had got used to being told what to do by the state, and had no idea how to organize against big corporations when they thought they were flouting the law.

We bought the local daily newspaper whose front page carried a story about a British diplomat welcoming a predicted exodus of half a million Poles to work in Britain, even as back in the UK the government's official estimate of workers that might arrive from that country remained at 13,000. Marek had high hopes for the economy – he reckoned Poles would indeed migrate in large numbers, driven both by the collapse of the old regime and by the ruthless economics of the new one, but he was confident they would then return to a richer home. Many of them would be migrants from those rural areas that currently provide a livelihood for such a large proportion of inhabitants but which were in EU and American eyes backward and needed urgent development. The EU plans for agricultural reform assumed that half of Polish farmers would have to go out of business.

We drove off along the poorly surfaced main road out of Poznán into the flat agricultural lands of Wielkopolska, or great Poland, and settled in for a slow, fuel-efficient but time-consuming progress behind agricultural vehicles and new transcontinental supermarket juggernauts all sharing the narrow arteries of the transport infrastructure that so far remained single carriageway.

Eventually we reached a small village called Kiełkówo that found itself on a new frontline, facing the invasion of American industrial pig farming. The houses of Kiełkówo ran in a dreary ribbon along a narrow road, but hidden behind each was a scene from a 1950s Ladybird book. Of the fifty-six households, fifty were family farms, each with its yard of tumbledown red-brick barns, where stacks of hay stood next to piles of firewood, on which cats were basking in the sunshine. While dogs dozed on lazy guard, chickens foraged for last year's grain, and white storks nested on telegraph poles. Each barn housed a few pigs being fattened on the families' waste, and a cow or two for milking. Stretching further back in a medieval pattern of strip farming, cherry and apple orchards gave way first to plots of vegetables, then to narrow fields of wheat or a fallow furlong. Everywhere there were the sounds of a lost world, wood pigeons cooing, swallows darting under eaves, children calling from quiet roads, dropping their bicycles unlocked, tractors bringing hay in to the yards, and the echoing fall of an axe on wood. Poland has preserved some of the greatest biodiversity in Europe.

The idyll of spring and summer here, however, often gives way to the bleakness of a subsistence winter. No one was suggesting that changes were not needed to make life easier, but Marek was clear that the wrong kind of change could definitely be for the worse.

'We have great national pride as we enter the EU. I hope we can teach the West something. It is such a big moment this coming together of Central and West in Europe, but we don't just want to adopt your attitudes to consumption, and always think we need more. We don't need an American culture shock.'

We were visiting the leader of the village, Małgorzata Nawracała. Her family had farmed there for generations, surviving first the Prussian empire, then the German invasion and the Soviet control. She and her husband grew onions and sent the surplus to the local market, and also harvested cucumbers and asparagus for export with the help of their six daughters. They cultivated wheat to feed their cows, whose manure fed their crops. Their animals were slaughtered at the small local abattoir. Some of their neighbours were also small-scale pig farmers. Under new CAP rules subsidies would be paid not for volume of output as other European farmers had been paid in the past but per hectare farmed. The Polish government had joined forces with the French to block more radical reforms that might have switched more money into environmental protection schemes. Małgorzata knew there would be a financial incentive to switch to certain cash crops, but she didn't like the risk that would bring. She explained that because they were practising mixed farming everything was in balance and they paid almost nothing for agricultural inputs such as fertilizer and pesticides. If she altered one part of her farming, she'd have to buy in more and become more dependent on the market, which would be fine when prices for what they produced were good but could mean debt and bankruptcy if they weren't. And, thanks to agribusiness, they had recently had a taste of what falling prices meant with pigs.

One of the villagers in Kiełkówo was negotiating a deal with Prima Farms, a front company for the world's largest producer of industrial pigs, the US agribusiness giant Smithfield Foods. Large factory units had already been installed on his land, capable of holding up to 4,500 pigs, and he had applied for a permit to bring in 2,000 pigs immediately, the other villagers said. They had protested and he had backed off, but now they had been alerted that Prima Farms was about to deliver vast quantities of feed, even though his current permit was still for just 150 pigs. The rest of the village had used their tractors and trailers to block access to his farm that morning and the police had been called. Now they were feeling militant. Małgorzata had called a crisis meeting in the village hall.

Smithfield Foods is the largest and most profitable pork processor in the world. It slaughtered 26 million pigs in 2006, generating sales of $11.4 billion and operating profits of $421 million. It already controls 26 per cent of the US processed pork market and is expanding by acquisition in Europe. It has bought subsidiaries in the UK, France, the Netherlands and Romania, as well as Poland.

Its Polish acquisitions were a bargain. Under Polish law foreign based transnationals were not allowed to buy former state farms. So Smithfield bought 70 per cent of the state-owned pork production company Animex and worked through that. It started buying up bankrupt state farm buildings, the old latifundia that had fed the Prussian military machine, and had been collectivized in a subsequent wave of empire. It was turning them into pig fattening factories and working through the front company Prima Farms to contract other farmers to raise pigs for its processing operations. The Polish government had invested millions in Animex shortly before the takeover, using a $100 million loan from banks, including $25 million from the European Bank for Reconstruction and Development, leading Smithfield's then chairman to boast to investors that he had only paid 'ten cents on the dollar' for it.

Smithfield was exporting large volumes of Polish pork to the UK, with Tesco one of its main customers. For some time, British importers exploited the loophole that allows meat that is imported but processed in the UK to be labelled as produce of the UK. Intense pressure from British pig farmers has however largely stopped the practice and most pork from Poland is labelled as Polish or as of EU origin, unless it is going into ready meals or other meat products such as sausages. Tesco labels the country of origin of its meat clearly, and says that any Polish pork it sells is sourced from farms that have been carefully and independently audited and comply fully with British standards of production.

Smithfield was not the only transnational hoping to build up a dominant position in the European pork market through Poland. Dutch companies and Danish Crown invested heavily too, driven in part by increasing regulation in their own countries as their governments try to clamp down on the enormous environmental degradation that accompanies industrial pig farming. (Denmark which has only 5.4 million humans raises 24 million pigs a year, which produce enough slurry to fill 90,000 swimming pools. The extraordinary concentration of livestock has created a problem. In twenty years, the number of farms has halved while the number of pigs produced has doubled. It is this scale that is the problem: pig waste in small quantities is useful manure, in large concentrations the land cannot cope with it. The stench in some areas of Denmark has become so unbearable the tourist industry has suffered, and Danish Friends of the Earth has taken to handing out leaflets to visitors on its beaches asking them to boycott Danish pork. The Dutch have tackled the slurry problem by exporting some of their waste to Africa.)

Not surprisingly, the expansion of large-scale international pig farming in Poland quickly produced a crisis of over-production there. In 2006 over a quarter of a million piglets were imported to Poland for fattening from Germany, the Netherlands and Denmark. By early 2007, prices were tumbling. This is one of the reasons why prices to British pig farmers can fall below their cost of production. Rather than raise the price they pay to British producers, supermarkets and processors can just threaten to buy elsewhere if farmers won't accept what they offer. Small and medium sized Polish farmers were suffering devastating losses too and began protesting outside Parliament. The government agreed to intervene by buying up surplus pork – a move that is illegal under EU rules, so it said it was using the pork to build up its 'national reserves'. The new industrial farms of course benefited from the state's efforts to support prices as well.

The progress these transnational companies were offering was the Western industrialized model of factory farming and processing. On its website Smithfield explains that its strategy is to 'capitalize on our vertically integrated protein model' and to 'evolve packaged meats to deliver higher profits'.

The vertically integrated protein model, perfected in the US, is this: as well as fattening pigs itself on large factory farms, Smithfield contracts farmers to raise pigs for it. It owns these pigs, known in the industry as modern genetically improved pigs designed to fatten fast, and controls their feed, the antibiotics and drugs they may have to be given, and their slaughter, processing and packing. The contractors provide the capital investment for the land and buildings – often taking on bank loans and debt to put them up – and are responsible for disposing of the prodigious quantities of faecal waste intensively reared pigs produce.

Campaigners argue that this model, which is essentially the same as that used in the industrialized chicken sector, has reduced farmers to little more than serfs and has been a prime engine of corporate dominance of the food sector. The contracting farmer is lucky to make a return of 1–3 per cent a year, while the processing giants enjoy returns of 20–30 per cent on their investments. The farmers are paid according to a set formula based on pounds of meat delivered minus the cost of the big company's inputs, as calculated by the latter. Although the contracts may start out looking favourable to both sides, as the big processor squeezes out local abattoirs, it gains more and more control and can force the farmers' terms down. The model has seen thousands of farmers go out of business in the US and has allowed the emergence of vast pig factories, where animals are raised in unprecedented concentrations, and require intensive feeding and routine drug use.

The processing stages generate substantial profits. By moving up the chain from fresh pork to convenience pork products Smithfield, for example, reckons it can increase its margins eight-fold.

The company has however been at the centre of bitter disputes between the industrialized meat sector unions, human rights groups and environmental campaigners in the US. They argue that if companies like Smithfield had to pay for the cost of disposing of their pig waste safely they would not actually make money at all. Pollution is built into the business model. Smithfield won notoriety ten years ago when two of its US subsidiaries were given the largest ever environmental fines by the government's Environmental Protection Agency, having to pay $12.6 million for illegally discharging pollutants from their operations into the Pagan River. They had committed more than 5,000 violations of permit limits for discharging phosphorus, faecal coli forms and other pollutants, including ammonia, cyanide, and oil, over more than five years, destroying fish stocks. They were also found guilty of falsifying documents and destroying records.

Campaigners also argue that the economic model only works because it uses cheap labour, and in effect imports the working conditions of the Third World. A Human Rights Watch report in January 2005 called 'Blood, Sweat and Fear' focussed on Smithfield Foods as one of three meat giants which violated workers' rights to form unions, put workers' health and safety at risk, and denied them compensation for injuries. At Smithfield's largest factory in Tar Heel, North Carolina, where its mostly migrant workers kill 32,000 pigs a day, or one every two seconds, staff turnover is 100 per cent annually. Various courts of law have ruled against Smithfield for its illegal action against workers. In a 400-plus-page ruling on its violations at the Tar Heel factory, a US judge in 2000 found that Smithfield had engaged in 'egregious and pervasive unfair labour practices' and had conspired with police to instigate violence at a vote among workers on joining a union. The 2000 ruling was upheld in the final court of appeal in 2006. In 2007 Smithfield agreed to pay over $1 million in compensation for the violations, although it said it still disagreed with the rulings.

Smithfield says it has learned from its mistakes and improved its environmental record, and that in addition to environmental awards it has received excellent results from more recent international health and safety inspections. It denies being anti-union and points out that 40 per cent of its workforce around the US is unionized. In its view the campaign against it by the unions is politically motivated.

Marek and the villagers of Kiełkówo were not inclined to give them the benefit of the doubt. 'The American corporations will take the subsidies from the EU for the land here. It's like feeding a cancer. They can sell pork very, very cheaply, and will grow and grow, no one will be able to stop them, the small farmers can't compete and won't survive. They'll buy everything up or reduce the Poles to contractors. Many people will have to migrate. But the true cost is paid by us all in the impact on the environment,' Marek said.

We joined the villagers of Kiełkówo with Małgorzata in the church hall and she tried to bring order over the raised voices of twenty-five angry men. They were sitting the length of a rough wooden table, tea in glasses in front of them, a crucifix on the wall behind them, trying to work out what to do.

'Where is he planning to put all his pig slurry?' one asked. 'He's already lost most of his land; he has nowhere to store it. Who will be responsible when it poisons our land?' another shouted.

'You are only allowed two pig units per hectare, so that waste can be disposed of safely, he only has eleven hectares. It will stink,' a third chipped in.

'The authorities are in cahoots; why are the police summoning us to the police station for blocking his farm when they saw he has no permits and is not allowed to bring these things in?' The bare hall echoed with their indignation.

They decided to guard the entrance to the farm day and night in a rota and to join forces with villagers in Wieckowice, where another Smithfield operation was already running an intensive pig factory, fattening up to 13,000 pigs.

In Wieckowice, villagers were complaining of nausea, asthma attacks, rashes and stomach upsets which they believed were caused by the factory's slurry. Children at the local school had

137

been vomiting. The litany of complaints followed the pattern of those made by residents near industrial pig factories in the US. The company wasn't controlling its waste properly, they said. The stench was so awful they couldn't open their windows. The shore of the lake nearby from which they had always swum in summer was now polluted with manure. They had formed a committee of activists to monitor the company.

Smithfield said it took the issues raised very seriously and would investigate thoroughly, but had no indication of such problems at its sites. It told me that its US operations are certified under international environmental management systems and these were being used in Poland 'to address deficiencies that were identified in 2003 relating to lack of operating permits for certain of our operations'.

From Smithfield's point of view, campaigners like Marek would hold back Poland's development; whereas it was investing heavily in a country with antiquated facilities and poorly capitalized industries. It told me its aim was to help secure Polish farmers' future in a global market by offering them access to capital and new technologies.

'Smithfield is continually investing to develop its sites to the highest European standards,' it said in a statement. It also says that its production sites are all British Retail Consortium approved, and that it is 'committed to being the industry leader in animal welfare practices'. Prima withdrew from its plans for Kiełkówo shortly after my visit.

Marek and I drove on, to meet government ministers in Warsaw. On the outskirts of the city of Wrocław, we passed a procession of gleaming tankers coming and going from the great multimillion-pound factory built by US-owned Cargill. Cargill had set up animal feed production and distribution in Poland and from this site the global grain trader hoped to build its position as leading supplier of isoglucose to EU markets. The isoglucose, made from Polish wheat, is like corn syrup and is used to sweeten drinks and confectionery. The plant had a greater capacity than all the facilities in Germany, France and Italy combined. When the Polish government, required by the EU on accession to stick to European sugar industry quotas, gave an allowance to Cargill that only accounted for a fraction of the factory's potential output, Cargill began legal proceedings against the Polish government for $130 million compensation for breaches of bi-lateral US investment treaties. The case was still going on at the time of writing.

We caught up with the Polish environment minister Krzysztof Szamałek at Warsaw's London Steak House. He was bullish about the future but thought it would involve great upheaval. 'Small farms will disappear – it's economically inefficient. You have to be a bigger producer. There will be a process of concentration and people from small farms will have to move to find work. Of course unemployment will rise, of course there will be migration, and of course there is a link between rural employment and the rise of the populist movement.'

Next day, as our journey came to an end and I headed back for home, the road took us past a ring of giant Western hypermarkets around town and a new Tesco. The car radio gave the result of latest polls in the election campaign. The party leading was the ultra-right nationalist party, Self Defence, headed by Andrzej Lepper. He had made the fate of the Polish peasant farmer one of his rallying cries. He subsequently became agriculture minister in the new coalition government.

The road from Warsaw was deeply rutted, giving way under the sheer weight of the newly arrived foreign juggernauts. The lorries of food hauliers ahead of us, familiar from our own crowded motorways – Willi Betz, TransAmerican Leasing and Tesco – were all taking their toll. The infrastructure had not been built to withstand them. 'You see, we are in danger of swapping one Big Brother for another. Why should this be the only model of economic development?' Marek wanted to know.

5. Sugar

I was struck recently by a scene at the school gate. It was the occasion of the Christmas Fair and the playground had been given over, with a typical twenty-first-century sense of priorities, to a car park. I stood and watched as small children emerged one after another from the school entrance only to explode in to tantrums. Irritable parents dragged them to their vehicles, their own tempers controlled with varying degrees of success.

Inside the school building the fair had been a consumption fest; more specifically a sugar fest, for sweet things had been thrust at the children at all turns. Brightly-coloured chews, with that lingering artificial fruit smell common to cheap confectionery, fabric conditioner and shampoo, had been consolation prizes in competitions; ten-penny lollipops on sticks had acted as irresistible lures to stalls; outsize American-trans-fat-style donuts washed down with fizzy drinks had done a roaring trade in the dining hall. These children had been as high as kites on sugar, additionally dosed with neurotoxic additives, and were now crashing back down to bad temper. The pleasure of the sugary excess had proved as brief as its outcome predictable. I found myself remembering a TV comedy sketch in which well-heeled suckers line up at a cash point, only to be robbed one after another by the yobs who are clearly standing waiting for them at the head of the queue. The parental exasperation in the playground was palpable, but why hadn't they seen it coming, or had they just felt they had no power to avoid the trap waiting for them at the end of the line?

On this occasion I was observing the comic performance,

but the scene has remained etched on my mind because I have been there myself, many a time.

To mention that there might be cause and effect between behaviour and junk food was, until recently, to have yourself marked down for a joyless bore – one of the reasons that it is indeed so hard to avoid the trap at the end of the line. What's wrong with a little sugar on a special occasion? Where's the scientific evidence of that cause and effect? Few culinary pleasures can match the rapture that comes from melting sweetened cocoa butter in your mouth. Why shouldn't we and our children indulge now and then?

In Shakespeare's times sugar represented innocence and purity – 'white-handed mistress one sweet word with thee,' says Berowne in *Love's Labour's Lost*. 'Honey, milk and sugar, there is three,' replies the Princess of France. But today sugar has formed an unholy trinity with fat and salt to become the devil incarnate, or at least the new nicotine. 'Sugar is as dangerous as tobacco [and] should be classified as a hard drug, for it is harmful and it is addictive,' a recent sounding in the distinguished *British Medical Journal* proposed. How have we managed to turn this sweet pleasure in to a habit as dissolute as the Rake's progress? Why can't we just say no? And if sugar really is addictive, how is that habit formed?

In fact we are born with an attraction to sweetness, taking our first gulps of it in the womb, when we swallow amniotic fluid. The evolutionary explanation is that this is how we learned to distinguish foods that are generally safe, since there is nothing in nature that is sweet and poisonous, from bitter ones that may contain toxins. Breast milk too is sweet, though, as mentioned earlier, flavours from the mother's diet during pregnancy and after birth are transmitted both to the amniotic fluid and to breast milk, so that breastfed babies experience not only sweetness but a wide range of tastes from sour to spicy.

A whole science has grown up to understand how our early taste buds are formed and how this may affect the way we eat later, with much of the cutting edge work being conducted at the Monell Chemical Senses Center in Philadelphia, a research establishment part-sponsored by industry. There Dr Julie Mennella has studied the formation of palates from the youngest ages and is currently exploring the relationship between early preferences for sweet foods and subsequent alcoholism. She has established that babies can detect sweet tastes at birth – and can even distinguish between different types of sugars. Sweet tastes can also act as analgesics and reduce the sensation of pain in children. She explained to me why she thought we were pro-grammed with this liking for sweet things. 'The heightened taste for sweetness occurs during periods of maximum growth and doesn't diminish until after adolescence, suggesting we crave sweetness when we have the greatest need for density of calories.' Bitter tastes on the other hand are learned. Before the mass industrialization of the diet, culinary traditions helped in the process of getting young children used to foods that are not sweet but are important sources of vitamins and minerals. 'If you mix salty, bitter and sweet in a solution, the solution tastes less bitter and more sweet – salt reduces the sensation of bitterness, which is why the rules of most traditional cuisines match salt with bitter things.'

But we have abandoned culinary traditions. Instead when we wean our children on manufactured baby foods today we take their palates in a different direction. Most graduate from the sorts of powdered baby rice my health visitor recommended to bottled jars of baby food. Before the 1970s, processed baby foods were a minority sport. Now they are regularly served up by large numbers of new parents as their confidence in what is safe and wholesome has disappeared. Although few baby food manufacturers supplying Europe add sugar as sucrose to their products these days, they are still often very sweet, making use of sugars processed from concentrated fruits such as apple and sweet vegetables such as sweet potato instead of more readily identifiable refined sugars.

Going through the baby products in my supermarket I found a 213ml jar of junior baby food apple and blueberry with 33g of sugars for example – that's the equivalent of eleven sugar cubes. Baby vegetable purées were noticeably sweet too, 12g of sugars in a jar of sweet potato; the meat dishes also had an underlying sweetness, a vegetable, beef and spaghetti I found in the supermarket had 4g of sugars a jar.

The way baby foods are processed plays a part as well. Gerrie Hawes, who used to work for Heinz and now runs her own baby food company Fresh Daisy, persuaded me to try some home-made dishes pureed in a blender alongside bottled equivalents to see the difference. 'Nearly all baby food jars are long-life products. The process involves cooking the food once, putting it in jars and then cooking it again in the jar under pressure to 121 degrees Celsius or more for up to forty minutes. The high temperature achieves the desired sterilization of the food but also changes the taste, texture and colour; it caramelizes the sugars in fruit and vegetables. Babies acquire a taste for that caramelized flavour.' It was true; the home cooked food had a graininess and cleaner mix of flavours even when pureed that the manufactured food did not.

The food industry is reluctant to surrender the power this sweetness gives them over its young customers. Global standards for foods are set by the Codex Alimentarius Commission and these are increasingly used as benchmarks in World Trade Organization meetings. At a meeting of Codex in November 2006, the Thai government introduced a proposal to reduce the levels of sugars in baby foods from the existing maximum of 30 per cent to 10 per cent as part of the fight against obesity. The proposal was blocked by the US and the EU.

Patti Rundall, an indefatigable promoter of breastfeeding and policy director of the Baby Milk Action group, is convinced such early exposure to refined sugars is how babies get hooked on sweetness at the point at which they would otherwise be weaned off it. Follow-on formulas are often incredibly sweet, and can contain 60 per cent more sugars than regular milk. Rundall points out that several research studies have shown correlations between bottle feeding and subsequent obesity. 'A bottle-fed baby consumes 30,000 more calories over its first eight months than a breastfed one. That's the calorie equivalent of 120 average chocolate bars. It's hugely important to obesity.'

The taste, once acquired, is maintained by sweetened snack foods and processed meals. Even salty snacks are sweetened – Pringles Originals are flavoured with dextrose while some children's crisps are sweetened with the artificial sweetener aspartame. The process of sweetening is often hidden: I found in my local store up-market crisps with 'sea salt and black pepper flavouring' that turned out on detailed inspection to contain the milk sugar lactose, and a variety with 'sea salt and West Country cider flavouring' that contained not a hint of West Country cider but milk sugar, sugar and flavouring instead. A whole new marketing language has been created to signal subliminally the sweetness of supposedly savoury foods: spicy Moroccan, Thai sweet chilli, caramelized onion, balsamic vinegar.

As well as the sugared breakfast cereals (see Chapter 1: Cereals), others foods purporting to be healthy are often so heavily sweetened they might as well be confectionery. Fruit-flavoured yoghurts have not simply had their sourness reduced; they can be sweeter than a chocolate mousse and be up to a fifth sugar. A 'light' strawberry yoghurt I found boasted that it was virtually fat-free but it was 7 per cent sugars, with not only added fructose but extra artificial sweetening too. In general as manufacturers have lowered fats to attract shoppers who are becoming more health conscious, they have replaced them with increased sugars, leaving you no better off. They've got to get in cheap bulk somehow.

The staples are not immune either. Look at the nutritional label on a traditionally made cheese and the line for sugars will read zero. Pick up a cheese spread or processed children's cheese and you can find it contains 6 per cent sugars, thanks to the milk sugars in the skimmed milk powders from which it is manufactured. Pizzas, buns for burgers, sausages and ready meals all get sweetened. Beer is the same: learning to like the bitter taste of ale is no longer an adult rite of passage. Industrial global beer brands have been dumbed down. They are not necessarily sweeter but they are less bitter and blander, even as they become higher in alcohol. Manufacturers use fewer hops and rather than using malt, bulk them out with brewing sugars, according to the Campaign for Real Ale.

Not even fresh unprocessed food has escaped this relentless sweetening of our palates. Wondering why so many of our traditional fruits have become hard to find in the cosmetically perfect world of the supermarket, it occurred to me it might not just be a question of shelf life. Many of those that have all but disappeared from the high street are the sharp tastes that require more effort whether it be gooseberries, rhubarb, bilberries or damsons. Pineapples are now all super sweet – which feels like progress – but where are the more subtle depths of flavour? I wondered whether even the pleasure of a ripe berry was in danger of forming a continuum that travels from blameless fruit to calorie-laden junk and on to obesity.

I decided to go to the East Malling research station, in Kent's Medway valley, one of the world's leading plant breeding centres, to find out if everything really was, as I feared, getting sweeter. Taking my coals to Newcastle, I carried a bag of supermarket-bought fruit to the labs set among its orchards of fruit trees gnarled by expert pruning. Vicky Knight, one of East Malling's raspberry breeders, Dave Simpson, a strawberry expert, and Ken Tobutt, an apple, cherry and rootstock man, had agreed to check the sugars content of my bag, which contained samples of the recently registered variety of apple Pink Lady and the long-established Cox's orange pippin, along with grapes with novel names and punnets of raspberries and blue-berries. It was the end of January but I had been able to purchase unseasonable fruits from around the world. The industry tests for sweetness in fruit using a small instrument called the Brix refractometer – it measures the density of liquid by the degree to which light is bent as it passes through its prism. The higher the score, the denser the juice and the greater the concentration of sugars.

The breeders all agreed that the taste of fruit in general had got sweeter, and our palates had altered, but it wasn't necessarily as simple as the levels of sugars in them being higher. Perception of fruit varieties and their taste is affected by acid levels. Sometimes what's happened is that fruit has had its acid levels altered by breeding so it tastes blander. The key thing about bland fruit is that you can consume it in larger quantities, and so you tend to come back for more of it than of richer varieties, and that helps increase sales, Tobutt explained.

Sweetness is also of course affected by how much sun fruit has seen in a particular year – fruit grown without sun or under plastic is not so sweet. How mature the fruit is when harvested obviously makes a difference to sweetness too but now most crops are mechanically harvested within a short space of time, and there's not usually the chance to come back for a second pick over fruit that is ripening more slowly. Since these factors determining sweetness must bend to forces that are not easily manipulated – supermarket logistics and climate – genetics has been enlisted to do much of the work instead.

Vicky, with thirty-five years' experience as a breeder, cast her trained eye over the plastic trays of cling-wrapped fruit I had pulled out. After years of not buying my fruit this way, the volume of packaging seemed phenomenal. She reached for the apples and read the label.

'Cox's orange pippin, British, grown in Kent, 68–73mm. Sell by January 31st. They'll be over four months old, picked mid-September I'd guess, kept in modified atmosphere to switch off the ripening mechanism. The storage is in a controlled atmosphere where carbon dioxide and oxygen levels are altered to inhibit respiration, they reduce the oxygen to remove ethylene which is a ripening gas; they call it scrubbing.'

She opened the pack and sniffed.

'Zero aroma.'

Dave took them, and shook them knowingly. The pips rattled. Was that significant, I asked, impressed. 'No, it just means that one's a Cox. And it's got pips.'

He added to the fascinating picture they were building up of modern production. 'They are testing a new gas at the moment that binds to receptors in the fruit and switches off the ripening process. Once you remove the fruit from storage it disperses and after a few days it starts ripening again. A day difference in sell by date will make a big difference to the sweetness and taste, if it means a day longer out of modified atmosphere storage.'

'Pink Lady, Italy, 70–75mm, sell-by date January 30,' Vicky noted. We nibbled both samples and agreed the Cox had more flavour but that the Pink Lady tasted sweeter if more bland.

A new variety of grape came out of the bag next. 'Ooh, half price, I like "half price to clear" – they might actually be ripe,' Vicky said. 'Hmm, they are very, very sweet. Sweet and nothing else really,' she decided.

Many breeds of raspberries are now a lot sweeter, they also agreed. 'A new variety, the Canadian Tulâmeen, was released in 1989,' Vicky explained. 'It has a higher Brix score for sweetness than some older varieties, so all new varieties being tested for market are now compared with a sweeter standard than ten years ago, and supermarkets will reject them if they are not sweet enough.'

Now for the proof. Vicky crushed a handful of the raspberries I had brought in a pestle and mortar. 'There's no smell at all, but a slightly bitter undertow to the taste as though you could be chewing the leaves of the plant,' she commented. But they were sweet on the Brix measure, showing as 10 per cent sugars – about the same sweetness as a milkshake.

Next she tested the apples. The new variety, Pink Lady, had what breeders call good crunch, the liquid bursting out of it when I bit into it. Marketed aggressively and grown under strictly controlled licence, it has been highly successful commercially, but it tasted unpleasantly, cloyingly, sweet to me. According to the Brix measure it was 12.5 per cent soluble sugars, high but not that high, but it probably tasted so sweet because there were few other flavours to counteract it. The Cox tasted much less sweet but had more depth and complexity of flavour. Its sugar levels were surprisingly higher on the Brix measure, at 16 per cent, but were balanced by greater acidity.

The blueberries, enjoying a fruit fashion moment, and popular with retailers because they can be sold for high margins, were crushed next. All the colour was in the skin, the flesh itself was pallid with a vague medicinal smell when pounded in the mortar. They were fourteen on the Brix scale.

Red grapes turned out to be the sweetest of the fruits I had bought. A new trademarked variety called Absolutely Pink from South Africa were indeed very more-ish, little explosions in the mouth of sweet liquid with no clearly identifiable flavour, more like a sweetened drink than a fruit. 'Ooh, they are absolutely tasteless,' Vicky said, handing me the refractor for inspection. 'But look, they are staggeringly high on the Brix. Twenty per cent soluble sugars. Exactly what we said, all sugar and no real flavour.'

I later asked David Thomas, the geologist cum nutritionist (see Chapter 3: Milk) who has studied changing nutrient levels in common foods to check how our results at East Malling compared with sugar levels in fruit sixty or so years ago. Thomas does his research by comparing data in wartime editions of the official bible of food analysis *The Composition of Foods* with more recent editions. (The Food Standards Agency which is now actually responsible for compiling and publishing *The Composition of Foods* was remarkably unable to help with this, not possessing a full set of earlier editions to track what has happened to our food.)

The 20 per cent in the new grapes compared with an average of 16 per cent sugars recorded in red grapes in 1940. My admittedly very unscientific collection of samples did all indeed seem sweeter than the average tested back then. Thomas' more detailed research on a wide range of foods, from dairy to vegetables and meat, has suggested that levels of many key minerals such as iron, calcium and zinc have fallen over that period. Intensive farming and fertilizing practices that fail to replenish minerals in the soil must be linked to this but changing breeds may also be playing a part in the decline in nutritional content of our food. The East Malling researchers were not sure about nutrient levels; this not being something supermarkets required information on in their otherwise phenomenally detailed prescriptions for the fruit they sell. They may want to specify size down to the last millimetre or percentage blush, but how much nourishment your food actually contains has not so far been on the list.

Changing sugar content and perception of sweetness like this, say its fans, helps make new foods palatable. East Malling Research's chief executive, Colin Gutteridge, who worked for Cadbury Schweppes for twenty-three years before joining the research station, told me he had seen a 'taste evolution' but it didn't trouble him. 'I remember being presented with yoghurt for the first time when I was nine. It was acidic and I thought it was repulsive. If there is a trend over the past 100 years, it is taking products that are marginal in taste and making them more acceptable to a wider range of people by adding in sweetness. Does any of this matter? Personally, I don't think so. Without it I would never have enjoyed yoghurt.'

He has a point. If fruit has been bred to be more appealing and as a result reluctant consumers eat more of it, that would surely be a good thing. However, a leading French wine maker I met at a Bordeaux wine fair had a different take on this constant raising of the sweetness threshold and its consequences. David Skalli worked as adviser several years ago to French president Nicolas Sarkozy before returning to help with his family wine business. Like his political master he was a free marketeer, a liberalizer who wanted French wine makers to stop depending on subsidies and get on and compete in a globalized world of new wine. But we also had a long conversation about the growing corporate concentration in the wine business and its impact on taste. He described graphically to me the difficulty of catering to the palates of the cola generation. 'Wine is a universal culture. For over 5,000 years drinking it has been rooted to settlements and civilization. But now people want high sugar and increasingly intense flavours in their wines. They expect to be shaken by the wine. It's like an audience that has been going to horror movies since the seventies; they are now so hardened, you have to keep giving them something bigger. More ripeness, more intensity of flavour, more residual sugar or a reduced acidity, and, of course, they want a higher percentage of alcohol.' The alcohol content of wine has been creeping up, and where a wine would typically have been 10 to 11 per cent proof a few years ago, now 13 to 14 per cent proof is the norm.

The problem of course is that these changes are part of a dramatic cultural shift that is not as benign as the odd sweeter raspberry. All this manipulation of our senses has led us into a diet that is good for profits but damages our health.

I thought again of the peasant cookbook that the people of Lampeter had sampled that night in their search for a kind of food that was both sustainable and nourishing. Its recipes, handed down through centuries and designed to make frugal use of what was available, were notable for their complexities of flavouring and texture. Bombarded with the bland and the sugary, today we have instead trained ourselves and our children for the sweet shop, for an instant gratification without effort, which promotes unconscious overindulgence. We train ourselves too in a pattern of highs and lows, accustoming ourselves to the hits that can lead seamlessly into binge drinking.

The driving force behind this shift is a mismatch between our food supply and our biology. Sugar in its various forms is coming at us from all quarters. (Fat is too, as the next chapter shows.) Record sugar cane and sugar beet output from the world's largest producers, Brazil, China, India and Thailand, in the early 2000s have joined subsidized US and EU sugar production. The vast global vat of sweetness has been filled still further by a huge growth in production of sugars from grains such as maize and wheat.

Sugar has become plural. It has so many incarnations today that you have to use the clumsy but more accurate 'sugars' to describe the sweeteners added to our foods. As well as sucrose, the centuries' old form of sugar derived from sugar cane or beet that consists of molecules of glucose and fructose combined, you may now see on the label high fructose corn syrup, dextrose, fructose, maltose, glucose or glucose syrup. All that subsidized dairy surplus does its bit too. It not only provides concentrated fats for manufacturing, its sweetness can be extracted in the form of lactose. In Britain we consume about 2.25 million tonnes of sugar a year. We only buy a fraction of that as table sugar – three quarters of what the country gets through goes directly to industrial users.

Sugar production from cane and beet is a highly concentrated business, just like the trade in the other agricultural commodities highlighted in previous chapters. In many cases, the players are the same. Governments around the world have long subsidized sugars and protected their domestic markets in them, and in doing so have fostered the interests of a handful of transnational corporations. The global sugar trade is, in other words, yet another fine example of corporate welfare funded by taxpayers. Our habits have not been formed by chance.

Production of sucrose in the UK is a legally sanctioned duopoly. British Sugar, a subsidiary of Associated British Foods (which is also a leading player in baking), controls 60 per cent of the UK domestic market and has held the entire quota for production of sugar from beet in the UK under the EU sugar regime. Tate & Lyle meanwhile is the sole refiner of imported sugar cane in the UK and controls the other 40 per cent of domestic consumption. Tate & Lyle interestingly describes itself as 'a world-leading manufacturer of renewable food' that helps 'add taste, texture, nutrition and increased functionality to everyday products used by millions of people around the world'.

The major global traders are highly integrated too, controlling both production and processing. The big three traders in sugars internationally are US-based Cargill (yes, them again), which trades and ships over 6.5 million tonnes of raw sugar each year; the French privately owned transnational Louis Dreyfus, which handles over four million tonnes annually, and Tate & Lyle, which accounts for four to five million tonnes a year. Dreyfus, as well as being one of the world's leading grain traders, is the largest supplier of sugar to American cane refiners and has annual global sales in excess of $20 billion. Tate & Lyle grew from a merger in 1921 of Henry Tate and Abram Lyle's sugar refining companies.

Cargill also controls a huge chunk of the global market in sweeteners derived from grains. Cargill and ADM each have about 30 per cent of the US market in high fructose corn syrup used to sweeten American soft drinks and processed foods. Glucose syrups or isoglucose blends are the preferred sweeteners for many European and British food and drink manufacturers. Isoglucose is a blend of glucose and fructose; when the fructose in the blend reaches 42 per cent it matches the sweetness of traditional sugar. Glucose syrups are similar to high fructose corn syrup although the glucose to fructose ratios can vary, as can the type of grain from which they are produced. Demand has been growing dramatically. They are handy because they supply not only sweetness but add cheap bulk and viscosity or thickness.

Production of sweeteners from grain in Europe has been limited until recently by EU sugar quotas, but as they are liberalized, isoglucose is taking off. Cargill has been building up its already powerful European presence. The Cargill isoglucose factory I had driven past in Poland with Marek was built as a bridgehead into the EU market.

In 2001 Cargill also acquired the French sweetener and starch processing company Cerestar for $1.1 billion. The merger was referred to the competition authorities but cleared, although it gave Cargill control of 38 per cent of the total EU production of glucose syrups and blends and nearly half of UK production, while also reinforcing its position as the leading supplier of glucose in North America. A Tate & Lyle subsidiary holds a further quarter of the UK glucose market.

Cargill makes its glucose syrups mainly from corn and in total about half the glucose blends in Europe are currently made from corn, although wheat is also used. Tate & Lyle for example makes glucose blends from wheat at its factory in Greenwich.

The Competition Commission inquiry that gave Cargill the go ahead for the merger gives the details of how most glucose blends in Europe are now made: first the grain is 'wet milled' to produce a starch slurry. The starch molecules in the starch slurry are made up of long chains of glucose molecules. Acids or enzymes are then used as catalysts in a process of hydrolysis to break down the starch chains to produce glucose.

Once the glucose syrup is made, it can be processed further into a range of other sweeteners. It may be hydrogenated to produce polyols or sugar alcohols such as sorbitol, mannitol or maltitol widely used in toothpaste, chewing gums and confectionery. Or a further enzyme process can turn it into maltodextrins or dried glucose. Maltodextrins are only moderately sweet and are often used in baby foods or sports drinks.

Until its recent reform, the EU sugar regime paid European farmers three times the world price for their beet-derived sugar and imposed production quotas and import controls on other sugar. The cost to the EU taxpayer was over €1 billion a year. EU sugar traders and processors as a result enjoyed huge subsidies in the form of export refunds from the Common Agriculture Policy for the difference between the artificially maintained EU price and the world price. They have also been able to dump their subsidized surplus on world markets at an artificially low price, undermining less developed countries' economies and promoting sugar consumption.

The largest recipient of CAP payments in the UK has been Tate & Lyle. If you remember it was not the farmers but the transnational manufacturers who topped the list of individual CAP payments we managed to get published under Freedom of Information legislation (see Chapter 3: Milk).

Tate & Lyle collected a whopping £358 million of taxpayers' money between 2002 and 2005. The second largest recipient of public funds in the UK was an old sugar trading company called Czarnikow Sugar, which banked £73.5 million over the same period. It likes to keep a low profile; I was told when I rang it to ask for more details of why it qualified for such largesse from the CAP. The sugar cartels compete with the dairy and barley barons in this form of wealth creation.

These figures just relate to payments made under CAP in the UK. Campaigners against EU agricultural subsidies have been able to identify further payments to Tate & Lyle subsidiaries in Belgium, and the Netherlands too, but many countries have still not published full lists of recipients. Dreyfus would no doubt be high on a French list of CAP payments were the French ever to release one.

Just as US government and its corn subsidies have promoted

a surplus of that commodity to be turned into sweeteners as well as animal feed, so has it supported its domestic sugar production with protectionist policies since the Great Depression. Overproduction then was causing prices to fall, and a system of price supports was introduced with the Sugar Act of 1934. They remain today. The effect has been to subsidize continued overproduction. Sugar refiners and growers in the US have benefited to the tune of $2 billion a year, according to an estimate in 2000 made by the US Congress's General Accounting Office.

No surprise then that sugar has been the largest agricultural donor to political campaigns in the US. In the 2003/4 election campaign the industry gave nearly $1 million in direct contributions to candidates. This was par for the course – in the fifteen years from 1990 its political donations to federal politicians came to more than $20 million.

One of the most generous donors has been the Fanjul family, whose sugar cane growing and refining operations are based in Florida. Florida is one of a handful of key swing states in US presidential elections. Both Republicans and Democrats are keenly aware of the need to keep its business interests on side.

The sugar industry manages to play it both ways. One of the Fanjul brothers is one of George Bush's top fundraisers. Another Fanjul brother has been a substantial donor to the Democrats. The access these sugar barons enjoy in Washington was highlighted when Bill Clinton famously interrupted an Oval Office assignation with Monica Lewinsky in 1996 to take a phone call from Alfonso Fanjul Junior.

The sugar industry has been amply rewarded for this support. Bush's US farm bill in 2002 committed to continue its sugar subsidies despite international pressure to cut them. And when the US has negotiated new free trade agreements with countries such as Australia and the Dominican Republic, which were supposed to liberalize markets and remove protectionist import quotas on both sides, sugar was simply omitted on US insistence.

The EU sugar regime was finally reformed in 2005 after the World Trade Organization ruled it illegal. The price support was cut, but not by the 50 per cent originally proposed. It was reduced by 36 per cent only, and thanks to determined lobbying, the sugar industry managed to extract €6 billion in compensation from taxpayers in return.

Sugar is a key commodity for many of the world's poorest countries, but thanks to these distorting subsidies, and the dumping of surplus that they encourage, they have not been able to benefit from the comparative advantage they have of climate and lower production costs. Meanwhile our money has been used to encourage overproduction of a bulk ingredient for manufacturing that is damaging our health.

Most people know instinctively that eating too much sugar is likely to make you fat and rot your teeth. The idea that consumption should be cut, and that we therefore need to produce less, probably doesn't seem very controversial. But that is to underestimate the scale of the vested interests. When the World Health Organization dared to suggest sugar consumption around the world should be reduced because it is causing chronic disease, the US sugar lobby provided an extraordinary show of its determination to fight off all threats.

In 2003 the WHO together with the UN's Food and Agriculture Organization published a final draft report spelling out the dangers of excess sugar, fat and salt consumption. For the first time it said that added sugars were a likely cause of obesity. Obesity, a serious health problem in its own right, is also a cause of diabetes, cardiovascular disease and some cancers. The report, known as '916' in WHO's technical series, recommended that people should eat no more than 10 per cent of their calories as added sugars.

It also warned that as developing countries switched to the highly processed high-sugar, high-salt, high-fat diets adopted earlier by industrialized countries, they were soaring up the obesity leagues and acquiring the diet-related diseases more associated with the affluent West. By 2025, for example, it predicted that India would have one of the highest rates of Type 2 diabetes, a diet-related form of the disease that has exploded in the subcontinent since it opened its markets to the big global brands of carbonated drinks and their advertising in 1992.

The report was based on advice from thirty independent experts whose names are a roll call of the great and the good of international nutrition science. It was meant to form the basis for a global strategy that individual national governments could use to tackle obesity and these diet-related diseases. But this limit of 10 per cent of calories from added sugars presented an enormous threat to the food and drink industry.

Boys and girls aged four to fourteen in the UK today are getting between 16 and 17 per cent of their daily calories from processed sugars according to the official National Diet and Nutrition Surveys. By the age of seven children are eating an average of half a kilo of sugary foods a day. By the age of fifteen boys typically have a 40kg a year habit, the equivalent of 1,000 cans of cola or 11,800 sugar cubes, and that's only counting what gets owned up to in food diaries. (In fact research has shown that these sorts of food diaries significantly under-record consumption. The sugary snacks eaten on the hoof, sometimes illicitly, tend to get forgotten from the lists.) Taking into account under-reporting, our teenage boys are matching or exceeding the consumption of impoverished manual workers of the nineteenth century whose requirement for calories was determined by fourteen hours or more of hard physical labour a day. And these are averages – those who live on junk food diets can easily get 30 per cent of their energy as sugars.

Although people reduce their consumption as a percentage of energy as they get older, all age groups get more of their calories from sugars than the WHO recommended 10 per cent, except older women. When over fifty, women just meet the target, unless they are unfortunate enough to have to go into an institution, when their consumption of processed sugars shoots up again.

British children are the gluttons of Europe in this. A child in the UK aged five to nine years gets through an average of £106-worth of confectionery a year, and roughly the same value of carbonated drinks. In France they consume only the equivalent of £60-a-year-worth of confectionery and £32-worth of fizzy drinks. In Italy confectionery spending for young children is limited to £31 a year and fizzy drinks to £49. By the time they get to the tweens, British ten- to thirteen-year-olds outdo their Continental peers in sweets and sugary drinks by an even greater margin. Once again, Britain, with its early severing of connections with the land and traditional food culture, seems to have been peculiarly susceptible to junk food compared with its Continental neighbours.

Only the Americans surpass us. In the US sugars average 16 per cent of calories in the diet, with children pushing the figure up to 20 per cent. Cutting sugars back to 10 per cent of calories, in other words, would mean a significant drop in consumption. The managing director of Tate & Lyle Clive Rutherford had already articulated what this would mean for the industry in 1997. He told a meeting of the International Sugar Organization: 'Perhaps the greatest threat to internal sugar consumption comes from the anti-sugar lobby who promote fake and misleading opinions on sugar in relation to diet and health. These activists seek to reduce consumption [of added sugars] to less than 10 per cent of calorie intake. To achieve this would mean a reduction in consumption of approximately 25 per cent in most developed countries, equal on a European basis to three million tonnes.'

Big sugar was having none of it. It set out to block the WHO strategy. The US industry's lobby group the Sugar Association wrote to the director general of the WHO threatening to 'exercise every avenue available to expose the dubious nature' of the report, including pulling in its political markers to challenge the organization's future funding – WHO is dependent on the $400 million-plus a year that the US government contributes to its budget. 'If necessary we will promote and encourage new laws which require future WHO funding to be provided only if the organization accepts that all reports must be supported by the preponderance of science,' it wrote.

The sugar industry also urged the American Secretary of State for Health Tommy Thompson to use his influence to get the report withdrawn. As the report proceeded through the protracted UN consensus system, it continued its ferocious lobbying, enlisting poorer producing countries to its side. Then just as the strategy was due to be presented to the WHO's executive board, the US health department weighed in. A letter was sent to the head of the WHO disputing the report's scientific basis and challenging the idea that some foods were good and some bad, in words that bore remarkable similarity to the industry's own arguments. The letter came from a special assistant to the US Health Secretary, one William Steiger, godson of George Bush Senior.

The scale, blatancy and sheer clumsiness of the lobbying left nutrition experts open-mouthed. They recalled nothing like it since the tobacco industry tried to block action on smoking. We should perhaps not be so surprised. To reduce sugar consumption would force the food industry to move away from precisely those 'added value' foods and drinks they build their profits on. It would have to abandon its economic model: which is to take cheap commodity ingredients and process them into products that can be sold for much more than the sum of their parts.

Official surveys show that the main sources of excess sugars in the diet for people of all ages are soft drinks, chocolate and confectionery, preserves, biscuits, breakfast cereals and cereal bars. But if you wanted to change the picture at a stroke, particularly for children, it is what the Americans have dubbed liquid candy that stands out.

British teenagers take in nearly half their sugars each day as soft drinks and derive nearly a quarter of their total calories from them. Half the increase in calories in the US in the last few years has come from soft drink consumption. And research has confirmed that for every extra daily helping of sugary drink, the incidence of obesity is significantly increased. Researchers at the Boston children's hospital demonstrated the causal link in a randomized controlled trial in which half the children were encouraged to stop drinking sugar-sweetened drinks by home delivery of alternative drinks. During the course of the trial their consumption of sugar drinks was almost eliminated which led to significant weight loss, particularly among those who started overweight.

Again most people are now aware that sweetened drinks are best kept limited, even if they weren't until recently. Sales of sweetened soft drinks overall have fallen slightly in the past couple of years, as people switch to fresh fruit juice, but they still remain far higher than a decade ago. In 1992 we drank 1.5l of soft drinks per person per week; that rose to about 1.8l in 2003/4, and dipped down to about 1.7l in 2004/5. But of course the fruit juice is getting sweeter. Sainsbury's has started selling a fresh pressed, not from concentrate, red merlot grape juice that is delicious but contains a breathtaking 44g of sugars per modest serving, that's more than fourteen sugar cubes. It's also more than is in a can of cola, albeit in a different form. A traditional pressed apple juice next to it on the shelf has 27g of sugars per serving.

We have no physiological need for refined sugar. In fact as the economic historian Henry Hobhouse has pointed out, before the sixteenth century the whole of the European world had managed on minuscule quantities of it, and all the glories of the Renaissance were created on just a teaspoonful per head of sugar per year.

Our physiology is geared to eating food in its whole, natural state rather than concentrated form. Refined sugars, and highly refined carbohydrates generally, are converted very rapidly to blood sugar which gives you a burst of energy and a high – rapidly followed by a low as the pancreas releases insulin to reduce blood-sugar levels, leaving you hungry for yet more sugars. This is why all these processed sugars are both attractive and potentially pernicious. On a diet high in refined sugars, you quickly slip into these swings of high and low that keep you coming back for more sugary foods. Stimulant drinks such as tea, coffee and colas or caffeinated sports energy drinks help lift the blood sugar in an additional way. They trigger the release of adrenalin, the flight or fight chemical and associated stress chemicals such as cortisol, which in turn trigger the release of glucose into the blood.

Intriguing evidence is also beginning to emerge that explains why high sugar consumption becomes quite so addictive. In animal experiments at Princeton University, Carlo Colantuoni has shown that rats that have been fed a diet of 25 per cent sugar and then have it removed show signs of opioid withdrawal. 'The indices of anxiety and other symptoms were similar to withdrawal from morphine or nicotine,' he reports in the journal *Obesity*. Others have linked sugar consumption to major depression and mental health problems.

The blood sugar curves are quite different when you eat whole foods. They are metabolized slowly so that energy is released steadily over a longer period. Their sugars come bound up with fibre so that they give you a feeling of fullness and satiety and you are less able to overeat.

Soft drinks on the other hand are the epitome of energy dense and nutrient light food. You can drink them without feeling full. Even fruit juices are the same – they are con-centrated calories. You can down a large glass of concentrated apple juice and still have room for more, yet it is the calorie equivalent of three or more fresh apples and you'd be pushed to eat more than three apples on the trot. Unlike fizzy drinks, fruit juices are at least a good source of vitamins, but this is why the official recommendations suggest only one portion of fruit juice a day. (The same applies to processed snack foods like crisps. Two packs of potato crisps are the calorie equivalent to half a kilo of boiled potatoes. Chomping through the latter would leave you feeling pretty replete, where the crisps would not.)

Refined sugars are not only stripped of the fibre that helps you feel full. Separated from their original plant source, they contain no micronutrients such as vitamins and essential minerals either, but provide only empty calories. Brown sugar retains traces of minerals but not enough to write home about.

Foods with lots of added sugars in other words have lots of calories but precious little nutrition. Moreover, if up to a quarter of your energy is coming from the empty calories of refined sugars, the sugars inevitably displace whole fresh foods with vitamins and minerals. If the fresh fruit and vegetables have also been engineered for sugar and sweetness rather than for nutrients levels and have been grown in depleted soils, it is even harder to get the vitamins and minerals you need.

This was vividly illustrated by a survey of pre-school children in 1997 that looked at intake of sugars and sugary food and relative nutrient intake. The children eating the most sugars were getting the lowest levels of nutrients, apart from vitamin C which is often added to sugary soft drinks as a preservative and to justify their sale. The children who were the highest sugar eaters were getting the lowest levels of dietary fibre, and not surprisingly, eating fewer wholegrain foods and fruit and vegetables. Those regularly eating chocolates, sweet biscuits, and sweetened soft drinks were getting significantly less vitamin B1, B2, B3, folic acid, vitamin D, calcium, zinc and iron. Their iron and zinc intakes in particular fell well short of the level considered the minimum for health. These minerals are found in seeds, nuts, wholegrains, pulses, well-reared meat and green vegetables.

As you expose yourself to sugar, your liking for it increases. Your sweetness threshold is raised, just as with salt. That's why, quite apart from all the controversies surrounding their safety, artificial sweeteners don't work. Their sweetness is also intense, so if anything they increase the threshold of sweetness. Aspartame, for example, is about 200 times sweeter than sucrose. Sucralose is about 600 times as sweet.

The use of artificial sweeteners has grown as people have tried to switch away from sugars to products they perceive as more healthy. But they have not displaced sugars. About 800,000 tonnes of artificial sweeteners were used around the world in 2007, and consumption has been growing 3 per cent in volume every year since the late 1990s. Yet all these extra sweeteners have not dented sales of sugars – we just keep managing to absorb more and more sweetness.

But then the same political drivers have been at play in the past with artificial sweeteners. Aspartame has a highly controversial history but writing about it tends to land you in hot water. A British Liberal Democrat MP Roger Williams drew attention to what he said were worrying elements in the regulatory process whereby the artificial sweetener had been approved. He told the House of Commons in 2005 that 'crucial questions that have been largely repressed since the early 1980s hang over aspartame's safety. When journalists attempted to tackle those questions, their newspapers were threatened with intimidating letters from the industry's lawyers. I am duty-bound by the immunity afforded to me under parliamentary privilege and as a servant of the public to initiate a debate that has been silenced for over two decades.'

In 1977 Donald Rumsfeld, later George Bush's Defence Secretary but then chief executive of the pharmaceutical company GD Searle, publicly stated that he would 'call in his markers' to win a licence for aspartame, the sweetener that had been discovered by chance in Searle's laboratories, Williams told the House of Commons in an adjournment debate in December 2005. There was much controversy about aspartame's safety at the time but 'Rumsfeld appears to have honoured his pledge'. In fact, 'the history of the approval of aspartame puts public health regulators and politicians to shame,' he ventured.

The sweetener is used in about 6,000 products, from crisps such as Walkers prawn cocktail, to soft drinks including Diet Coke and Robinson's fruit squash, chewing gums such as Orbit, and vitamins pills and medicines. Yet the science on which it was given approval was 'biased, inconclusive, and incompetent', according to Williams. 'There is compelling and reliable evidence for this carcinogenic substance to be banned from the UK food and drinks market,' he believed.

On the day of his inauguration as President in 1981, with Mr Rumsfeld on his transition team, Ronald Reagan personally wrote an executive order suspending the head of the US Food and Drug Administration's powers on aspartame, Mr Williams further claimed. One month later Mr Reagan appointed a new head of the regulatory authority, Arthur Hayes, who granted a licence for the sweetener. 'The history of aspartame's approval is littered with examples showing that if key decision makers found against aspartame's safety, they were discredited or replaced by industry sympathizers, who were recompensed with lucrative jobs.'

Searle had originally submitted a host of studies to the FDA in the 1970s in the hope of getting aspartame approved. But when flaws were revealed in the science behind another Searle product, Flagyl, the FDA set up a taskforce to investigate fifteen of the key studies submitted by Searle on aspartame. Dr Jerome Bressler was commissioned by the FDA to investigate three of these studies. He had found fifty-two major discrepancies in Searle's clinical conduct of the studies, Mr Williams told the Commons. Tumours contracted by rats were removed before dissection but not reported; one record shows an animal in the experiment was alive, then dead, then alive again, then dead again.

MPs were told that because it lacked funds, the FDA submitted the twelve other studies to be analysed by a research body that was under contract to Searle at the time and therefore had a conflict of interest. It declared all twelve studies authentic. Doubts about aspartame among FDA scientists were overruled by the FDA's administration and it was given approval. Many other countries soon followed suit and approved aspartame on the basis of the same flawed studies, Mr Williams said. In 1996 a review of aspartame research found that every single industry-funded study found aspartame safe. But 92 per cent of independent studies identified one or more problems with its safety.

Mr Williams outlined to MPs the evidence that the breakdown products of aspartame include suspected carcinogens and toxic molecules that damage nerve cells. But the final nail in the coffin for the sweetener, he told MPs, was a new, 'monumental' peer-reviewed study, that should have 'set alarm bells ringing in health departments around the world'.

This vast study, conducted by the Italian-based independent European Ramazzini Foundation, demonstrated that aspartame caused a significant increase in lymphomas and leukaemias, malignant tumours of the kidneys in female rats and malignant tumours of peripheral and cranial nerves in male rats. These tumours occurred at doses that were well below the acceptable daily intake recommended by the regulatory authorities in the EU and US.

The MP said he was highlighting 'the strong scientific evidence' that the components of aspartame and their metabolites can cause very serious toxic effects on humans, and that long-term aspartame use can cause cancer in rodents.

The public health minister, Caroline Flint, responding for the government, said it took the issue very seriously and would look at any new evidence. But she added that the use of food additives was very strictly controlled at EU level. The safety of aspartame had been very extensively reviewed many times and the current advice remained that it does not cause cancer and is safe.

Artificial sweeteners help in the control of obesity, she said. Acceptable daily intakes were set at a very conservative level. Moreover, the UK's expert committee on carcinogenicity had reviewed the initial data from the Ramazzini Foundation and had not been convinced by its interpretations, but the European Food Safety Authority would conduct a review when it had the full data.

The European Food Safety Authority did indeed conduct its review. But that too attracted controversy. The reassessment of aspartame was the first big test for the recently-formed authority, which had already lost its first director and 10 per cent of its staff. Over 1,000 people were waiting for the webcast of its judgment on the Italian research. When its expert scientists gathered at a press conference in Rome to give their opinion on the latest research on the sweetener and whether it might cause cancer in May 2006, the acting director of the European Food Safety Authority, Dr Herman Koëter, adopted an unusual opening gambit. He wanted, he said, to tackle the persistent controversy that has swirled around the artificial sweetener aspartame head on.

Aspartame is eaten every day by millions of people around the world – any review of its safety has enormous political and economic implications. But first, Dr Koëter said, he wanted to clear up misunderstandings about 'conflicts of interest' among his advisory panel overseeing the review. MEPs had complained that the scientist who chaired the advisory panel, Dr Susan Barlow, works for the International Life Sciences Institute, a body funded by sweetener manufacturers and major aspartame users such as Coca-Cola, PepsiCo and Nestlé, and Monsanto. The European Commission was also told by MEPs of other 'conflicts of interest'. One scientist involved in the review had declared a research grant from Ajinomoto, the leading Japanese manufacturer of aspartame, they said. Other panel members listed links with food processors such as Nestlé in their declarations of interest. But to say that these scientists therefore have a conflict of interest was a misunderstanding, Dr Koëter explained to the Rome conference. 'The expertise required [to judge any new study on whether aspartame causes cancer] almost inevitably means having a previous involvement.' Eliminate the scientists who had worked in the area before or who had worked for industry and there would be no scientists left, he said. The panel had been 'fully impartial'. Its members had no direct or indirect interest in the particular issue of aspartame. Dr Barlow's work for industry had been generic and had not related to sweeteners. The research grant from Ajinomoto related to a student project on flavourings, not sweeteners.

Then the news that the press conference had been waiting for was delivered. The European Food Safety Authority (EFSA) reconfirmed that aspartame was safe. Having reviewed the new Italian study, its scientific experts decided that it had a number of flaws that undermined the validity of its findings.

The panel therefore concluded: 'There was no need to further review the safety of aspartame nor to revise the previously established acceptable daily intake for aspartame.' The British Food Standards Agency immediately welcomed the judgment, which it said raised similar concerns about the Italian study to those expressed by the UK's independent expert advisory group, the committee on carcinogenicity. Three experts at its meeting to consider the new aspartame study made declarations of interest related to the industry. The industry said the review closed the book on the safety of aspartame. 'The opinion from EFSA is completely consistent with the global scientific consensus that aspartame is safe. Extensive scientific research over decades and regulatory reviews conducted by numerous national and international food safety authorities, together with a history of more than twenty years of safe use, support the conclusion that aspartame is safe,' the Aspartame Information Service, an industry website said. I asked the AIS if it wished to make any further comment, but it said that the EFSA judgment spoke for itself.

The Ramazzini Foundation however refused to close the book on aspartame. Its director, Dr Morando Soffritti, told journalists at the Rome conference that it stood by its research finding that aspartame causes cancer. The decision to reconfirm the safety of aspartame hinged on the complex details of the Italian study.

The foundation's work on the sweetener had begun over seven years previously. A not-for-profit cancer research organization, it uses unorthodox methods in its testing. In the palatial surroundings of a fifteenth-century castle near Bologna, it conducts 'mega-experiments' on rats, in which thousands of animals are treated with suspected carcinogens until they die spontaneously, typically at around three years. The aspartame study involved over 1,800 rats fed a wide range of doses. Other studies typically use only twenty to fifty rats and sacrifice the animals after a fixed period, at about two years. EFSA's panel acknowledged that the new study 'represented a substantial effort' but noted that the methods did not conform to inter- nationally agreed protocols. The foundation argues that its method mirrors the human condition, since over 80 per cent of cancer is diagnosed in people over the age of fifty-five. It adds that its previous studies using the same methods have led to major changes in international regulations several times. But EFSA said that lifetime studies have their own difficulties – animals are likely to suffer more background disease, for example. There may also be postmortem changes in the tissue samples before analysis of animals allowed to die in their own time rather than at a fixed point.

The expert panel's conclusions on the Ramazzini study revolved around three key areas. The Italian researchers reported a significant dose-related increase in blood cancers known as lymphomas and leukaemias in the rats fed aspartame. EFSA scientists decided this finding could be attributed to a high incidence of lung inflammation and infections in the rats rather than to aspartame, and therefore could be dismissed. Dr Soffritti countered that both groups of animals, those treated with aspartame and the control group, had higher rates of inflammation because that is what happens in ageing and dying animals, but the aspartame group had significantly more blood cancers.

The study reported an increase in cancers of the kidney, urethra and bladder. EFSA decided that these were probably related to feeding the rats aspartame but felt they could be explained by imbalances in calcium metabolism, which were specific to the rat and therefore not relevant to humans. In response the Italian researchers said these cancers were found in rats where there was no problem of calcification.

The Italians also found an increase in cancers of the peripheral nerves, which are very rare. This finding depended on diagnosis, according to the EFSA panel. It said there was uncertainty about diagnosis in one case and that the finding could only be evaluated if independent pathologists reviewed the laboratory slides. The Ramazzini researchers, who reported sixteen cases of these types of cancers, said the US national toxicology programme had already given a second opinion on the diagnosis where there was any doubt.

The EFSA panel was unanimous in its decision that the Italian study on aspartame provided 'no scientific basis for reconsidering its use in foods', according to Dr Koëter, but 'if any new information becomes available in the future, EFSA will review these as a matter of priority', he said. As the Rome conference wound up, I asked the EFSA acting head if he himself ate aspartame. 'Yes, I would. In chocolate, I would.' Did that mean he did actually eat aspartame? I persisted. 'I don't drink aspartame in soft drinks, but that's because I don't like the taste.'

He then revealed that he had learned this while working on artificial sweeteners in the past. 'Aspartame has an aftertaste, you know,' he added.

At the time of writing EFSA was reviewing further results from Dr Soffritti's studies which once again suggested a link between aspartame and cancer. Aspartame's manufacturers subsequently commissioned a huge review of studies by a panel of experts who were not aware who was funding the work. 'The authors are an international group of highly respected scientists who have reviewed more than 500 studies dating from before aspartame was approved for use as a food ingredient in 1983 to the most recent studies. The study concludes that aspartame is safe for people of all ages and with a variety of health conditions,' representatives of the manufacturer Ajinomoto wrote, drawing the work to my attention.

The link between disease and diets high in sugars and cheap fats and low in fresh fruit, vegetables and fibre was established nearly 100 years ago. In the early 1900s Robert McCarrison, a British surgeon working in the Indian Medical Service in the North-West Frontier area that now borders bin Laden country, was struck by the extraordinary health and longevity of some of the remotest mountain tribes of the region. He was particularly impressed by the people of Hunza. The Hunza valley in the high Karakorams is also said to have been the inspiration for the mythical paradise of Shangri-la in James Hilton's 1933 novel *Lost Horizon*.

Intrigued by McCarrison's work, I took the chance to visit the valley when I was living in Peshawar working with Afghan refugees in the late 1980s. It is still cut off from the rest of the world by snow for months at a time, sitting as it does at 8,000 feet above sea level, with some of the world's highest and most breathtaking peaks towering above it. To reach it, you must first negotiate the Karakoram Highway that threads a dynamited path, redrawn each year by landslides, along ledges above deep and desolate desert gorges. Eventually the road opens out and you can turn into a side valley of ethereal beauty. Tiny plots, pinned to the hills by dry stone walls, form a cascade of terraces down the mountainside. In late autumn in falling light, the evening leaves of apple, peach and pear orchards turn a blaze of crimson and vermillion against the rose pink of the snow peaks. The soil of the Hunza fields below the retreating glaciers is highly mineralized and irrigated by icy waters channeled with careful husbandry from the spring and summer snowmelt, so its fruits have more than average goodness in them.

The people of Hunza were legendary for living to a great age and for being free of the diseases of industrial nations such as tooth decay, dyspepsia and ulcers, cancer, and heart disease. McCarrison noted that they were 'a race unsurpassed in perfection of physique and in freedom from disease in general'. He set about studying the effect of the Hunza diet on large colonies of experimental rats and comparing it with that of southern Indian peoples whom he found sickly and prone to early death. The Hunza ate wholegrains and pulses, lots of vegetables, often consumed raw, but only a little meat and no sugar or white flour. They also flourished on the famous Hunza apricots and their kernels. The southern Indians were subsisting on a diet of polished rice, vegetable fats and meats with few vegetables or fruits. In later studies McCarrison fed colonies of rats the diet of poor Britons at the time: white bread, margarine, cheap jams, tinned meat, potatoes and sweetened tea. The rats on the Hunza diet thrived, suffering no illness or infant mortality and living long lives. Those on southern Indian food were stricken with diseases of vitamin deficiencies, and also with heart disease, infections, ulcers and cancers. Those on the poor British diet also ailed, and in addition to their physical deterioration, their mental state was affected. 'They were nervous and apt to bite their attendants; they lived unhappily together, and by the sixtieth day of the experiment they began to kill and eat the weaker ones among them,' he wrote. McCarrison concluded that food of 'improper constitution' was responsible for a large proportion of ill health in Great Britain, with refined carbohydrates, sweetened foods and extensive processing being the main culprits. (I recall wanting to add a few small caveats to this pioneering research during my breathless scramble up into the thin air of the Hunza mountains all those years ago. As our party came into a village, a cloud of black flies rose off the legendarily nourishing apricots sun-drying on the roofs of its half-timbered houses. Everyone there certainly looked ancient, but they were rather vague about their actual ages, and the ravages of sun and high altitude may also have made their contribution.)

Although McCarrison's work was widely published and he was honoured at the time for his discoveries, he was ignored by the medical profession. It was setting off on a different path. Just as the vital role of nutrition in health was beginning to be understood, antibiotics were discovered, allowing medicine to ignore prevention of disease through good diet and become preoccupied instead with miracle cures and technical fixes, and allowing intensive farming of animals to take off. It is only now that obesity has reached crisis levels that the mainstream is having to recognize that it must go back to the first links in the food chain.

Because we have no need of sugar and because it was the first commodity to change what had until then been a fixed pattern – that the staple of the diet for civilizations was always a complex carbohydrate – it makes the perfect study of how those first links work. In the history of sugar, you find the conditions that are replicated in subsequent periods of food empire, the exploitation of resources and of people that nearly always underlie the creation of new forms of mass consumption. As Sidney Mintz describes in his definitive history, the sugar trade was the engine of both the first consumerism and of emerging capitalism.

Until mass sugar consumption, maize, rice and wheat had provided staples, with other types of food, vegetables, oils, nuts and seeds used as supplements, and meat, spices and herbs added as flavourings. It was only with the sugar trade that a whole society turned this idea upside down, making sugars, with fats, and meat the dominant elements in the diet.

We tend to think of economic globalization as a phenomenon of the 1990s and beyond, but in fact it began with the growth of the triangular trade between England, Africa and the West Indies back in the seventeenth century. England sent its manufactured iron tools, guns and cloth in its ships to Africa to trade for slaves. In Africa, human cargoes of slaves were loaded with brutal efficiency for the next leg of the ships' journey to the Caribbean; there the British sugar plantations had an insatiable demand for labour and they produced sugar that was then shipped for the final leg of the triangle back to Britain.

From the time when the Arabs first developed its commercial cultivation, building the first mills and refining factories and establishing plantations in the eighth century AD, sugar was a labour-intensive crop and depended on slaves. The Arabs spread sugar through Europe following their conquest of the Spanish peninsula. The crusaders brought sugar back to Europe from their campaigns. Christopher Columbus then took sugar cane to the New World from the Canary Islands. The Portuguese carried it to Brazil and were for a while the major producers in the sixteenth century. But it remained a luxury, compared in worth to pearls and spices, and the preserve of the rich.

Then in the early to mid seventeenth century the English, Dutch and French established their colonies in the Caribbean. The British introduced sugar to Barbados in 1627 and with the invasion of Jamaica in 1655 were able to expand production and establish their West Indian territories as virtual monopoly suppliers of sugar until the Napoleonic wars.

The price of sugar dropped dramatically at the beginning of the eighteenth century and in the hundred years between 1700 and 1800 the mass market in sugar developed. Consumption in Britain increased from about 4lbs per person per year to 18lbs per person per year. Sugar became a necessity. Produced by slaves and imported from the colonies, it was the fuel of the industrial revolution back home – along with cheap bread, it fed the factory workers of the late eighteenth and nineteenth centuries.

The rural poor, forced off the land by the Enclosures, migrated to the towns and became urbanized workers in the new factories of England. With women and children as well as men working in the mills, there was little time for the preparation of slow-cooked vegetable broths that had previously supplemented the diets of the poor, nor was there access to the fresh milk and porridge oats that had added nutrition to the rural diet. Bread washed down with heavily sweetened tea provided the equivalent of today's microwave meal – a semblance of an instant hot meal. Paradoxically even as their incomes increased, the quality of their diets deteriorated. Then from the mid nineteenth century consumption rose exponentially again as free-trade victories made sugar cheaper still and more and more available. By the 1890s each person in Britain was on average eating their way through nearly 90lbs of sugar a year. Here, in our history as the first nation to industrialize, is a large part of the answer to why we have been so much more susceptible to junk food than others. The colonies provided the cheap calories. Crucially for economic development, they also provided a market for manufactured British goods.

In 1848 the philosopher and political economist John Stuart Mill wrote of the sugar colonies: 'There is a class of trading and exporting communities ... hardly to be looked upon as countries ... but more properly as outlying agricultural or manufacturing establishments belonging to a larger community. Our West India colonies, for example, cannot be regarded as countries, with a productive capital of their own ... The West Indies ... are the place where England finds it convenient to carry on the production of sugar, coffees, and a few other tropical commodities. All the capital employed is English capital; almost all the industry is carried on for English uses; there is little production of anything except the staple commodities, and these are sent to England . . . to be sold in England for the benefit of the proprietors there.'

The availability of sufficient cheap labour was vital to the sugar industry. Initially the British sent indentured servants and deported Irish Catholic workers to the West Indies under Cromwell's Western Design to attack Spanish trade. But they suffered such a high mortality rate the owners had to turn elsewhere. Africa became an easier place for procurement.

Between 1670 and 1807 the British carried at least 3.5 million Africans into slavery across the Atlantic. One of the most graphic images of the horror of the trade is perhaps the picture of the slave ship *Brookes*, produced by abolitionist Thomas Clarkson and his fellow campaigners in 1789. It was a diagram purporting to illustrate how slaves might be stowed on board ship for greatest profit. Hundreds of Africans lie dehumanized, crammed into every inch of hold and deck as though they have been forced into a mass grave.

The slaves that survived the middle passage laboured to create wealth that mostly returned to Britain. Sugar became the single most profitable legal cash crop after tobacco and began its extraordinary upward curve. Slaves, who paid with their lives, were the biggest external contribution to Europe's economic growth, contributing to the accumulation of capital back home. This was the beginning of the creation of a system of world trade and of capitalism. It underpinned the growth of empire. 'Sugar led all else in dramatizing the tremendous power concealed in mass consumption. This remains true . . .' Mintz points out.

The mercantile system at home protected the planters' markets, defended the slave trade, supported the growth of the British fleet, and protected factory owners from foreign producers of finished goods as capitalism developed, until it was eventually challenged by the new economic philosophy of free trade in the nineteenth century. By then the working classes depended on sugar and lots of it and free trade would provide it even more cheaply.

Plantations provided the early push for industrialization and intensification of farming. The first stage of processing had to take place near the fields where the cane grew because its chemical composition changed very rapidly after harvesting; so planters had to build labour-intensive boiling houses, distilleries and storehouses on the land – in this, sugar production foreshadows today's pack-house system where farms are turned into industrial complexes attached to fields, needing an infinitely flexible labour force. Slaves on the sugar plantations worked in continuous shifts through the day and half the night, driven by the needs of production rather than of man. Those who fed the cane into the mill were liable to have their fingers caught between the rollers since they had to feed the mill with cane at ceaseless speed. A hatchet was kept nearby to cut off the arm which was always drawn in to the rollers when this happened.

The colonial planters were also the first to work out elaborate staggered patterns of planting to ensure a constant supply of raw material to the boiling houses for processing, precursors to the methods of today's industrial agricultural production.

In Britain, the quayside warehouses that all that nineteenth-century sugar passed through hint at the power of storage and transport in determining markets. The West India Dock in London, completed in 1802, was the world's biggest engineering project at the time, and involved excavating two huge dock basins and constructing half a mile of warehousing along the Thames-side quays. Powerful sugar merchants, who acted not just as slave traders and commodity sellers, but as bankers and insurers too, had the ear of 300 MPs and successfully lobbied the government into not just building the dock but granting them a monopoly over sugar coming into the port of London. The new warehouses, some of which now house the wonderful Museum in Docklands, enabled them to store sugar on an altogether new scale, and thereby manipulate the market. They persuaded the government to make the warehouses bonded, that is secured under joint locks of the Revenue and Customs and the dock companies, so that the duty on the sugar they imported only fell due once they had sold it. With this tax break, they were free to stockpile sugar and control when it was released and at what price. London and the Thames was able to establish itself as major refining centre – the profits from the finished goods accruing to the home nation rather than those countries producing the raw commodities. Transnational commodity trading corporations today understand this vital connection between control of storage and shipping and power over the market. They too have become financiers.

As well as unlocking the power of mass consumption and being the engine of capitalism, the sugar trade provided the first example of ethical shopping. A sugar bowl from the early nineteenth century on display in the Museum in Docklands' new galleries on slavery and sugar was sold with a novel marketing message. Inscribed on the reverse of the Wedgwood design are the words: 'East India sugar not made By Slaves. By Six Families using East India instead of West India Sugar, one less slave is required'. Like so much about so-called 'ethical consumption', it exposes its own limitations. If the system is wrong, you have to change the system, and although the way you shop can send powerful messages, it cannot on its own undo the wrong.

Consumption of sugars today remains a function of price, availability and production, as it has been for centuries. Barry Popkin at the University of Carolina has looked at the food disappearance data for more than 100 countries going back to 1962 – this is the total amount of food available including both what is consumed and what's wasted. In his report 'The Sweetening of the World's Diet', he shows that as populations have become urbanized, dependent on processed foods and exposed to advertising, the number of calories they get from sugars has increased by a third. As the gross national income per capita of a country goes up with industrialization, so too does consumption of sugars. Then the patterns of disease change. The rhetoric of the free market and free choice has obscured the fact that our food choices today are highly manipulated, just as they have been for three centuries and more.

In the early 1980s I had reason to visit a family who were living in Bulgaria a couple of times. I have a vivid memory of the soulless shops of the capital Sofia. Soviet central planning had provided the city with enormous quantities of tinned Vietnamese grapefruit to line the shelves but almost nothing else. Each day you could see the socialist model's notorious queues for the most basic of provisions – grey bread, a little sausage, grey pickled cabbage. In the early autumn it was possible to drive through a village in the country's fertile rural plains where there was a glut of tomatoes, but an hour down the road find the nearest town quite empty of anything fresh to eat, since without a market there was no incentive to get the goods to where they were wanted. You could not but be struck by the dismal failure of the system.

Post communism, the shortages have gone, and the market appears to have responded to consumer demand. Despite my Polish guide Marker's reservations about a new kind of big brother, many of the people of the former Soviet bloc are only too pleased with the arrival of a Western-style food system. Capitalism has given people plenty and the apparent freedom to choose what they want to eat. It has in fact succeeded to the point where there is little argument about any possible alternative system.

The genius of contemporary globalized capitalism, however, has been not just that it gives consumers what they want but that it is able to make them want what it has to sell. Capitalism has done this since its earliest days and the triangular trade. But now it continues to do it even to the point of destruction.

For the inescapable logic at the core of this manufacture of desires is that our desires must be ever expanding.

Even when we have become saturated with sugars we must consume still more. So now a new class of additives has been developed to disguise them. 'Sweetness modifiers', which may be labeled as 'flavouring', prevent the taste receptors in the mouth registering sweetness. They are recommended in trade catalogues for processed foods such as cheese, meat and salad dressings where sugars are being added at levels that 'taste wrong', even to our bamboozled senses.

Our desires may know no limits or at least none that may be recognized by business, but we are reaching the limits of biological and environmental capabilities. The unfettered market, moreover, reduces everything to a financial transaction but puts no value on some of the things that are most important to us. It does not charge for the social cost of slave labour, nor for the exploitation of resources and despoliation of the environment.

The guilt associated with sugar consumption used to arise out of the enslavement of fellow man. 'When we work in the sugar mills and catch our finger in the millstone, they cut off our hand; when we try to run away, they cut off our leg . . . it is at this price that you eat sugar in Europe,' the native of Surinam protests in Voltaire's *Candide*. With the current food system there is an added anxiety, that we are dealing in self-harm.

6. Fish and Tomatoes

Unless we radically change the way we manage the seas, there will be no fish left for our grandchildren to eat. Wild seafood will be gone in fifty years, if exploitation of the oceans continues at its current rate.

This prediction, published in the journal *Science* in 2006, came from a large team of international researchers from leading EU and American marine institutes. In coming to their shocking conclusion on the state of fish stocks, the researchers looked at historical records and current data on more than a dozen marine ecosystems, and found that about a third of the fisheries off coasts that used to feed populations around the world are now useless, fished to the point at which nearly half of their marine species have collapsed. This decline has been long and steady and began over 200 years ago.

But when you look at what has happened to catch records from the open ocean, the decline has been much more recent. From 1950 on, it has been rapid and widespread. As coastal waters became fished out, fishermen took to going further and further afield to find their catches. Until the fifties their ability to inflict damage on the oceans was restricted by the physical limitations of their boats and the elements but since then highly capitalized, often subsidized fleets, with more and more advanced equipment, have been able to exploit every last depth. The decline of fish stocks accelerated, and it is accelerating still. By 2003 just under 30 per cent of open-sea fisheries were in a state of collapse, with collapse defined as a decline to less than 10 per cent of their highest recorded yields.

Projecting current fishing levels into the future, the researchers predicted that all stocks will have collapsed by 2048.

The lead researcher Professor Boris Worm of Canada's Dalhousie University commented: 'We asked, "If this trend which has been very strong and very consistent over the last fifty years were to continue, where ... would we end up?" And the answer is you end up with no seafood.'

There is one glimmer of hope. Where marine reserves are introduced and no-catch zones enforced before areas collapse, biodiversity can recover quite well, and fish stocks around the exclusion zones can increase, giving fishermen better catches. It is nearly, but not completely, too late.

We could save fish stocks, but as with climate change, it will require an unprecedented act of co-ordinated and collective political will. It requires us individually to give things up, to consume less, and it requires politicians to take long-term unpopular decisions. So far there is little evidence of where the will may be found.

Although I can manage the exuberant optimism that oil expert Rob Hopkins described when I think about the coming energy crisis, I'm afraid it is the other reaction he warned of, nihilism, which tends to overwhelm me when I think about the state of fish stocks. Here is a true tragedy and yet we are given so many dire warnings about environmental devastations, always delivered with a battery of worsening statistics, that it's easy to feel punch drunk. I was given a powerful antidote to this feeling of helplessness however, in the form of a slideshow by one of the world's foremost experts on marine conservation, Professor Callum Roberts of York University, recently.

I was at a Greenpeace gathering of celebrity chefs, who had come together to launch a campaign to turn 40 per cent of the world's seas into marine reserves closed to all fishing and waste disposal. Professor Roberts produced his collection of early photographs of fishing fleets, fishermen and their catches to bring the dry statistics vividly into focus. Here were pictures of Irish fishermen in the early twentieth century standing next to common skate caught near their shores that were nearly twice their own size; the common skate as its name implies was abundant then but is now extinct in many areas because of overfishing by trawlers. The hold of a 1905 Lowestoft fishing boat employing over a dozen men is so bursting with mackerel that the fish fill the decks to the gunnels too. Anglers of the time stand after a leisurely day's fishing next to their trawl: prize specimens so large and plentiful that they are strung up row upon row, recalling the now-shocking old photos of Victorian colonialists standing proud by their profligate bags of then-common tiger and other game from a day's hunting in Africa.

Photos of the seabed where bottom trawlers have not dragged their destructive beams show a rich and colourful fauna of coral, sea fans, sponges and a myriad other invertebrate species cloaking underwater slopes, but where the industrial fleets have bulldozed their way through, nothing is left but a desolate wasteland of gravel and mud.

Professor Roberts was optimistic though that we need not 'sing a requiem for the sea' quite yet. As his pictures showed, the wholesale wrecking has been quite recent. It could be reversed so long as we are prepared to introduce marine reserves and change our habits as consumers.

There is a certification scheme for sustainable fish. It's run by the Marine Stewardship Council which was originally set up by Unilever and the World Wildlife Fund in 1997. Unilever, then owner of the Captain Bird's Eye range and one of the world's largest buyers of seafood, realized that it would not be able to make its leading brand fish fingers for much longer if it didn't support efforts to prevent the collapse of the fish stocks on which it depended. The stewardship charity became independent from both its founder organizations in 1999 once it was established. Working with scientists and fisheries experts it has developed standards for sustainable fishing. Fisheries can apply to it to be assessed and win the right to use its eco-label.

Some environmentalists have criticized some of its certifications as too easily granted, in particular the ones given to large trawler-industry fisheries that catch New Zealand hoki and Alaskan pollock. But as Charles Clover points out in *The End of the Line*, his ground-breaking and impassioned book on saving the world's fish, if they are only to certify perfection, there will never be anything certified. The MSC scheme is a great deal better than most of the other ineffectual efforts to intervene or than no action at all.

At the moment, about 7 per cent of world fish stocks are certified or are being assessed under the MSC schemes. The fishing industry is in places changing to less destructive methods of fishing to win accreditation.

But you hit your first obstacle if you want to marry fish sustainability with other environmental considerations, such as buying locally where possible, cutting down on fossil fuel-heavy transport and processing. If you go to the MSC website, to the section 'Where to buy', and click UK, a long list will come up of supermarket products, but many of them are tinned or transmogrified via a freezer into a 'fresh' ready meal. You can also have fresh MSC-certified Alaskan salmon from Sainsbury's or MSC-certified New Zealand hoki from Tesco. M&S can do you MSC Pacific halibut, and Waitrose will bring you MSC rock lobster tails from west Australia or scallops from Patagonia. But the list of sustainable fish from the waters off our own extensive shores is shorter than a half pint of prawns. There's Cornish mackerel, but only in season, Burry Inlet cockles in a polybag, Thames herring in season, creel-caught langoustine from Loch Torridon, the catch from the fisheries in Hastings, and that's about it.

I decided to try the last of these one autumn day, Hastings being an easy train journey from my part of London. As I walked to the beach from the station, the rain that had started as a dreary mizzle turned into a driving horizontal sheet. Along the front a few locals, umbrellas blown inside out, were battling their way through the amusement park puddles towards the eastern end. As in so much of Britain, the main economic activity has become ersatz entertainment. Fishing boats have put out from the stony working beach here for centuries but today the tiny Hastings fleet consists of just twenty-five or so boats that are certified by the MSC as a sustainable mackerel, herring and sole fishery. If you know the times of the tides, as the locals do, you can buy the catch from the boat sheds as they land it. The fish is so fresh it smells only of the sea.

Paul Joy, who heads the cooperative of Hastings fishermen, has been fishing for nearly forty years himself and reckons his family has been casting their nets and lines from the same beach since the 1200s. All the boats here are less than ten metres; they stay close to shore and only fish for a few hours at a time, assuming the weather allows them out. I caught up with him once he'd unloaded his early morning catch, over a post-fish breakfast at the Angling Club on the beach where all the local fishermen congregate. With the steam rising from mugs of tea, runnels of condensation flowing down the windows, and the rain lashing the roof, this felt like a tight community bound together against the elements and the rest of the world.

The sole was 'teeming' he told me. But it turned out they had had to stop catching their sustainable mackerel at the beginning of that month because the mackerel quota for these British waters had run out, the lion's share of it allocated to large, distinctly unsustainable trawlers. The herring season had not started. In the past cod might have seen them through the periods in between. But the North Sea cod quotas imposed to save cod from extinction meant they could average only one kilo of cod per boat per day, about a fish each, before going over the limit. He and most of the other boats had thrown back hundreds of kilos of cod that morning because it would be illegal to land it. 'We have the MSC certification on mackerel but we're not allowed to catch it because nearly all the quota is allocated to the big boys who destroy it. The large boats have about three quarters of all the quotas. We have to waste the

184

cod. We were buzzed by spotter planes today, logging our positions; the navy board us regularly; the sea fisheries committee send out their patrol boat to board and check us; when we come ashore, the fish is checked again. Oh to be a Frenchman,' Joy sighed.

Joy, now fifty-eight and a fisherman for over thirty-five years, has fought the system long and hard and fallen foul of the law in the past. In a case taken up in parliament and in the press, he and a fellow Hastings fisherman were taken to court for breaching cod quotas in September 2003. They had caught mature cod as bycatch while fishing for plaice. They argued that the quotas had not been intended by the EU to apply to boats under ten metres since they were not required to keep logs. They lost, despite going to appeal in 2006. But Joy remained indomitable. As well as acquiring the MSC certification for its sole, herring and mackerel, he said the Hastings fleet was going to try to have its cod allocation removed from the quota for the North Sea since they thought they could show that the cod off Hastings, which are currently abundant, are endemic to the channel and do not migrate back to the North Sea, staying instead within its western approaches. It was immoral to throw back good fish, and he didn't want to do it.

He was also exploring whether he could use ancient Sussex bylaws to stop the damage being done to the seabed by vast beam trawlers that had moved in to drag their five-tonne chains over the seabed and rocks up the coast, destroying local mussel beds that used to feed plaice and 'obliterating the food chain in two days' work'. He was particularly vociferous against armchair skippers who used their wealth to buy up quota and lease it out to such trawlers without ever going to sea themselves.

With the rain still driving down, we dived back along the steeply shelving beach, through the winching gear, past a shack with its sign saying 'Gone fishing' to Joy's office next to the tall, narrow net huts. He wanted me to see the mountains of paperwork now required of them. Like the dairy farmers I'd met, Brussels bureaucracy had burdened them without protecting them. A gull's nest blocking the gutter was sending a fountain of rainwater back up the façade and, under a heavy sky, huge rollers from the blue-grey sea were dashing against the shore, their constant tow dragging down its pebbled slopes with a thundering roar. Everything seemed such a struggle.

I wondered where you could buy the Hastings MSC fish if you didn't happen to live in Hastings. He shrugged. You couldn't really. In fact, nearly all the catch goes to Holland or France, where people seem to care more and will pay a higher price for knowing that the fish they eat are sustainable. All the big retailers in Holland have recently signed up to a commitment to source only sustainable, MSC-certified fish by 2011. M&S and Asda have made a commitment to switch to sustainable fish over the next five years; but so far no British supermarket has agreed to stock MSC Hastings sole.

The MSC scheme is on the cusp of becoming mainstream, but it's not there yet. The story is familiar: look back to the same point in its development and you would have seen the Fairtrade movement struggling to achieve critical mass. The breakthrough for fish will probably only come if individuals persuade shops and restaurants they mind where their fish come from, before stocks run out, and if, by asking, they persuade the big processors that they cannot afford not to care.

I promised to write a call to action, and found myself mourning the cod with Joy, the single fish of that species that his boat might safely land each day. 'Would you like some fish and chips for lunch?' he quickly asked. So it was that I ate that cod. It was battered for me in Maggie's Café of food guide fame, over the fish market next door to the office, by Maggie herself. For every 100 jobs in fishing here there are about 1,000 more in associated trades, Joy said. Fried to a creamy, melting perfection, it made the best fish and chips I'd had for years. How would I explain its loss to my grandchildren?

★

As with the livestock revolution, technological advance and economic empire provide much of the explanation, as Professor Roberts points out in his beautifully written study, *The Unnatural History of the Sea*. The first great expansion of trawlers came with the advent of steam and growing demand in the mid nineteenth century. Already in the 1850s, there were violent protests by fishermen using lines, nets and traps against these trawlermen who were destroying their livelihoods. Even back then small boatsmen were complaining that industrial trawling was despoiling the seabed, netting and destroying invertebrates that were essential to the food chain. They were also catching juvenile fish before they had matured enough to spawn and ensure future stocks. The decline continued through the turn of the twentieth century. The enforced moratorium of two world wars gave fish some respite and a chance to recover, but they were quickly overexploited again soon after. Fishing fleets from industrialized countries responded to falling yields by fishing further afield.

It was after the Second World War however, just as in agriculture, that industrialization of fishing achieved a new scale and ecologically disastrous force. Factory ships were developed to cut costs – they were able to freeze fish on board, allowing boats to stay out longer. They could extract oil from cod liver at sea and process fish waste into meal. Instead of fishing nearer to home and returning at regular intervals to offload their catch, long-distance fleets could stay out for weeks at a time, exploiting stocks further and further away. The fish might not be as fresh as previously but there were hi tech ways round this. As much as a third of tuna imported to the USA for example is now flushed with carbon monoxide which makes it retain the bright reddish hue associated with freshness, although the tuna that is landed in less than thirty days from catch is rare. The EU has banned the technique, but since tropical fish is frequently transhipped at sea – that is, moved from one ship to another, and laundered with other catches – CO-treated tuna finds its way in to EU markets too. (It was a UK supermarket fish buyer who taught me how to spot a tuna treated this way: watch out for a slightly unnatural raspberry jam tint to the colour. The main concern is not a health one, but that the practice deceives shoppers as to the freshness of what they are buying.)

The factory fishing fleets of the Eastern bloc were just as ruthlessly efficient as the Western Europeans at extracting from the sea. Then in the 1970s, just as everybody was beginning to recognize that overfishing was leading to the collapse of certain species such as herring and countries such as Iceland were fighting cod wars for the principle that individual nations had the right to preserve sustainable fishing in their own waters, the EU began to set up its Common Fisheries Policy, moving in the opposite direction, towards a scheme of sharing stocks and allowing its fishermen to trawl the waters of any member state, while subsidizing their ability to do so.

Small local fleets tend not to foul their own waters, since they know that to do so will kill their own future. But intensive international trawlers have had few such scruples. Where they operate, parts of the seabed may be hit as much as ten times a year, destroying habitats and giving them no chance to re-grow.

New and apparently ever more egregious examples of careless greed are reported. I thought I had lost my ability to be shocked by such accounts until I read of the largely unregulated and previously unknown fleet of Spanish ships, most of them registered in Britain, that have been laying thousands of miles of semi-permanent gill nets on the seabed in the north Atlantic west of the Hebrides and around Rockall. Gill nets form a near invisible wall of fine nylon that traps fish by the gills. An investigation at the end of 2005 discovered that this fleet was taking monkfish and sharks, mainly for the oil from their livers rather than their flesh, which often goes to waste, and has managed to reduce shark stocks to about 20 per cent of their original numbers in just ten years.

Sharks, extraordinary creatures with seven instead of our five senses, are particularly vulnerable to overfishing because they are slow growing – they can live for up to 200 years – and have low reproductive rates. These boats sometimes leave their nets in the water for weeks at a time while they go back to port to land their catches, and when they finally return to harvest their vast trawls between half and three quarters of the catch may no longer be usable and is discarded. The trawlers are thought to deliberately abandon up to eighteen miles of net each trip, since the nets are just too big to stow on board at the same time as a full load. The abandoned ghost nets continue to entangle sharks for years.

I have more sympathy for those fishermen who, faced with this sort of rape of the ocean, find their livelihoods at risk and break the law themselves. The skippers of almost the whole of Whitby's fishing fleet – ten captains, nine ships and two trawler companies – were in just this position a couple of years ago and were fined for mass breaches of quotas at Whitby crown court shortly after this shark fishing scandal came to light. The North Yorkshire fishermen said they had been driven to desperation by EU restrictions which had left their trade 'on its knees'. None was earning more than £20,000 a year and all had failed to declare half the fish they were landing, putting North Sea stocks of cod, haddock and whiting at risk by fishing beyond their quotas. This is the fishing industry committing suicide.

Fish farming is often held up as the solution to the intractably gloomy news about the state of fishing. Aquaculture is booming and expanding at a huge rate around the world, and is seen as offering developing countries in particular a way of meeting their growing populations' need for protein. But as many questions are raised by fish farming as by industrial trawling. The trends in fish farming have followed those in intensive agriculture. The drive is nearly always to maximize production and cut costs.

Just as with factory animals, keeping fish in unnatural and overcrowded conditions leads to disease. Sea lice thrive in densely stocked salmon farms and the industry depends on chemical treatments to control them. Now sea lice have become resistant to some of the older treatments and some have to be replaced with chemicals that are even more toxic. Organophosphates and other nerve toxins are often used as chemical baths or the fish may be fed insecticides which are controversial because they persist in the environment or in the flesh of the salmon. Four of the commonest chemical treatments for sea lice in salmon are said by some experts to be both carcinogenic and hormone disrupting. Parasites from farmed fish have, moreover, infected wild populations around them.

Salmon farms have been plagued not just by parasites but also by epidemics of disease, from infectious salmon anaemia to kidney disease and vibriosis, a bacterial infection that causes ulceration in fish and gastrointestinal illness in humans if they eat fish infected with it, unless it has been thoroughly cooked. Fish farming has depended on antibiotics just as factory animal farming has.

I have personally never felt the same about farmed fish since discovering the 'SalmoFan'™ – a little fan of colour charts that looks for all the world like a sheaf of Dulux paint charts. The SalmoFan specifies how much food dye a salmon farmer should administer with his feed depending on how strong a pink colour he wants his end product to be. In the wild salmon acquire their pink colour from the shellfish they eat. In captivity, they have to be artificially coloured to have the same hue.

The ills of salmon farming have, like those of the poultry industry, been well aired and parts of the business have made big efforts to clean up their production. Some fish farms now use hydrogen peroxide baths to kill parasites, which are relatively environmentally benign according to Sustain, the alliance for better food and farming; and others use a fish called wrasse, which feeds on the parasites, but stocks of these fish are now themselves under threat because of demand from salmon farming. The best fish farms have also reduced stocking densities to tackle disease and cut down on antibiotic use although the worst still carry on as before – shipments of salmon are regularly rejected by port authorities around the world for illegal levels of antibiotic residues – and even the best have not been able to eliminate their use.

Organic fish farming is better than most, although critics within the movement have argued against certifying farming a migratory species like salmon as organic at all. Stocking densities on fish farms certified as organic by the Soil Association are only allowed to contain half the density of fish that non-organic farms consider normal. The feed for the fish has to come from recycled waste from the processing factories that prepare fish and shellfish already caught for human consumption. Salmon pens can only be sited in areas where tides flush the waters strongly enough to reduce the build up of waste from fish faeces, which can drain surrounding waters of oxygen and create dead zones. Chemical treatments are restricted and the toxic anti-foulant chemicals used conventionally to keep cages and nets free of seaweed and barnacles may not be used. When medicines are needed to treat outbreaks of disease, longer periods of withdrawal are required before the treated fish can be sold, and although natural colourings are allowed in feed, artificial colours are not.

But even where fish farming has cleaned up its act on pollution and disease, there appears to be no way as yet of answering the unbalanceable equation at the heart of all current aquaculture. Farmed fish are fed other fish, and typically for every 2–3kgs of wild fish in the form of fishmeal or fish oil you feed them; you get just 1kg of farmed fish back. The industry argues that most of the fish fed to farmed fish are bycatch or waste from other fishing. But this in effect just rewards the industry for negligently killing marine life with the wrong kind of nets or overfishing, and contributes to the overall problem.

The very best organic fish farms have managed to reduce the conversion ratio to just over one to one. But even so there is no net increase in the amount of fish available.

It is true, you can feed fish grain and soya, and the grain and soya industry, led by the American giants of agribusiness, have not surprisingly been keen to develop such feed, but vegetarian fish do not grow so well and the flesh of those fed this way does not contain so much of the long-chain fatty acids that we want. They start to lay down the wrong kind of fat and more of it, their composition becoming more saturated, just as that of grain- and soya- as opposed to grass-fed cattle does.

The organic part of the industry hopes to get to a point where all the feed for its operations will come from the filleting wastes from fish caught in fisheries that have been certified as sustainable by the MSC, but we are not there yet. Meanwhile, insanely, 30–40 per cent of the world catch is still converted to fishmeal and oil, largely for the production of animal feed, fertilizer and food manufacture of products such as margarine.

The loss of cod, and the many other fish stocks threatened with collapse, would not just be an ecological and economic disaster, though it would unquestionably be that. It could have profound consequences for human biology. For the terrible irony is that we are hurtling towards the end of seafood, just as we are beginning to understand how vital the nutrients found in fish are to our brains.

Health experts have long recommended that we eat more fish. Increased fish consumption would improve cardiovascular health, reducing the incidence of strokes and heart disease. It is also known that fish consumption during pregnancy benefits foetal growth and in particular the growth of the nervous system.

The UK government's Scientific Advisory Committee on Nutrition recommends people eat two portions of fish a week, one of which should be oily fish. It had to calculate the benefit of eating fish against the risk from pollutants however. Disposal of industrial waste at sea has led to dioxins, polychlorinated biphenyls (PCBs) and mercury building up in the fatty tissue of oily fish, particularly those predatory fish such as marlin, sword-fish and shark, at the top of the food chain. Because mercury is known to be toxic to the brain development of foetuses, the official advice to women of childbearing age is to avoid these particular fish. The mercury content of tuna is lower, and up to two portions of fresh tuna or four medium sized cans of tinned tuna a week are judged unlikely to harm the developing foetus. Pregnant women are also advised to avoid having more than two portions of fish such as salmon, trout and mackerel a week because of the dioxins and PCBs they contain. New research however has suggested that this advice may be wrong. It found that even above these intakes of fish there is a greater health benefit to foetal brain development than risk from pollutant damage; the more fish and seafood the mother had eaten while pregnant, the higher the IQ, fine motor skills and social development of the child at the age of eight, even when other factors such as social class were taken into account.

Fish are rich in essential fatty acids. Essential fatty acids are called essential precisely because humans cannot make them but must obtain them from the diet. Every cell in the body depends on essential fatty acids for its construction, and essential fats are particularly important in the vascular system, in the eye, in sperm, and in the brain. The long-chain omega-3 fatty acid DHA makes up part of the brain's structure. More recently the links between a diet high in fish and reduced risk of depression, dementia and other mental health and behavioural problems have been emerging.

The essential fatty acids in seafood come served up not only in the elongated form that our bodies use for cell construction but also wrapped up with a complex of other essential nutrients and co-factors such as zinc, iron, selenium, iodine, copper, manganese and vitamin E that we need to metabolize them. Oily fish such as mackerel, salmon, tuna, and sardines have the highest concentrations, but even a low-fat white fish like cod has significant amounts of the long-chain omega-3 essential fatty acid DHA. It may have relatively little oil in its white muscle but what it does have is 47 per cent DHA. A portion of 100g of white fish muscle gives you about 700mg of DHA (that's about twice what you'd get in a good quality omega-3 oil supplement that costs a fortune).

Tinned tuna sadly is not a good source of omega-3 fatty acids. Most of the beneficial oil is squeezed out of the fish during the process of canning. (It often goes to feed pigs and other animals instead of us, only to be replaced in the tin by subsidized US soya oil.) So health experts and government advisory bodies want us all to eat more fish, but they don't say how we might save our supplies of it. The truth is if we destroy any prospect of sustainable fishing, we may find we have also destroyed the food for our brains.

This link between essential fatty acids and the brain has become the fashionable area for study, not just for scientists but for the food industry. It's not only my cat food that has jumped on the bandwagon. Omega-3 anti-dementia products are said to be the next big thing. The fashion for marketing the benefits of essential fats may be new, but the work is not; some of the proponents of this area of diet and health have been working away at it for decades, through the 1970s and 1980s when they were rowing against a tide that promoted omega-6 poly-unsaturated fats, which had often been hydrogenated, instead.

Several of the leading experts came together for a seminar on the latest thinking on the impact of nutrition and omega-3 on human behaviour in February 2006. The venue was the Society of Chemical Industry in its grand headquarters in London's Belgrave Square.

I had interviewed several of these experts for my last book *Not on the Label*, but in the few years since then, their hypotheses have gained ground as new work makes them more compelling; and agribusiness has stepped in, quick to spot and to exploit the commercial possibilities. The academic scientists, confronted with apparently unaccountable rises in behavioural and learning disorders such as attention deficit and hyper-activity disorder (ADHD), dyslexia, dyspraxia and autism, in aggression and depression, and other mental health problems in children – one in ten children are now thought to have a mental health problem at any one time – were trying to find explanations, often complicated and depending on an inter-relation of nutrients, for what had gone wrong. The industry scientists and marketers were keen to isolate individual fixes that could be reduced to a profit-generating slogan.

Two researchers based at Oxford University's department of neuroscience, under the supervision of Professor John Stein, brother of the more famous fish-cooking Rick, presented their work. Dr Alex Richardson had conducted clinical trials with children suffering from dyspraxia, which causes learning difficulties and often disruptive behaviour. Those treated with long-chain fatty acid supplements experienced major improve-ments in their reading ages. Three trials have shown that attention and behavioural problems could be helped by fish oil supplements with some vitamin E where children had been diagnosed with dyslexia, attention deficit and hyperactivity disorder or dyspraxia. But in two other studies where ADHD had been treated with DHA alone there had been no benefits – our understanding of deficiencies and how to correct them is still young.

Bernard Gesch, a former probation officer now also based at Oxford University, had begun his work on nutrition when helping persistent criminal offenders. One had been sentenced by UK courts on thirteen occasions for stealing trucks in the early hours of the morning, and had been sent to prison three times. Gesch recorded his diet:

Breakfast: Nothing (asleep).

Mid-morning: Nothing (asleep).

Lunchtime: 4–5 cups of coffee with milk and two and a half
teaspoons of sugar.

Mid-afternoon: 3–4 cups of coffee with milk and two and a half
heaped sugars.

Tea: Chips, egg, ketchup, 2 slices of white bread, 5 cups of tea or
coffee with sugar.

Evening: 5 cups of tea or coffee with milk and heaped sugars,
20 cigarettes, £2 worth of sweets, cakes and if money was
available 3–4 pints of beer.

This was all he ever ate. A large proportion of his calories were
coming from sugar, there was no obvious source of essential
fatty acids, little protein and fibre and very few vitamins and
minerals. He was given education to improve his diet as part
of his court order. He eventually trained as a chef. He never
reoffended again.

Gesch was told this happy ending might have been down to
his devoted attention as a probation officer rather than changes
in the boy's diet, so he set out to test the idea that poor diets
might cause antisocial behaviour and crime with a randomized
trial in the maximum security Aylesbury prison. 231 prison
volunteers were assigned either to a regime of multivitamins,
minerals and essential fatty acid supplements or to placebos.
The supplement aimed only to bring prisoners' intakes of
nutrients up to the level recommended by government as the
minimum daily requirement.

Aylesbury was at the time a prison for young male offenders
aged seventeen to twenty-one, convicted of the most serious
crimes. It was where prisoners were sent when they had already
assaulted staff and the rest of the prison system hadn't been able
to cope with them. I spoke to Trevor Hussey, who had been
the deputy governor at the time, and he had been sceptical
about the study when it started. He reckoned the food was

quite good, although prisoners on the whole chose the white bread, meat and confectionery rather than fruit and vegetables. But quite quickly staff noticed a significant drop in the number of reported incidents of bad behaviour in the prison. 'We'd just introduced a policy of earned privileges so we thought it must be that rather than a few vitamins and fats but we used to joke 'maybe it's Bernard's pills'.

When the trial finished it became clear that the drop in incidents of bad behaviour only applied to those on the supplements and not those on the placebo. The results showed those receiving the extra nutrients committed 37 per cent fewer serious offences involving violence. Those on the placebos showed no change in their behaviour. Once the study had finished and the supplements were no longer being administered, the number of offences went up by the same amount. Ironically the office the researchers had used to administer nutrients was restored to a control and restraint room after they had left.

Gesch was not suggesting that nutrition is the only explanation of antisocial behaviour but did think it might form a significant part of the explanation for the rise in crime that has mirrored industrialization of the diet. If the brain is deprived of the nutrients it needs for its construction it makes sense that it will not work very well and that will affect behaviour. But nutrition is not pharmacology. It involves a complex interaction of many nutrients, some of which we still do not fully understand. Take depression: people who are depressed often have reduced levels of omega-3 essential fatty acids in their blood and tissues, but they also tend to have a low zinc status. Eating lots of fish seems to protect against depression; so does getting lots of folic acid from green leafy vegetables.

In the audience to hear all this were representatives from the major food and drug transnationals – Bunge; Nestlé's patent, licence and brand holding subsidiary Nestec; Unilever; Dow Agrosciences; and pharmaceutical and supplement companies – who could turn this new emerging understanding to commercial advantage; and from Chelsea, one of the world's richest football clubs, the man who advises some of the world's top players on how nutrition affects their performance. Yet at least three of the academics present were struggling to get funding for their ground-breaking work.

Professor Michael Crawford, chairing the seminar, was the first to establish that DHA was structural to the brain back in the 1960s. He is now head of the Institute of Brain Chemistry and Human Nutrition at London Metropolitan University, but was based at London Zoo when he did some of his early work on essential fatty acids. He predicted in 1972 that unprecedented changes in the type and quantity of fats in the Western diet would not only be associated with the epidemic of heart disease that was already visible then, but that a dramatic rise in mental disorders would follow. His view is that the degenerative diseases of the cardiovascular system that you find today in most developed countries, but not in societies that have not industrialized, is caused as much by a lack of essential fatty acids as by an excess of saturated fats. In particular he thinks the problem is the imbalance between omega-3 and omega-6 essential fatty acids. We don't get enough omega-3 and we are drowning in omega-6. It is a view that is gaining weight in relation to cardiovascular disease and is increasingly accepted in relation to mental health.

It was a group of primates that sounded one of the early warning bells. Crawford was experimenting in the early 1970s with feeding monkeys diets with different ratios of omega-6 to omega-3 fatty acids to discover the effect on the brain. The different groups had normal diets except that the type of oil in the feed was manipulated. One group that was receiving safflower oil which has no omega-3 in it started hurting themselves. The result was quite unexpected and took Crawford by surprise, this being an era before the phenomenon or even the phrase 'self-harm' had been heard. One of the group even started trying to eating his own testicles. The experiment was stopped and the animals fed their old diets including oils with omega-3 in them. They became calm again. But when the experiment was repeated and primates were once again fed a diet from which omega-3 was removed, they started to self harm once more.

Crawford, who has done much further work since, believes that a very high proportion of our children are omega-3 deficient, and that because the omega-3 to omega-6 fatty acid ratios in industrialized diets are so out of kilter, what we are witnessing in the rise of disorders such as depression, dyslexia, dyspraxia and ADHD is the effect of that deficiency, particularly on maternal nutrition and early foetal brain development.

One of the most important dietary shifts over the last century in industrialized countries has been the change in the types and quantities of fats we eat. A flood of industrial vegetable oils from corn and soya, which are high in omega-6 fatty acids, is added to thousands of processed foods, and have skewed the balance, so that instead of a ratio of omega-6 to omega-3 that should be 2:1, as it was in earlier times, people now consume in ratios that are closer to 20:1.

Animal husbandry started with grass and green foods which are rich in omega-3 but has moved to corn and soya feeds high in omega-6. The beauty of fish and seafood is that it is still largely wild and living in an omega-3-rich environment, (green algae providing the nutrients at the bottom of the marine food chain). But fish farming disrupts that. Fed a high-energy cereal diet mixed in with fishmeal, the omega-3 fatty acid content of the fish goes down while the omega-6 fatty acid content of their flesh goes up – it's typically 20 per cent omega-6 in farmed salmon compared with 3–7 per cent in wild salmon.

It was at the same seminar at SCI that I first met Joseph Hibbeln. Hibbeln is a distinguished research scientist and practising physician and psychiatrist. Thanks to his research on diet and mental health the American Psychiatric Association now recommends that all adults should eat fish at least twice a week and that patients with psychotic, impulse control, and mood disorders should eat more omega-3 long-chain fatty acids. It advises doctors to use supplements of fatty acids to complement psychiatric treatment for patients suffering from depression and bipolar disorder (what used to be known as manic depression).

In reaching this advice the scientists are finally catching up with several millennia of cultural wisdom, Hibbeln points out. The Chinese belief that good mental and physical health is maintained through a balance of yin and yang, symbolized by the fish, dates back to 3,000 BC. Seafood was prescribed for anyone who had become too aggressive or agitated. In Christianity fish is a sacred food, and became the symbol that represented gentle Jesus; eating fish on specified days became part of religious duty. Fish is associated with purity and moderation in the Koran too, while Jewish people are told that the pregnant woman who eats fish will have graceful children in the Talmud. The association of fish and peace is nearly universal, emerging in early Chinese and Middle Eastern civilizations and lasting for millennia.

Hibbeln's most recent study had, like Gesch's, looked at links between poor diet and violence and crime. It involved a clinical trial with volunteer violent drunks, advertised for and found through the *Washington Post*. He presented the early results briefly at the SCI seminar and their cases sounded so challenging, the idea that nutrients could solve their problems so contrary to all our notions of personal accountability, that I persuaded him to let me interview some of them at the end of the research.

So it was that I found myself at a US government base in Bethesda, near Washington, that is home to the prestigious state-funded National Institutes of Health, seeking to closet myself away with as many violent drunks, reformed or other-wise, as would be interviewed.

Hibbeln, as well as being a doctor, biophysicist and epidemiologist, is a lead clinical investigator in the US Public Health Service, an employee of the US government; and it was in the uniform of a commander, with braided epaulettes, military peak cap, and decorations for service – during hurricanes Katrina and Hugo and for outstanding academic work – pinned to his chest, that he steered me through the tight security at the base. Post 9/11 no one was taking any chances over the threat of attack to society from without. I handed my passport in to the guards and we were put in line to wait for the X-ray machine. While we queued we talked about the enormous but largely overlooked new threat to society from within.

Hibbeln's hypothesis is also that modern industrialized diets have changed the architecture and functioning of the brain. Like Crawford, he believes we are suffering from widespread diseases of deficiency. Just as vitamin C deficiency was eventually shown to cause scurvy, he thinks that deficiency in the essential fats the brain needs are emerging as a cause of a host of mental problems from depression to aggression. The consequences are as serious as they could be – the pandemic of violence in Western societies may be attributable at least in part to what we eat or fail to eat.

If that's right, it challenges our whole notion of criminal justice. For if mood, behaviour and achievement are affected by whether the brain has enough of the right kind of nutrients to function properly, it throws into doubt how far anyone from the disruptive child to the convicted criminal can actually control their behaviour. 'Well, it challenges the whole basis of psychiatry too, which used to be all Jung and Freud and then moved on to psychopharmacology, but the idea that it might be diet, well that is just too simple . . .' he pointed out.

I met Dwight Demar a few hours later in one of the windowless meeting rooms of the outpatients' clinic. That he was able to sit in front of me, sober, calm and employed, was 'a miracle' Demar declared in the cadences of a prayer meeting sinner. He was rocking his 6ft 2in bulk to and fro while delivering a confessional account of his past into the middle distance. He wanted me to know what had saved him after twenty years on the streets: 'My dome is working. They gave me some kind of pill and I changed. Me, myself and I, I changed.' Demar had been in and out of prison so many times he had lost count. 'Being drunk, being disorderly, trespass, assault and battery, you name it, I did it . . . And then I tried to kill a person and I knew something need' be done, cos I was half a hundred and I was either going to kill somebody or get killed.'

When he came out of jail after that, he bought a can of beer and seemed headed for more of the same, dossing under a bridge where a colony of other down and outs, many mentally disturbed, had made their home. But then a case worker saw Hibbeln's ad in the *Washington Post* and persuaded Demar to take part in the clinical trial. After an initial month voluntarily locked on a ward for detox, with valium to help him through, the pill that had effected what Demar called his miracle was nothing more than a large dose of fish oil.

Demar had been out of trouble and sober for a year when I met him. He had recently been made employee of the month at his company. Others on Hibbeln's trial had improved dramatically too, including some who also had long histories of violence and blighted lives – not just their own lives blighted but blighting all those they touched. They had been able to control their anger and aggression for the first time thanks to omega-3 fatty acids to correct deficiencies.

Patients helped ranged from convicted criminals to respectable teachers to an ex-secret service agent. Just as our failure to manage the resources of the seas has pushed us to the environmental limits, so our neglect of diet appears to have taken us to the biological limits. Diseases of deficiency, caused by our industrialized, highly processed diets, are emerging and they have profound social implications.

For Hibbeln the results of his study with violent alcoholics were anything but a miracle, more what you would expect if you understood the biochemistry of the brain.

The brain is mostly made of fat – essential longer-chain fatty acids are what make up its structure. The membrane of nerve cells is 20 per cent essential fatty acids. The synapses or junctions where nerve cells connect with other nerve cells contain even higher concentrations of essential fatty acids – being about two thirds made of the longer-chain omega-3 DHA.

As humans we eat two kinds of essential fatty acids in plants: the omega-3 alpha-linolenic acid (ALA) found mostly in leaves and a few seeds such as flax, and the omega-6 linoleic acid (LA) found in oilseeds such as soya, corn and safflower. These parent fatty acids are short chains of carbons which mammals then metabolize and build on to make longer chains.

What kind of longer chain you end up with depends on which parent fatty acid you started with. Say you eat lots of leafy plants and you start with the omega-3 alpha-linolenic acid. Enzymes can then convert it into the longer-chain EPA and then into the yet longer fatty acid DHA, that omega-3 fatty acid beloved of marketing men these days that is concentrated in the brain, retina and testes. If you start instead with soya oil, corn oil or safflower oil and are therefore eating lots of the omega-6 linoleic acid, enzymes will convert it to a different longer-chain fatty acid, arachidonic acid.

These two fatty acids, EPA from the omega-3 line and arachidonic acid from the omega-6 line are both essential and used by the body to make highly active hormone-like substances called prostaglandins which act as the brain's messengers. The prostaglandins are also the precursors of a substance that promotes blood clotting and constriction of the blood vessels. The omega-6 arachidonic acid produces prostaglandins that are highly inflammatory – which is important if you've suffered an injury for example. The omega-3 EPA on the other hand produces prostaglandins which are the opposite; they switch off the inflammatory response.

But crucially, the two different families of fatty acids compete for the same enzymes and metabolic pathways. If you get too much omega-6 it blocks the conversion of omega-3. And if you aren't getting enough omega-3, the inflammatory response doesn't get switched off. It is this mechanism that is now believed by many experts to be one of the crucial factors in many immune and degenerative diseases, including cardiovascular disease.

The brain's signalling system depends on essential fatty acids. Communication between the nerve cells takes place when neurotransmitters such as serotonin, dopamine or insulin dock with receptors in the nerve cell membrane. But they can only dock properly if the receptors are the right shape. And the shape of the receptors is determined by the fatty acid composition of the membrane. DHA is long, electrically active and highly flexible. When it is incorporated into the nerve cell membrane it helps make the membrane itself elastic and fluid so that signals pass through it efficiently. If omega-6 fatty acids supplant it and are picked up to build the cell membranes, they are more rigid and they don't function so well. That leads to low serotonin and dopamine levels. Low serotonin levels are known to predict increased risk of suicide, violent and impulsive behaviour, and are associated with depression. Many antidepressant drugs work by boosting serotonin levels. Dopamine is what controls the reward processes in the brain; if dopamine is deficient, the ability to learn from reward and punishment is impaired.

Laboratory tests at NIH have shown that the composition of tissue and in particular of the nerve cell membrane of people in the US – with their heavy use in processed foods of oils high in omega-6 – is different from that of the Japanese with their diet rich in seafood. The Americans have cell membranes far higher in omega-6.

Evidence has been building that deficiencies in DHA/EPA at crucial times when the brain is developing rapidly – in the womb, in the first five years of life and around puberty when the brain has another tremendous growth spurt – can affect its architecture permanently. Studies have shown that when animals are deprived of omega-3 ALA over two generations their offspring are left with a residual deficit in their ability to release dopamine and serotonin. The extension of all this is that if children are left with low dopamine as a result of early deficits in their own or their mother's diets, they cannot experience reward and punishment. If serotonin levels are low, they cannot inhibit their impulses or regulate their emotional responses. Here is a biochemical explanation for so many of the behavioural disorders that seem to be prevalent in industrialized societies, and for the cycles of deprivation that accompany crime and poor educational performance.

'There are critical moments in prenatal and later brain growth when you have to have the nutrients,' Hibbeln told me. 'You can get the essential fatty acids in short chains from plants, but not everyone is good at converting them to the longer chains of omega-3 that are so vital to the brain.' The easiest way is to get them from fish but where is the fish to come from?

Over 80 per cent of the fish we now eat in Europe comes from outside EU waters. Having destroyed our own resources, we have taken not just to partaking of other people's but raiding them wholesale. Most often those resources are the stocks of poorer countries and our exploitation of their natural capital echoes that made in previous eras. The rules of the current food system ensure that developed countries see the benefit but leave little in return for developing nations. In the modern globalized economy, however, the consequences catch up with us faster than they used to. For the effect has been to drive a new tide of migration, much of it from the parts of Africa that were at the centre of that first abusive exchange of commodities, the trade in sugar and slaves. Today the trade is in fish and the slavery has found a new form in migrant labour.

Senegal is one of the major exporters of fish to the European markets. I went there at the end of 2005 just as the African delegation was preparing to go to the ministerial summit of the World Trade Organization in Hong Kong, because Senegal might have been written as a case study in what is wrong with today's globalized food system. In the sprawling docks of the capital, Dakar, where the smell of half-rotten fish is as intense as the glare of the equatorial sun, you can see world trade in action: Senegal's rusty national fishing fleet now shares the crowded quays of the port with satellite-navigated Spanish trawlers, passing oil tankers and visiting US naval carriers. European skippers oversee black African labour landing tuna and other prized catches from African waters in front of a Chinese-owned fish processing factory. Vast container ships with their ubiquitous Maersk crates loom over them. Cheap subsidized US rice, Dutch poultry and Italian tomatoes are unloaded from gantries to flood the local market, while sub-Saharan cotton and tropical fish are prepared for export to Europe. Sole, tuna, bream, monkfish, octopus, grouper and prawns are among the high value seafood that starts its journey to British fishmongers and restaurants here.

It was from Dakar, and the tiny Ile de Gorée a kilometre out from the port, that some of the first African slaves were shipped to the plantations of the Americas and Caribbean in the sixteenth century. The trade boomed through to the nineteenth century, as successive waves of traders and colonizers, Portuguese, Dutch, French and British, gained control and shipped their human cargoes from West Africa's coast. You can still visit the slave house that is said to have been their point of departure.

Modern empire has modern instruments of command, however: military occupation, colonization and enslavement at the point of a gun have been replaced with the force – far less

206

draining to the economic powers – of unequal trade rules and unfair protections, of debt and structural adjustment programmes. The cheap labour on which the industrialized West's food production has always depended comes from the same places as ever. But now it is the World Trade Organization and the international financial institutions it controls, such as the World Bank and the International Monetary Fund, that provide the framework for economic domination by agribusiness, with expansionist China more recently bringing its money and influence on to the scene. Debt has been the chain that dragged and held poor countries in.

With the US government's Marshall Plan making sure that free trade became the terms of engagement after the Second World War, a steady reduction in protectionist taxes and tariffs among countries that were members of the General Agreement on Tariffs and Trade followed over the next quarter of a century. Through the 1950s and 1960s, once Europe had recovered, food aid played a central part in promoting US political interests through its disposal of American agricultural surplus which became a tool of the Cold War in Africa and Latin America. But in the 1970s American interests shifted. Bad weather had hit crops in 1972. The Soviet Union was facing shortages too, and wanted to import wheat. The Soviets moreover had oil. Grain took on a new role, and became an important element in the US administration's policy of political and commercial détente with the communist bloc. In the summer of 1972 the US announced an agreement with the USSR, which was to become the largest grain deal between two nations in history. The Soviets would be allowed to buy US grain; although it was only after they had purchased $1.1 billion of US-subsidized agricultural produce at artificially low prices that just how much they had taken emerged. They had managed to acquire one quarter of the entire US wheat crop. Dramatic spikes in the price of food followed in the US, causing a huge political storm.

When the oil shock of 1973 and the subsequent global recession hit in the mid to late 1970s countries started moving back towards protectionism. The US was under pressure from its farmers to do the same but instead led a drive to revive free trade among GATT members, with eight years of negotiations through the 1980s, which became known as the Uruguay round. From those negotiations at the end of 1995 the World Trade Organization emerged. The WTO extended the areas in which free trade was to be negotiated, adding agriculture, intellectual property, textiles and services to the areas that had been negotiated under GATT. Poorer countries agreed to open up their agriculture as the price of participating in the global market, allowing transnational agribusiness to move in, even though richer ones managed to retain their supports for their own farmers and fishermen.

This was the historic context in which Africa had joined world trade. I was met in Dakar by Moussa Faye, regional director of both the Global Campaign against Poverty and Action Aid's West Africa operations, who was a member of the Senegalese delegation to WTO summits, and who had promised to show me how the rules looked from the African side.

As we sat in the hot dusty snarl of Dakar's traffic, aiming for the elegant grid of its old French colonial heart but trapped instead in the featureless squalor of its random and explosive urban growth, he tried to explain how this imbalance in global trade and debt had stymied his country's recent development. The way the food system worked and in particular the crisis with fish were at the heart of the problem. We had plenty of time: Dakar was experiencing one of its frequent power cuts and the computers in the office were down so there could be little other work done anyway . . .

Senegal had become a net food-importing country and heavily indebted. But it wasn't always like this, he insisted. After the end of the slave trade, French colonial rule had brought groundnut plantations to West Africa, and groundnuts for oil had been the major export. In the early years of independence from France, the Senegalese government ran a programme of support for the economy, providing subsidized seeds and fertilizer to farmers while maintaining prices. Growth had failed to keep pace with the growing population but at least there had been improvements in education rates and health. Unlike some of its neighbours it saw democratic transfers of power; it had a relatively well-educated population and an internationally acclaimed cultural scene.

But the combination of severe drought, falling agricultural commodity prices and the oil shock of 1973 led to a severe downturn and spiralling debt. When the global recession of the late 1970s hit and the flow of credit was turned off, Senegal couldn't afford to pay back. It was forced to turn to the IMF and World Bank for loans, and sign up to their vision for development. This vision, part of the so-called Washington consensus, and based on the World Bank's 1981 Berg report, was that development must be based on free trade using the private sector not inefficient state interventions. It was, in other words, the economic vision of the US. The conditions they imposed were a series of structural adjustment programmes that removed protections and opened Senegal's markets to imports. The government had to end its subsidies to key food staples and support to farmers. As aid organizations repeatedly point out, none of the industrialized countries of the rich West developed in this way, instead they protected their fledgling industries and economies while they developed. But African beggars could not be choosers.

Cheap subsidized goods from the US and EU started to flood in, undermining the country's own farmers and radically changing diets in just two decades. Senegal became ever more dependent on imports.

The result however was not the intended development but regression. The agricultural and industrial sectors experienced massive job losses. More than 70 per cent of the Senegalese population live in rural areas and depend on farming or fishing for their income but food production per capita actually fell. By the turn of the millennium the country was meeting only half of its food needs.

Moussa and Action Aid, along with other aid organizations such as Christian Aid, had tracked the impact of these policies on Senegal's food industries and consumption patterns. As we diverted to a restaurant to try the culinary legacy of former rule, local fish drowned in a heavy cream sauce, Paris haute cuisine-style, circa-1970, Moussa reminded me that, as with most developing countries, this wasn't just a question of who made money out of the food chain, but whether people could live and survive at all. They were finding it increasingly difficult.

Until 1994 the government had protected the tomato industry with tariffs and quotas to discourage imports. Before liberalization, tomato production had thrived. With deep cuts in import tariffs however, the EU was able to export its triple concentrate tomato paste at prices that started to undercut local production. There is not much free trade about EU tomato production. About 80 per cent of it is subsidized. The support given to EU farmers and processors in the last few years has represented as much as 43 per cent of the price. This is what small African farmers were supposed to compete with. The effect was as devastating as it was predictable. By 1997 Senegal's tomato industry was producing barely a quarter of what it had done six years before. It moved from self sufficiency to dependency on imports in just four years.

The story had been the same with the Senegalese poultry sector. The EU chicken industry, able to take advantage of heavy grain subsidies when buying its feed, had been able to dump cheap poultry in West Africa, sending the Senegalese the bits no one in Europe wanted, thighs and wings at rock bottom prices. Seven out of every ten Senegalese chicken farms went out of business in the five years to 2003.

The reforms imposed on Senegal didn't just lead to job losses; they led to a disintegration of the Senegalese social fabric. Twenty years of IMF and World Bank intervention were accompanied by an increase in poverty and malnutrition. The step from here to migration has been but a short one.

Many of the ruined farmers have taken to fishing to replace their lost livelihoods and to feed their families. Recurring drought has further swelled the numbers of subsistence farmers migrating from the interior to the coast. With the structural adjustment programmes' drive to produce food for export, fish, a key part of Senegal's natural wealth, was supposed to provide the answer to bringing in foreign currency for growth. But it is foreign boats that have reaped much of the benefit, and now West Africa's stocks, like most of those around the world, are under threat.

The waters off the coast of West Africa have been among the richest fishing grounds in the world, with over 1,000 species of fish identified in what is known as the Sahelian Upwelling. Fish of infinite variety, and dolphins and whales, move through these waters, followed by fishermen of many nationalities.

Over the last quarter century, the EU has bought licences for its trawlers to fish in Senegalese waters, as have the Chinese and Japanese, bringing in much-needed revenue to the government in the short term but at the cost of the sustainability of fish stocks.

Maps of fish densities off West Africa show a dramatic decline since 1960, and a sharp acceleration in losses through the 1980s and 1990s as hi-tech trawling intensified. In a short period, Senegal's natural capital has been plundered.

I visited the Spartan office of the Senegalese government's director of industrial fishing, marooned at the end of an unmade road on the outer fringes of Dakar port, to ask how he viewed the deals with the EU and their impact on West Africa's resources. While outside carrion crows fought each other over the remains from the morning's fish market, Dr Papa Namsa

Keita expounded on the new colonialists. The EU signed a series of four-year deals from 1979 to allow its boats to fish in Senegal's waters, currently paying the government about €16 million a year for the privilege. For years there were no limits on what they could catch. The most recent deal has, under international pressure, introduced a sustainability element. 'The latest EU licences give them about 20,000 tonnes a year. It's forbidden to factory ship. The big trawlers may not process on board, and we have a division for surveillance. This does not mean there is no fraud,' he smiled wearily.

The predominantly Spanish and French EU trawlers that come are double the size of the Senegalese industrial fishing vessels, some of them over forty metres. As stocks decline, highly capitalized Western fleets have deployed technologies originally designed for military use, to exploit areas of the sea previously considered too inaccessible to fish. Sonar mapping systems can reveal every crack of the seabed; precision satellite navigation systems and tracking of surface temperatures together with depth sensors enable them to target fish when they are most vulnerable.

Dr Keita reckoned that the small local boats were responsible for overfishing too but the EU trawlers are heavily subsidized and in unfair competition with Senegal's own industrial fleet.

Professor Callum Roberts puts it more bluntly than Dr Keita. He says that while local fishermen are frequently blamed, in fact 'foreign trawlers are strip-mining African waters of their fisheries resources. It is a scandal.'

The plundering of resources does not stop there. The US and the EU have other ways of tipping the trade to their advantage, Dr Keita explained. 'They create other barriers to trade, some of them based on prejudice. At the moment most of what we export goes unprocessed – that's a great loss of potential earnings, but the EU imposes Draconian safety and hygiene rules on us when we want to export fish to you. We invested millions to upgrade our fishing processing facilities to meet them. Two of our local tuna-canning factories went out of business. But even with all that investment, the price we got for fish was no higher.'

On the outer edge of the port, a Spanish company Vierirasa has its processing factory. Pass through the security gates here and you enter another world. Inside the giant chilled warehouse, rows and rows of Africans work shifts in surgical whites and face masks, preparing the most valuable fish for export to the EU. Highly prized species are washed gently in a large tumbling machine and passed along the lines of filleters to be cut, before being dipped in a chlorine solution to kill any bacteria and hermetically sealed for freighting to the lucrative European markets, fresh on ice if by air, frozen if by sea. Facilities like this are capital, energy and labour intensive, and where they exist in Senegal they are mostly controlled by foreign capital, while African labour works them.

Outside on the docks it's the same story. The EU is limited in theory in the number of boats that can fish here, 200 trawlers in 2003 compared with fewer than 100 of all nationalities in the early 1970s. Any trawlers flying the Senegalese flag must be 51 per cent Senegalese-owned. In practice, foreign money is behind most of the latter with a Senegalese shell company for a front, and much of the profit is taken abroad. The number of boats has grown and the volume of catches declared in Dakar has more than quadrupled over the last three decades, putting intense pressure on stocks. But no one really knows how much fish is actually being taken out of these waters. Plenty of the catch is not declared at all.

Pirate fishing has become an enormous problem and the Senegalese can't keep up with it. The Environmental Justice Foundation together with Greenpeace tracked vessels fishing illegally off West Africa for two years in 2006–7 and recorded dozens of different infringements of the rules. They found foreign boats fishing without licences for the waters they were working, trawlers using much smaller and more damaging nets than allowed, and vessels discarding enormous quantities of bycatch or fish deemed too small or too worthless for the European market. The prawn trawlers in this region are among the most wasteful in the world, throwing away 10kg of marine bycatch for every kilo of prawns caught. Unlicensed boats were trying to pass themselves off as licensed ones owned by the same company, and refrigerated reefers were illegally transhipping fish at sea, mixing it with legal fish on board or taking it to Las Palmas in the Canary Islands where it was unloaded and mixed with legal catch before being passed into the European markets, including London's Billingsgate.

The season before my visit a large Spanish trawler had been caught red handed. It was illegally transhipping at sea rather than coming into Dakar to land its fish and pay its taxes. It was fined, but did not pay up; it had simply come back the following year, undeterred, to fish just outside Senegalese jurisdiction in bordering Mauritanian waters. There it would of course have been raiding the same fish stocks, along with the largest fishing supertrawler ever built: the infamous Irish-owned *Atlantic Dawn*, which under bilateral agreements with Mauritania was allowed to drag an unselective purse seine net behind it that was twice the volume of the Millennium Dome.

Faced with a decimation of stocks in which they have played a leading role, the larger trawlers have every possible piece of equipment to hunt down what is left in the ocean. The smaller local boats have no such help.

About 60km north of Dakar, the coastal town of Kayar is the third largest fishing centre in Senegal. I set off early to see it, hoping in vain to beat the permanent traffic jams, but instead stuttered and crawled for an hour through slums and potholes to reach the exit road from the capital. The route north eventually takes you in to bush country where children weave their footballs round chickens foraging in dirt tracks and fruit sellers sit in the shade of spreading baobab trees. I passed the Taiwan technical services station that had been closed down because now that China is making loans to Senegal, it is demanding its own price for help.

To the eye, the beach at Kayar has the colours and light of a tourist dream; a long uninterrupted stretch of sparkling sand, covered with brightly painted traditional fishing boats under a brilliant blue sky reflected in tropically turquoise waters. But the sounds and smells are more like those of a Dickensian estuary scene. The air is full of the din of pre-industrial activity, the hammering of nails into leaking keels, the beating out of old oil drums for metal, the scraping and chiselling of wooden oars. Women crouching over stick fires gut fish while shouting at small children to hurry, their scrawny knees buckling under the weight of water vats on their heads. Shrill-crying birds circle over the innards. A dead goat lies bloated by the scorching sun here; an exhausted horse hangs its head under the burden of its cart there. There is a stench of ordure overlaid with the reek of fish waste and burning. Hustlers and hawkers work the shadeless strand, and gangs of bare-backed men heave the boats down over rusty metal rollers into a sea so full it can take no more. A remorseless wind blows. It carries no cooling breeze; instead its hot biting breath is thick with sand as it whips up the Atlantic waves.

Over 1,000 pirogues were parked up on the 300-metre beach when I arrived, every inch of territory accounted for. Fifteen years before there were just a few locals. But now thousands of Senegalese move from inland to the coast here during the fishing season to try to earn a living. Once out at sea they compete not only with each other but with the foreign trawlers.

Mar Mbaye, a forty-five-year-old fisherman whose family has worked the sea off Kayar for five generations, told me about the pressures. 'The local fishermen are conscious of conservation because it's their future and their children's future. The others are not. Then at night the trawlers come into the zone six miles from the shore which is supposed to be just for artisanal fishermen. The pirogues cross the line the other way too because it is so crowded. The local boats fish with lines and throw back young fish, but further up, the trawlers have destroyed the seabed, you can see them do it, they damage the habitats.'

Mbaye who uses lines to fish for what he called the deep sea 'noble fish' such as monkfish, bream, squid, octopus, and grouper, helps oversee a management system to ration the number and length of trips each pirogue can now make from the beach. But tension inevitably flares up. The Kayar fishermen had recently tried to stop boats from further north leaving their nets out for prolonged periods; a fight had broken out, and a man had been killed.

Faced with this competition, entrepreneurial Senegalese fishermen have turned their boats over to a more lucrative albeit high-risk trade: people smuggling. The raiding of African waters by EU vessels has had an unforeseen pay back for governments in the West. It has driven a tide of young African men to migrate to their countries.

The coast that runs north and south of this key former outpost of the African slave trade is now the point of departure for the human cargo of our times, migrants desperate to work in Europe. Thousands of small wooden pirogues set sail from Senegal each year with Africans packed on board like sardines, turned into live freight just as their forebears were on the eighteenth-century Liverpool slave ship *Brookes*. The attrition rates are a shocking echo of the mass mortality of that earlier trade in people.

From Senegal's Atlantic coast, the pirogues aim for the first fall of European land, the Spanish Canary Islands, where so much of their fish is illegally landed. The Red Cross has estimated that one in five would-be illegal entrants die on the trip.

With dreadful irony, many of the people displaced by the pressure from EU interests on Senegal's fishing and tomato industries have ended up as illegal migrants in Italy working on the tomato harvests. If they survive the dangerous pirogue journey, they often pass briefly through detention camps and then out into the labour market of southern Europe, where they provide the illegal cheap workforce used to harvest and process the very EU-subsidized crops that have put paid to their own livelihoods back home.

I caught up with some of those who had become the West African fishing boats' alternative cargo at the end of 2006, in Rosarno, a small town in the mafia-controlled toe of Italy. Every dawn hundreds of migrants gathered along its litter-blown streets, recreating a map of Africa's troubles, as they queued in the hope of work. They were joined by Eastern Europeans, many of them refugees from the 'backward agriculture' that the EU and transnational business reckoned needed reforming. On that December morning, Moroccan men had formed a large gang in the middle of Rosarno's main street, their pale skins giving them an advantage in the brutal pecking order. Opposite, a group of Bulgarian Roma women were taking their chances, huddling a young child close to them. Chain-smoking Romanians, both men and women, had marked out their territory slightly away from the Roma, whom they said they despised; next to them was a solitary Russian. Back across the way a knot of newly arrived Egyptian youths said they were dreaming of England; and at the end of the road were the black Africans, always last to be chosen, dozens of them, from Senegal, Ghana, Nigeria, Mauritania, Ivory Coast, Burkina Faso, Mali, Togo, Eritrea and Sudan.

About eighty of the migrants had taken shelter in a burned-out paper factory on the edge of town. Most of them had worked the tomatoes before moving here when that season came to an end and the olive and orange seasons started. The main hall of the building was empty by day but for a few tents patched with cardboard where a handful of Senegalese men slept the sleep of the dead, laid out straight and wrapped in thin cloths like shrouds. Shafts of light pierced the broken windows. The roof was mostly gone, though patches remained with their asbestos threads exposed to the air. Around the bare concrete floor were the remnants of fires from the night before – the migrants cut down trees to cook their one meal of the day each evening. There was no sanitation. Outside, the rubbish heaps had attracted a healthy population of rats. Most of those I spoke to were from West Africa and they were desperate and angry.

In another derelict factory building I met Yasir, who had arrived from Morocco also via West Africa. He was living in a damp, dark store where the light barely penetrated. Daubed on the walls over the remains of the plaster were the names of the places the shifting population had called home and their routes of illegal entry: Dakar, Rabat, Tunisie, Maroc, Mombasa, Lampedusa, Paris, Milan, Barcelona. There was no sanitation or access to running water here either. Yasir was haunted, by the memories of home, and by the trauma of his voyage. He had come on a small Senegalese pirogue, loaded to the gunnels, at a price of £1,000 per person. He had started the journey with a group of fifteen friends, but once at sea they had been hit by a storm. The waves washed over them; most could not swim. 'I was crying and crying, I thought I was going to die. I still think about it.' All his friends drowned and he found himself alone, picked up off the Canaries by the Spanish authorities and later released from detention camp, free to disappear and work but only to live without papers, in fear.

The international charity Médicins sans Frontières, most famous for its emergency work in Africa and Asia, became so concerned about conditions among migrants in Puglia and Calabria that it sent a team to assess the situation in 2005. It found that most migrants were living in conditions that would not even meet the minimum standards set by the UN High Commissioner for Refugees for refugees in camps in Africa. Estimates put the numbers involved at around 20,000. Over 40 per cent were living in abandoned buildings, a further third in overcrowded houses sharing mattresses. More than half had no access to running water. Half also had no access to lavatories. Most of the migrants were young and should therefore have been in good health but of 770 examined by MSF, 94 per cent had a least one significant health problem. Three quarters had chronic disease. Skin diseases resulting from poor hygiene and exposure to pesticides were rife as were respiratory infections, including some resistant TB. Many of the workers could only afford to eat once a day and were consuming fewer calories than they needed to maintain their body weight during eight to ten hours of manual work. Nearly a third of those interviewed had been subjected to violence, mostly in the form of beatings by Italians.

Nine out of ten tins of tomatoes consumed in the UK come from Puglia. Oranges and olives from Calabria feed the north European markets. We have all eaten the fruit of this labour. I went back to the ruined paper factory in Rosarno as darkness fell and waited for those who had found work to return. From the road out of town, there came the sound of tired feet being dragged in step and a low African chant as they kept themselves going the last yard home. It was a sound that seemed to echo down the centuries.

I thought of those migrants again later. I was looking at the sugar bowl from the London's Museum in Docklands that had been an early example of ethical shopping, with its engraving promising that East India sugar would only cost five slave lives rather than West Indian sugar's six. Suddenly my efforts to buy fish with a little label that said 'sustainable' seemed pathetically inadequate. And yet. It was on such small tokens of concern that a political movement was built. If the early nineteenth century abolitionists could change things, why shouldn't we?

7. Fats

I remember well when the bizarre relationship we in affluent countries have with fat first struck me. I was watching an ad for polyunsaturated margarine. It must have been the late 1970s and the general message seemed to be that not only did real men not eat quiche, they really ought to give up butter too.

'Stop. Ought he to be eating Flora?'

'The Margarine for Men.'

'A Flora man knows what's good for him.'

'Isn't it time to change your husband?'

No doubt there were others for other brands but the Unilever ones were the cleverest, and they have stuck in my mind because they bothered me.

Later when they started to target women in a particular way, they bothered me even more.

'Isn't it time you changed your husband?'

'What does Mum do?'

'Polywassernames . . .'

They were all model families playing happily together in an outdoorsy sort of way thanks to the caring housewife, not too glamorous not too matronly, who shopped wisely for the right brand. What I heard was an unspoken subtext that if you didn't buy him the right fat spread he might keel over from a heart attack and leave you an unwaged widow with two children to bring up on your own.

These sorts of ads marked, too, my first awareness that instead of being allowed the pleasure of eating normal foods like butter that had been happily consumed for centuries before heart disease was ever an issue, we were being encouraged to think of food as something scary, potentially dangerous, that would need a magic new product to fix it. The official advice was that we should substitute saturated fats and cholesterol in the diet with polyunsaturated fatty acids, and manufacturers like Unilever were quick to find ways to help us.

Other cultures I have lived among still celebrate fat. The Afghan refugees we worked with in Pakistan's North-West Frontier always offered us as guests the choicest bits of any meal. At feasts we would be given the best slices of a slow-roasted lamb, which they considered to be those larded with a thick layer of sweet fat under a slice of crisp skin. Still hot from the fire, they were indeed delicious. But in rich countries, in our fear of becoming fat ourselves, we tend to shun fat on food where we can see it, only to consume all the more when it is invisible in processed foods.

Fat has joined sugar and salt as something to avoid, even though we need essential fats. Fats do have much in common with sugars. Both are energy dense; and sugars and highly refined starches are often the parents of fats, in that our bodies deal with excess glucose by converting it to hard saturated fatty acids for storage. But they are also different. While we have no physiological need of sugar, our brains and bodies depend on the long-chain omega-3 and omega-6 fatty acids. Instead of demonizing them all, we need to make sure we get the right kind in the right proportion. Unfortunately, thanks to modern processing, we mostly get the wrong kind.

What type of fat is eaten and absorbed in the body (or applied to the outside of the body, come to that) has been a function of price, availability, production, and power, just as with other agricultural commodities from the early days of mass sugar consumption on. As with so much of our food, the nature of our fat consumption changed radically in the second half of the twentieth century. The technological advances that made such change possible came from discoveries towards the end of the nineteenth century, and new advances are changing fat processing still. As usual, it has been a mix of economic and foreign policy interests that has determined when those technologies were applied to which fats, and what we end up consuming.

When it comes to sourcing fats, governments have worked to protect whatever the prevailing interest was seen to be at the time. For much of its recent history, fat supply has been about the competing interests of dairy farmers and vegetable oil producers. Within the interests of vegetable oil producers, there have been tussles too, between the competing needs of soap making and food manufacturing industries. The new twenty-first-century use of edible oil for engine fuel has added a further dimension to the dynamics of power.

One of the most important dietary shifts over the last century has been the change in the types and quantities of fats we eat. Experts in heart health have warned against the saturated fats that subsidized dairy and meat production have provided in prodigious quantities as cheap raw materials for manufacturing. Meanwhile, experts on mental health and the brain worry that a flood of industrial vegetable oils added to thousands of processed foods has skewed the balance of essential fatty acids, so we eat far too much omega-6 and don't get enough omega-3 fatty acids. This imbalance is increasingly implicated in heart disease too.

The food industry is the main user of fats and oils, not the consumer direct. The largest sources of fat in our diets, contributing nearly a quarter of the fat we eat are meat and meat products. Within this, processed meat dishes, meat pies, and sausages supply more fat than unprocessed meat. Next is the category of cereals and cereal products that account for nearly a fifth of our total fat intake (this includes all those cereal bars, cakes, biscuits and pastries, and factory breads too, a major use of industrial fats). The next largest source of the fat we eat is milk and milk products. Fat spreads and butter only make up about one eighth of our total fat consumption, although illogically what we spread on our bread rather than invisible industrial fats are what we often concentrate on.

The scale of the change in fat consumption is most obvious when you look at the American statistics. In the US, soya oil accounted for only 0.02 per cent of all calories available in 1909, but by 2000 it accounted for 20 per cent of available calories, a 1,000-fold increase. The figure is so astonishing it bears repeating: a fifth of all American calories come from one source, soya oil, a commodity ingredient that was not used in food in any quantity before the Second World War. In the UK, omega-6 fats from oils such as soya, corn and sunflower were 1 per cent of energy supply in the early 1960s, but by 2000 they were nearly 5 per cent. The politics and economics have been different in Europe. Palm from former colonies, and rapeseed that suited the climate of countries that benefited from EU subsidies, dominate consumption of vegetable oils here. Neither was eaten in significant quantities in the West before the Second World War either.

The first alarms over fat supply were sounded by scientists in the 1950s as they tried to explain the epidemic of heart and circulatory disease that hit the US and then Britain. By the 1960s these diseases had become big killers, and cardiovascular disease is still the UK's largest cause of preventable death, accounting for 39 per cent of deaths in 2002. Coronary heart disease, the main form of CVD, causes approximately one in five deaths in men and one in six deaths in women, even though death rates have been falling rapidly in the UK since the beginning of the 1980s, thanks to great advances in treatment and the prescription of drugs to tackle the main risk factors.

Those risk factors are widely accepted to be: raised blood pressure, being a smoker, being overweight, drinking too much alcohol, having diabetes or a family history of it, and raised levels of blood cholesterol. Excess salt in the diet, mainly coming from processed foods, is accepted to raise blood pressure. Taking lots of exercise, eating lots of fruit and vegetables and fibre and consuming fish regularly are agreed to reduce your risk.

It is also currently widely accepted that too much saturated fat in the diet raises risk, and the WHO 916 report that the sugar industry lobbied so hard to water down recommends that polyunsaturated fats be substituted for saturated fats from dairy and meat products.

But looking back, what's remarkable about all the advice on dietary fats and health is how subject to revision it has been as knowledge has increased, and how much is still being argued over. In particular the significance of raised levels of blood cholesterol and what causes them is still the subject of fierce debate, with a significant minority remaining sceptical of current orthodoxy.

In the early days of investigation into the epidemic of heart disease in the 1950s cholesterol in the diet was said to be part of the problem. This was the edict that demonized eggs, since they are high in cholesterol, and from which eggs have still not really recovered, even though this notion has been now discounted.

Cholesterol is a hard waxy fat that is essential for our health but we do not need to get it from our diet because the body can make it. It is carried around the body by lipoproteins. Low-density lipoproteins (LDL) carry cholesterol and other fats from our livers to our cells, while high-density lipoproteins (HDL) carry cholesterol and fats from our cells back to our liver, where excess cholesterol is converted to bile salts for excretion. LDL cholesterol is often referred to as 'bad cholesterol' while HDL cholesterol is characterized as 'good' in terms of risk of cardiovascular disease.

The sceptics of the dietary cholesterol theory pointed out that not only was cholesterol vital to the body but that we had ways to keep it in balance.[1] The body's feedback systems make sure that if the diet is high in cholesterol, the liver produces less and vice versa. It is now accepted that eating cholesterol has little effect on blood cholesterol. Some forty years on the WHO report notes that 'evidence for the association of dietary cholesterol with cardiovascular disease is contradictory'.

Now instead the experts' theories on fat and heart disease have been refined. It is high levels of blood cholesterol rather than dietary intakes that are said to be associated with a greater risk of heart disease. There are sceptics of this theory too however, who say that although the association is real enough, this may be because they are a marker of other things going wrong. They use the analogy of crime: areas with high crime may have a high police presence but that doesn't mean the police are causing the crime.

The current consensus is, however, that too much saturated fat in the diet raises blood cholesterol, particularly LDL cholesterol, increasing the risk of coronary artery disease. Evidence of the role of saturated fats in cardiovascular disease is strong and has been demonstrated in animal experiments, epidemiological studies and clinical trials in various populations. WHO advice is that they should be replaced with polyunsaturated fats. Sceptics of this view still argue that animal fats were consumed, often in large quantities, long before heart disease was widely known, and that too many pieces of the puzzle don't fit – why do the

[1] Cholesterol has several functions. One is to regulate the fluidity of cell membranes, as the work of Joe Hibbeln and others on the brain has highlighted. Highly unsaturated fatty acids make cell membranes more fluid, saturated fatty acids harden it. If the cell membrane becomes too flabby, cells synthesize their own cholesterol to stiffen the membrane, or if the cell membrane becomes too stiff cholesterol is removed from it. The body also makes cholesterol in the liver. Cholesterol acts as a precursor to various steroid hormones, including the sex hormones oestrogen, progesterone and testosterone and the flight or fight stress hormone cortisone, which promotes the production of glucose and suppresses inflammation. Mother's milk is especially rich in cholesterol.

French who eat large quantities of butter, cream and meat, not suffer high rates of heart disease, for example? Why have so many of the studies that switched people to low fat diets not produced the expected results?

What has become almost universally accepted, but only in the last few years and it took half a century to acknowledge, is that trans fatty acids, unnatural fats which are created by hydrogenating unsaturated fatty acids, are even worse than saturated animal fats in promoting heart disease. For decades now experts have been advising us to switch to vegetable oils and products made from them such as margarine for healthier hearts, but what they failed to take into account was that these polyunsaturated fats were so often hydrogenated during industrial processing. When hydrogenated, the polywassernames were seriously bad news. The official advice has in fact made things worse.

The food industry post-war has been built on these hydrogenated fats – it wasn't just margarine for the table, but margarine produced for factory baking, hydrogenated oils for frying fast foods and a thousand other processed products that depended on them.

In the early 1990s evidence was suggesting that trans fats affected foetal and infant growth by disrupting the production of the long-chain essential fatty acids for the central nervous system.

Then in 1993 Professor Walter Willett, the principal investigator in the Harvard Nurses Study, one of the world's largest epidemiological studies and the one on which much of current advice is based, not just for cardiovascular disease but also for cancer, published evidence that nurses in the study who ate significant amounts of trans fatty acids had a 50 per cent increase in heart disease. They were twice as likely to have a heart attack as those who consumed few trans fats. In 1997 he called hydrogenation 'the biggest food processing disaster in US history'. In 2004 he told an interviewer that the advice to switch from butter to vegetable oils hydrogenated into margarine had turned out to be 'a disastrous mistake'. The US Food and Nutrition board advised that the only safe intake of trans fats was zero.

Yet table margarine had put itself in popular perception at the forefront of the fight against heart disease. That it did so represents a cultural colonization that is truly remarkable for a product that has spent most of its brief life as a poor relation. The latest 'science' has always helped it on its way, but science could not have achieved this transformation of our diets alone. (Were that possible fruit and vegetables might be doing better.) It was economic expediency and commercial interests that supplied the force needed to conquer us.

Margarine was originally developed by a French chemist Hippolyte Mège-Mouriez in the years between the Paris World Exhibition of 1867 and 1869 in response to a call from the French government for a cheap and long-life substitute for butter. The French were preparing for war they feared was coming with Prussia, following the latter's stunning victory over Austria, and were concerned to ensure that there would be adequate supplies of fat to feed their army and working classes. This was an era of rapid industrialization and of applied chemistry celebrated by such institutions as the Society of Chemical Industry. Warfare and military provisioning were subjected to the same measures of progress as other factory production – armies no longer fed themselves on the land they marched through but needed supply chains that could move with them along new transport infrastructures. Fats that were cheap and didn't go off during prolonged storage were a more reliable source of calories than butter that tended in any case to be in short supply when agriculture was disrupted by war. Mège-Mouriez worked away on his fat chemistry at the imperial farm that was the property of Napoleon the Third and was duly awarded a prize for his efforts by the emperor.

Early versions of his 'oleomargarine' were made from beef

tallow mixed with skimmed milk. The margarine was patented by Mège-Mouriez in France and England, but it was a Dutch dairy merchant business Jurgens that took up the process for mass production along with rival butter merchants in the Netherlands the Van den Berghs. The first margarine factory was built in Germany in 1872 immediately after the Franco-Prussian war (in which France had been trounced), and other factories followed rapidly over the next decade around Europe and in the US. By 1886 Lever Brothers of New York were dabbling in margarine-making, along with more than thirty other manufacturing companies in the US. Lever Brothers was originally a company set up by William Lever in England to sell soap to Lancashire factory workers, and pursued its famously philanthropic production in Port Sunlight. There was a natural synergy between soap and margarine, both using the same raw materials – the cheapest and most readily available sources of fat.

But the Dutch manufacturers had already established a dominant position in margarine. Originally they imported cheap rendered animal fat from the growing meat-packing industry in the US for their European production. It was 1906 before vegetable oils were first substituted for animal tallow.

By 1910 the price of animal fats was rising thanks to increasing competition for them from soap manufacturers such as Lever. Early organization among workers in the notorious Chicago meat yards was helping raise wages and push prices up too. Hydrogenation provided the technological breakthrough that gave the margarine industry a new answer to its sourcing problems – it was a development that would have profound consequences for the food industry and public health, but that was not known at the time. A German chemist Wilhelm Normann, adapting a process discovered earlier by a Frenchman, Paul Sabatier, had worked out how to harden fats artificially. Commercial production of these new artificially hardened vegetable oils had begun at a company in Warrington in Britain that would later be absorbed into Lever Brothers, but it was at the Jurgens factory in Germany that Normann oversaw the building of production capacity over the next decade that would transform the whole nature of fat consumption.

The physical properties of fats reflect their chemical properties. Polyunsaturated vegetable oils are usually liquid at room temperature. Saturated fats on the other hand are relatively solid at room temperature. The process of hydrogenation allows manufacturers to alter oils' molecular structure to make them more solid and change their melting point. They can thus create different fats for different effects – chocolates use fats with a melting point designed to melt in the mouth; a croissant may use a harder, more hydrogenated fat to make sure it retains its crisp quality during baking.

Hydrogenation involves mixing vegetable oils such as soya, corn and rapeseed with a metal catalyst, usually nickel, and heating them up to 200 degrees Celsius. Hydrogen gas is then pumped through the hot oil in a high pressure reactor over a period of several hours. Fully hydrogenated fat is incredibly hard and is stored as plastic-like beads for use in manufacturing. The process can be stopped part-way when manufacturers want oils that are still liquid or soft but more stable and it is this partial hydrogenation that creates so-called trans fatty acids which have become the focus of so much concern recently.[2]

---

[2] The chemical process involved in hydrogenation is as follows. Fatty acids – the building blocks for the brain discussed in Chapter 6 – are chains of carbon atoms with hydrogen atoms attached and a carboxyl molecule on the end. When all the carbon atoms in the chain are linked to hydrogen atoms they are said to be saturated (filled with hydrogen). Where two carbon atoms are double bonded to each other rather than attached to a hydrogen atom, the fatty acid is unsaturated. Polyunsaturated fatty acids have more than one double bond ('poly' being from the Greek for 'many'). During the process of hydrogenation the hydrogen atoms penetrate the fatty acid molecules, causing the double bonds to become single ones as the carbon atoms are saturated with new hydrogen partners. Partial hydrogenation creates trans fatty acids because it twists the double bonds so that the hydrogen atoms end up on opposite sides of the carbon chain rather than in the original configuration on the same side ('trans' is the Latin for 'across').

Trans fatty acids are sufficiently similar to natural fats that the body incorporates them into the cell membrane. Once there, their altered chemical structure wreaks havoc with thousands of vital chemical reactions from energy release to prostaglandin production. Certain forms of trans fatty acids occur naturally in dairy fats. But these have a different molecular structure to the ones created by partial hydrogenation. The latter are entirely new to human physiology, and by the 1970s edible oil industry researchers were already expressing concern about what their effect was.

Back in Britain in the early twentieth century, before much of this was understood, the battle of the fats was an economic one. Lever Brothers had come to an agreement with three other manufacturers to limit competition for their raw material, the oils and fats needed by both soap makers and margarine producers. It was attacked by the *Daily Mail* which accused the company of running a cartel, which it dubbed The Soap Trust. The brothers successfully sued the *Mail* for the slur, winning £50,000 damages, considered massive for the time, as today's Unilever website records.

Van den Bergh and Jurgens took to importing vegetable oils from India, China and West Africa and cotton seed oil, a by-product of the cotton industry, from the US. They also set up a palm-planting venture in German Africa. William Lever looked to Africa too, and in the scramble for that continent turned to the Belgian Congo. He secured a concession there to plant palm for oil in 1911 and established 'Leverville'. When Leverville was visited by the Belgian King Albert and Queen Elisabeth on a grand imperial tour a decade and a half later, it was described by reporters as 'humming', 'a famed palm-oil extracting centre of Lever Brothers, the World's largest Soap Makers'. They also recounted how, earlier, Albert's predecessor King Leopold had been less than impressed by the new-fangled ingredient in his soap. 'Quaint was Mr. Lever's presentation to King Leopold II of an ivory box containing the first cake of soap made from Congo palm-oil extracted at Leverville. Leopold, whom no gift could dazzle, afterwards said that the presentation cake "stank cursedly and wouldn't lather", when he sought to use it "out of compliment to Monsieur Lever".'

The new hydrogenating technology opened the way for not just vegetable oils but other novel ingredients. Whale oil became useful for soap and margarine for a while, now that industry knew how to solidify it to the right degree, since it was very cheap. Ever quick to protect their interests, various fats businesses, including Lever, got together just before the First World War to form the Whale Oil Pool to regulate the distribution of this new commodity.

Alarmed by the threat to its supremacy in the fat business, the dairy industry fought back, largely through government intervention. In 1877 states in the US began passing laws to restrict the sale of margarine and to stop manufacturers using colours to help pass artificially hardened fats off as butter, as they tried to protect their milk producers. By 1886 sufficient momentum to fight the threat had been gathered for the US Congress to pass the Margarine Act, which imposed a tax of two cents a pound on margarine and required those wanting to make or sell it to be licensed. Individual states introduced bans on the colouring of margarine, so that its greyish undyed appearance might deter consumers. The federal tax was increased five-fold in 1902, and between 1902 and 1904 consumption of margarine halved as a result. The Americans were brought their first hydrogenated vegetable oils in margarine by Procter and Gamble which had bought the patent from Normann and launched Crisco shortening in 1911.

The First World War led to shortages of dairy fats and a rise in margarine again. The British and German governments brought the fats and oils industries under government control to secure supplies. Lever Brothers entered the margarine industry in Britain at the request of the British government.

Consumers ate what they could find. For most of the conflict Van den Bergh and Jurgens supplied both sides of the warring parties with margarine.

But once the war was over and butter became more available and affordable again, margarines sales dropped through the 1920s. During this decade, Lever Brothers were acquiring companies that made other uses of animal and vegetable fats – including Wall's sausages and ice cream. By the end of the 1920s its interests also accounted for 60 per cent of the total output of UK soap manufacturing.

The two Dutch margarine giants, Jurgens and Van den Bergh, had been working ever more closely together, buying up rival European manufacturers and entering at one point into profit-sharing agreements. In 1927 they joined together formally to create the Margarine Unie, or Margarine Union.

The Lever Brothers group responded to the challenge by negotiating with the Margarine Unie. At first the two parties aimed just to negotiate an arrangement to keep out of each other's principal interests, but in the end a full-blown merger was agreed between the Dutch Margarine Unie and Lever Brothers which created what *The Economist* at the time described as 'one of the biggest industrial amalgamations in European history'. Unilever, the corporation that emerged, processed more than one third of the total tonnage of edible oils and fats traded on the global market. It had become, in other words, the world's fat controller.

The Great Depression saw a renewed effort by several states in America in the 1930s to protect their dairy industries and desperate farmers, and by governments on the continent to impose taxes and production limits on margarine. So the see-saw between interests continued until the Second World War. With the world at war again, controlling the supply of fats for food and soap acquired strategic importance. In September 1939, Unilever found itself with major interests on both sides, its operations split between the British Empire and the Third

Reich. As war broke out it controlled 68 per cent of the margarine industry in Germany, and had twenty-five margarine factories in the country, as well as oil mills, refineries and hardening plants, and soap interests. It was also the dominant supplier of fats to Britain. Like most other transnationals caught up in the divide during the war, Unilever continued to operate, with subsidiaries in Germany being run almost autonomously.

After the war, Unilever was under attack as one of the largest concentrations of economic power in Germany, and a target for the Allies' 'decartelization and deconcentration policy'. The Americans were pushing to have monopolies broken up and vital sectors opened to competition from their business interests. The terms of the Marshall Plan made sure that free trade, backed by anti-trust measures and economic liberalization, would become the terms on which international commerce resumed in the post-war order. In the end the US decartelization policy fizzled out without Unilever's interests in Germany being dismantled. The US had achieved what it wanted anyway. It set the terms of trade for the post-war era that would see the entry of its giant agricultural traders into the European markets in primary fat processing and oilseed crushing.

The legacy can be seen today. Now the US is the largest producer of oils and fats and the largest net exporter of them too – soya oil is the largest vegetable oil traded over the globe – with Brazil recently catching up. Palm oil has come a major second, and 92 per cent of the world's palm comes from just two countries: Malaysia and Indonesia. The rush for biodiesel and to cut down on trans fats has given it new impetus. The UK, Netherlands and Germany are the main EU markets for palm, accounting together for more than half of the total EU consumption. The Mediterranean countries and France with their lower rates of heart disease use olive oil. The EU, the largest producer of rapeseed in the world, still accounts for over half of world margarine production. The largest net importer of fats is now China, and as its imports rise dramatically its patterns of disease follow ours.

With the new theories on heart disease being translated into dietary advice for the general population margarine entered its heyday after the Second World War. The medical profession approached manufacturers like Unilever to come up with products using polyunsaturated fats that would help the fight against premature death from heart attacks and strokes.

The 1960s saw a rush of new products. Flora was launched by Unilever in 1964 and advertised on TV in 1965. By 1970 Unilever had begun promoting its use directly to the medical profession. Through the 1970s marketing campaigns promoted it as the alternative fat for a healthier heart, particularly for men, based on the accepted expert advice at the time. The 'high in polyunsaturates' claim was allowed to be advertised for the first time in 1979. And so for more than a decade the brand built a following and a leading position in the market as the fat that was better for you.

As with the breakfast cereal market, fats and spreads have depended on heavy spending on advertising and marketing. In the UK in 2006, for example, £29 million was spent on advertising by the fat-spread makers and their butter-spread rivals. Unilever spent an estimated £9 million advertising its Flora range in 2005.

Although people tend to talk about margarines in fact there are strict EU rules about which description can be used on fats sold in shops to consumers. Margarine has to have a fat content of 80–90 per cent, anything with a fat content between 62 per cent and 80 per cent is a fat spread, under 60 per cent fat counts as a reduced fat or if under 41 per cent low fat spread or light spread. Recent years have seen a shift to the last of these. In reduced and low fat spreads, water, that cheapest and lowest of calorie ingredients, is substituted for a large part of the fat, together with emulsifiers to hold it all together.

Demand for industrial margarines and shortening, as opposed

to table spreads, also produced by partial hydrogenation of vegetable oils, began its exponential rise in the 1960s and 1970s too as new snacks and convenience foods were marketed to populations that had emerged from the privations of food rationing into growing affluence and leisure through the 1960s.

Between 1970 and 2005 consumption of liquid vegetable oils such as soya, rapeseed, and sunflower in the UK tripled to over 1 million tonnes a year. These were becoming the preferred fat stocks, as agricultural subsidies, for soya in the US and for rapeseed and sunflower in Europe, encouraged farmers to plant more and more acres with them.

The market has remained highly concentrated in the hands of a few transnational corporations. Unilever no longer dominates the primary processing – the first refining stages – of fats and oil, having sold its interests in that sector to concentrate on making consumer products, but it remains the largest oil and fat firm worldwide in terms of secondary processing. A handful of US-based corporations now account for most of oil refining. The names dominating the world markets in refining and primary processing will be familiar: Bunge, ADM and Cargill. Edible oil production is now highly integrated with the animal feed industry – since the crushing and processing of soya and rapeseed produce both oil for industrial fats and the high-protein feeds needed for intensive livestock factory farming. These three companies and their subsidiaries are estimated to account for 80 per cent of European soya bean crushing, and about three quarters of European feed manufacturing.

It was not just these oils that were being produced in ever greater quantities. Tropical fats have followed the same trajectory. After the Second World War, a new front opened in the fat wars, this time not between butter and margarine, but between palm oil grown in a former British colony and American soya oil. The Malaysians, independent from 1957 but still under British influence, were facing both loss of their main source of income – the natural rubber markets that synthetic rubber was overtaking – and a serious threat from Chinese communist insurgents. If they were to keep the hearts and minds of peasant farmers, they needed to secure them a source of income. So soon after independence the government began a major land development programme, persuading smallholders to join cooperatives, and clear the jungle – today it would be called rainforest but then it was savage jungle in need of taming – and plant palm trees for their oil. By the 1970s, the policy had begun to deliver large volumes of the new crop for export. But it was still relatively unknown as an oil. So the Malaysians set up a research institute to market their palm.

A key member of this institute was Kurt Berger, a 1944 Cambridge science graduate and food technologist who has been at the heart of the development of the modern fat industry. Berger had acquired an expert knowledge of bakery fats working for J Lyons & Company after the war, using his science to develop new raw materials as soon as controls on the food industry had been lifted after 1953. His new job selling Malaysian palm oil involved travelling the industrialized world, asking food industries what they used fat for and working out how they might be induced to use palm instead. He would take samples of their fats back to his lab and reproduce the same quality of fat for them using mixtures and fractions of palm oil. The attraction was that the palm substitute would be much cheaper. The Japanese and Chinese who had mostly fried foods in animal fats till then started switching to palm. As snack food markets grew, frying oils were needed in ever greater quantities. Palm withstood the high temperatures of factory production better than most alternative oils. Improvements in the refining process through the next two decades made it possible to remove some of the compounds that had previously made it unattractive.

Global consumption started to take off from 1970 onwards. This same decade saw improved methods of 'fractionating' the oil – a technique that enabled crude palm oil to be separated by cooling it until it crystallizes into different fractions, into olein which remains liquid, and stearin, a very hard, concentrated highly saturated fraction of the oil that could compete with the characteristics of hydrogenated soya oils.

The Americans were not about to surrender their markets to the East without a fight, however. US subsidies for soya and soya-oil refining tended to be pegged to a price that even after the additional process of hydrogenation made it just cheaper than palm oil. Hydrogenated soya oil was the preferred fat for US food processing, but palm was nevertheless a threat. Imports of palm and coconut oil were rising and the US fat export market was being challenged.

In the mid 1980s the tropical fats wars broke out in to the open. Berger recalled the form they had taken: 'A wealthy retired builder whose wife had died of heart disease many years before put adverts in the major papers saying that palm oil, which is relatively high in saturated fat, was killing Americans. At the same time the American Soybean Association [the soya farmer and industry lobby group] published a cartoon of a fat plantation palm farmer with a huge cigar in his mouth and a bomb in the shape of a coconut in his hand. Health campaigners started pushing the food and drug administration to introduce labelling of tropical fats as saturated on food packets. Palm oil is about 50 per cent saturated fat. Coconut oil is even more saturated: about 90 per cent saturated fatty acids. The strategy was to get America to label imported tropical fats and then the world would follow suit. The Americans were doing all sorts of things with subsidies too to persuade the Asian market we were developing to buy its soya.'

Berger was part of a palm industry delegation that visited the American Soybean Association to object to its activities. The ASA had begun its campaign in 1986 with a Fat Fighter Kit and letters to American soya bean farmers encouraging them to write to the US government and food companies complaining about tropical fats. In 1988 a congressional hearing into tropical fats was set up and Berger attended. 'The hearing decided there wasn't enough evidence against palm, and the FDA decided against labelling tropical fats as saturated. Of course the other major producer of tropical fats at the time was the Philippines; coconut oil was their only real export. It was effectively an American protectorate and of strategic importance. The US didn't want to clobber them . . .'

So palm and coconut oil were not given warning labels, but the damage was already done in public perception in the US. Tropical fats were killer fats. Soya oil, most of it hydrogenated, had won the American stomach.

Then in 1993 things got difficult for margarine and industrial baking fats made from soya and rapeseed. Willett's findings from the Harvard Nurses study were published and some of industry insiders' worst fears about trans fatty acids were confirmed.

In Britain, an entrepreneur started taking out adverts for a new 'Whole Earth Superspread' made without hydrogenated fat, presenting consumers with 'the facts that could save your life'.

The entrepreneur was Craig Sams, a macrobiotic Californian with a passion for sustainable consumption and a habit of finding ways of making money out of uncomfortable truths about food. He later went on to chair the Soil Association and to launch Green & Black's organic chocolate with his partner. Hydrogenation of fats had never been allowed in certified organic foods. The advert he ran in 1993 said that trans fats from hydrogenation were the biggest single dietary hazard of our time. 'The fats issue has been more clouded over than most with cholesterol panics and scientific gobbledygook serving commercial interests but the truth will always out.'

As well as the Willett findings that trans fats contributed to heart disease, the ad highlighted a series of studies and hypotheses that were new at the time but have since been confirmed. It quoted the view of Michel Odent the natural childbirth guru that trans fats were blocking the synthesis of prostaglandins that regulate the birth process leading to an increase in Caesareans. It pointed out that the level of trans fats in McDonald's French fries had risen enormously as the company, which had been targeted by health campaigners for its use of beef fat, switched to hydrogenated fat for frying. It said that high consumption of trans fats was associated with junk food and low income, explaining socioeconomic difference in obesity levels. And it noted that trans fats were implicated in low sperm counts. With all the trans fats in margarines, low fat spreads, bread, croissants, pastries, biscuits, meat substitutes, frozen meals, pastry, ice cream and pâtés and meat spreads, what you needed was Whole Earth Superspread!

Unilever, as manufacturer of Flora, complained to the Advertising Standards Authority. Sams lost and was told not to use his adverts again, not on the grounds that his information was inaccurate, for he had mounted a vigorous defence, pointing to the science behind each claim, but on the grounds that the advert appealed to fear to sell its products. Sams was monitoring commercial rivals, products at this point, and says his tests found that Flora contained 21 per cent hydrogenated fat at the beginning of his campaign for his new Superspread but that even as Unilever was complaining about his ad, it was altering its flagship product. The levels of hydrogenated fats were being reduced. His subsequent tests found trans fats down to under 1 per cent, at which point the company started putting a low trans fat claim on its labels. But for an uncomfortable period, the period during which it made its complaint to the ASA, Unilever found itself selling a product that was marketed as being good for your heart when it was heavy on trans fats that were known to be not just bad for your heart, but worse than the saturated fats of butter it was replacing.

I put the figures and this account Sams had given me to

Unilever in 2006 and asked why it had continued to market margarine with trans fats as healthy, when the evidence had come out against them. Its director of external affairs Anne Heughan told me that in Unilever's defence its work with polyunsaturated fats had begun when medics approached it in 1956 to come up with a product that would help in a practical way to achieve what scientists and public health policy makers wanted: for the population to cut its intake of saturated fat. It had thought, like everybody else, that it was doing the right thing. 'As a responsible manufacturer we can only go with the evidence at the time. When Walter Willett's evidence in 1993 indicated that trans fatty acids were as bad as saturated fats we felt that the weight of evidence had moved and we set about removing them. It took about two years.' Flora was free of partially hydrogenated fats by the end of 1994. Unilever changed its other brands Stork and I Can't Believe It's Not Butter slightly later. The company told me that before reformulation its spreads contained an average of 19.3 per cent trans fats. The average for Flora was 10 per cent and other brands around 25 per cent. By 2004 the level of trans had been reduced to less than 0.5 per cent in all its fat spreads. Unilever also says it has changed over 8,000 of its products, about half its total portfolio, as part of its goal to move to healthy and sustainable food. The result was a decrease of 30,000 tonnes of trans fatty acids in its products between 2004–2006.

Although Flora was not made with hydrogenated fat after 1994, a very large number of other fat spreads continued to be made in the same way until very recently. When I conducted a survey in 2005, together with a researcher, of what was on sale in UK supermarkets and asked manufacturers what type of oil they used and how it was processed, Unilever was clearly ahead of the rest in removing hydrogenated fats. Others were still in the process of removing them and several brands still used them unashamedly. A decade after science confirming there was a problem, parts of the industry were still dragging their feet. They had been finally pushed into action, but only by the threat of litigation in the US and by a requirement across the Atlantic that trans fatty acids be labelled from January 2006.

Without its preferred method of making margarine, the hydrogenation it had depended on for several decades, the food industry has had to find other ways to change fats that are naturally liquid into fats that are solid. It could of course in theory have just cut back on fats in its products, but for the most part that would defy the laws of economics. The price of fat has decreased by 50 per cent in the last fifty years, while the price of other healthier ingredients, of fruit for example, has gone up by a third. Fat and sugar are what get produced, fat and sugar are cheap, fat and sugar are therefore what get used, and fat and sugar are what we end up eating.

So rather than abandoning its props, industry now depends on two other ways of modifying fats. To explain them, I'm afraid I will have to inflict yet more polysyllabic modifications of our diet on you: interesterification and fractionation. The former is not allowed in organic production, the latter is. Margarine makers have largely turned to the former. Unilever, for example, told me it now produces Flora by interesterification using a blend of soya, rapeseed and sunflower oils. Fractionation is also being used increasingly to produce palm stearin, the fraction of palm oil that is hard as a brick but can then be mixed or interesterified with other liquid oils to reach the right consistency.

Inter-esteri-fication. I find it helps to get your tongue round this mouthful if you break it down. (The esters are the class of chemical substances that oils and fats belong to.) Remarkably, in my experience, many of the health groups or academic scientists studying nutrition and diet seem not to know about it. The process is not a new invention and so products made with it have not had to undergo independent safety tests. If you invent a new additive it at least has to be subjected to scrutiny by regulators before it can enter the food supply. But fat modification processes just don't get tested in this way. We have simply, quietly, been led into another mass experiment in molecular manipulation of our food.

A fat is made up of three fatty acids attached to a glycerol base. While hydrogenation works by altering the molecular structure within the fatty acids, interesterification works by chopping up and rearranging the order of the fatty acids on their base.[3]

Interestification does not produce trans fatty acids, but as one food technologist who has worked in the fats business for years but preferred not to be named put it to me: 'If we didn't know enough about hydrogenation, we know even less about interesterification. It is not as extreme as hydrogenation, but it is capable of taking a liquid and turning it into a solid so some fairly fundamental changes are going on at molecular level.'

There are two methods of interesterifying oils. The chemical method dates back to the 1940s when it was first introduced in the US. This process involves taking oils that have first been 'degummed' – that is stripped of impurities, proteins and unwanted types of fats such as lecithin – then bleached and dried, and then mixing them with a highly reactive strong alkali catalyst. The chemical reaction that takes place randomly reorders the fatty acids on the glycerol base. Afterwards the oil is bleached again and then deodorized at high temperatures to

[3] Industry insiders have described the process to me as follows: Imagine a fat is like your hand, with three fingers sticking up from the palm which acts as the base; imagine this is a triglyceride that forms the basic structure of most fats and oils. The three fingers represent three fatty acids (hence the tri-) attached to a glycerol base. Interesterification chops up the three fatty acids and puts them back on the glycerol base in a different order. While hydrogenation modifies fats by physically inserting hydrogen atoms into the fatty acids chains, interesterification works not by altering the structure within the fatty acid chains but by rearranging the chains. It can be achieved by processing either with chemicals or with enzymes.

remove the unpleasant smells. This was the original form of the process invented in the 1940s but its first commercial development coincided with advances in hydrogenation that made it possible to process soya oil more efficiently and cheaply so it never really took off. Interesterification also involved working with catalysts that could be hazardous in the factory. It destroyed the vitamin E in oils, and it was hard to control where the fatty acids ended up, so hydrogenation won out, until the problem with trans fats forced industry to think again.

Much more recently a process which uses enzymes rather than chemicals as catalysts has been introduced. Interesterification with enzymes is more controllable; manufacturers can decide exactly in which position the reordered fatty acids end up on the glycerol base. This has lots of advantages – food technologists know that we prefer the taste and mouthfeel of fatty acids in certain positions, and they have manipulated them for baby milk and chocolate for example. But it is also more expensive. There are other downsides: it is less easy to switch between different oils as feedstock and European industrial fats production has generally depended on manufacturers being able to substitute one oil for another depending on market price – that's one of the reasons you often do not see a full list of what sort of oils have been used declared in margarines. But with enzymes the vitamin E is not destroyed and although oil must arrive bleached and 'degummed' at the beginning of the process, it does not have to be bleached again afterwards. It goes through the same deodorizing process to get rid of off flavours and unpleasant smells at the end.

Unilever's highly expert research laboratories have conducted their own tests and shown that there is no difference in effect on blood levels of fats or other parameters between unsaturated blends of fats and interesterified blends.

A recent study, however, has suggested that interesterified fats may depress beneficial HDL cholesterol, raise blood glucose levels and decrease insulin production. It was conducted by scientists at Brandeis University in the US collaborating with researchers at the Malaysian Palm Oil Board. Both groups of researchers in other words could be said to have interests to declare.

Margarines and spreads for the table have tended to adopt interesterification as a substitute for hydrogenation. But the trans fat problem has also given new impetus to the palm oil industry, and palm fractionated to the very hard stearin is increasingly being used in other food processing.

Hydrogenation is the source of the vast majority of trans fatty acids that we consume. It is not the only one however. Today's oil refining process itself can produce small amounts of trans fatty acids. Advances in oil refining are what made it possible for soya, rapeseed and palm to enter the global food supply on an industrial scale. But the processes are still relatively new. And the use of these particular oils is recent. Although palm oil has been used for cooking by the West Africans for hundreds of years, it was exported mainly to be used for soap making since it had a very strong taste and dark colour that was considered unpalatable by everyone else. Soya oil was similarly considered unusable for food until after the Second World War because it smelled unpleasant and developed strong off flavours when used for frying. Rapeseed was thought entirely inedible, either by animals or humans – tests on rats fed with it in the 1950s found that they developed fatty degeneration of the heart; animals tended to reject it because it contained a toxin, glu-cosinolate. Although the Bengalis have a tradition of eating it, most cultures find it disgusting to taste in its crude state. It too used to produce strong off flavours when cooked.

Rapeseed's handicaps were solved however when the Canadians bred a new variety, called 'double zero' from which both the particular fatty acid that had troubled the rats' hearts and the toxin had been removed. It is this variety that opened up the rapeseed market. Double zero rapeseed is what is now planted in Europe and turns large swathes of England a very un-English smelly yellow just before harvest. Its oil is referred to in the Americas as canola, a coinage from 'Canada oil'.

These oils became usable only as refining techniques developed and industry worked out how to remove the terrible smells and tastes. Modern refining is not however a gentle process. First the oils in the palm fruits or oil seeds are extracted. Long ago, this would have been done by crushing them between millstones, which is how artisan cold pressed olive oil is still made. Now the crushing takes place, once the seeds have been heated, between steel rollers which also generate heat. Further oil is extracted by treating the crushed seeds with a chemical solvent, usually hexane, which is later removed in a further process of heating and steam. From this point on the crude oil extracted from the fruit or seeds can be further refined chemically or physically.

In chemical refining, the first step is degumming with hot water, to take out lecithin, proteins and pesticides and contaminants. Caustic soda is then added to the oil to neutralize free fatty acids – the fatty acid chains that have been broken free during the earlier stages and which go rancid. By reacting them with the caustic soda they can be converted to soap stock. These free fatty acids are either recovered by a further sulphuric acid treatment and used as animal feed or the soap stock goes to make soap and candles. All this is tremendously greedy of energy and creates large quantities of potentially polluting waste water.

Next comes a bleaching stage to take out colour and remove organic pollutants. Finally the oil is deodorized to remove unwanted smells and flavours.

In the 1990s Unilever developed a new process called 'superdegumming' which allowed liquid oils to be physically as opposed to chemically refined. The aim was to reduce environmental pollution and energy expenditure and create a process that was milder on the oil. This physical refining dispenses with the caustic soda step, and instead degums the oil more thoroughly at the beginning and then depends on a more intense deodorization stage at the end, which often takes place at very high temperatures.

Over the last fifteen years nearly all the major refining companies in Europe and the USA have changed over to this new method of physical refining. The only oils that are not refined in this way and are still consumed in their relatively raw state are olive oil, and a tiny number of special oils valued for their flavour such as walnut or hazelnut.

Some industry insiders have worried that this new form of physical refining produces trans fatty acids, particularly trans of the omega-3 fatty acids, unless the deodorization stage is very carefully controlled. The Food Standards Agency's view is that the amount of trans produced, which is only a fraction of what is produced by hydrogenation, is too small to be of concern. However the European Commission did commission a study of the metabolism of trans fatty acids formed this way. The study, conducted across three countries, noted that although trans polyunsaturated fatty acids are formed during refining of oil and are known to be taken up in tissue fats, 'their metabolism and potential effects on disease have been largely ignored'.

It also noted that while all reputable refiners would say that they do carefully control the deodorization stage, surveys of oils had found that up to 40 per cent of the omega-3 fatty acid in them could be turned into trans fat during refining. The findings of the study were not encouraging. In healthy men given high but 'not unrealistic' amounts of these trans fatty acids, after just three weeks' consumption, bad LDL cholesterol increased, and the ratio considered to be an important risk factor for heart disease, of bad LDL cholesterol to good HDL cholesterol, was altered for the worse. The formation of these trans fatty acids can be minimized but at a financial cost to the manufacturer. Unilever, for example, specifies a limit of 1–2 per cent trans on the refined and deodorized oils it buys from refiners such as ADM. The American Food and Nutrition Board may have judged that the only safe level of trans fats is zero, but it would not be possible to achieve that zero without abandoning the vast majority of today's refining plants.

Exposure of the perils of hydrogenation and trans fats failed to sound the death knell for margarine as a health product. Consumers, perhaps weary of endlessly changing expert advice, were slow to react to the trans fats issue, particularly in the UK. It was a full decade before campaigns to have them banned reached sufficient crescendo to affect eating habits. By then the top end of the industry had moved on, reduced trans fats to a minimum, and found new 'clinically proven' ways to sell itself.

The latest advance is the addition of high doses of plant sterols to margarines to lower blood cholesterol. The Finns were the first to develop these, extracting sterols from waste wood pulp from their paper industry. Benecol was the first fat spread with sterols in the form of sitostanol ester obtained at first from pine tree pulp, and later from rapeseed oil. It was launched in Finland in 1995 and was developed by one of Europe's larger oil refining and feed companies Raisio, in collaboration with Finland's public health institute. It arrived in the UK and Ireland in 1999, marketed under licence by a subsidiary of the US-based pharmaceutical company Johnson and Johnson.

Unilever came out with Flora with added plant sterols in 2000, having been delayed by new EU legislation that required novel foods such as plant sterols to be given regulatory approval before going on sale. The two have since fought a long legal dispute, which was only settled at the end of 2007, when they finally agreed to share and license the rights to the global plant sterol and stanol they had patented.

Phytosterols are plant compounds – alcohols of the steroid group to be more precise – derived from oils, trees and leaves. ('Phyto' just means 'plant' in ancient Greek.) They are naturally present in small quantities in many fruits, nuts, seeds and plants containing fat. Stanols are fully saturated phytosterols. Plant sterols have a similar chemical structure to cholesterol so that when they are eaten they seem to partially block the uptake of cholesterol from the gastrointestinal tract; the stanols seem to block uptake completely. This leads to a reduction in cholesterol levels in the blood. Phytosterols are naturally present in vegetable oils, but they are systematically stripped out by oil refiners during the refining process because they are a nuisance to industry, along with the other nutrients that help us metabolize oils. Just as with cereals, manufacturers have found a way to sell back to us what they took out in the first place.

Unilever introduced its first plant sterol-enriched range with Flora pro.activ® in the UK in 2000. Its sterols come from hydrogenated soya oil. The product is 'clinically proven to lower cholesterol*' it says, with a little asterisk that leads you to small print on the back of the pack. The claim is qualified there with the advice that you should eat it as part of a balanced diet including lots of fruit and vegetables and that it might not be right for everyone. The product is endorsed on the front by the World Heart Federation, with which Unilever recently signed a three-year sponsorship deal, giving the charity half a million Swiss francs in 2003.

The manufacturers point to over forty studies to show that plant sterols taken in sufficient quantity can actively reduce blood cholesterol levels in people with both normal cholesterol and raised cholesterol levels. The products have been taken up enthusiastically by the medical profession, which has been targeted with generous marketing budgets. The WHO 916 report on diet and health says that 'the cholesterol-lowering effects of plant sterols have been well documented and commercial products made of these compounds are widely available'. It sounds a note of caution however. 'But their long term effects remain to be seen.'

The UK government's expert committee on novel foods also

concluded that plant sterols were effective in lowering cholesterol but advised that foods to which they have been added 'are
suitable only for "at risk" groups, namely those who have been
advised by their GP to reduce their blood cholesterol levels by
altering their diet'. The committee also emphasized the other
ways of lowering blood cholesterol – cutting down on biscuits,
cakes, pies, sausages and dairy fats, taking regular exercise and,
if necessary, drugs. For those without high cholesterol, sterol
products are less suitable, it concluded, as they can interfere with
the absorption of key nutrients. The carotenoids, needed to
make vitamin A, and to a lesser extent vitamin E, are affected.
Pregnant or breastfeeding women, and children under five,
should be warned not to eat products with added plant sterols,
it concluded.

'It cannot be said that Unilever developed this product in
response to a particular demand from margarine users, but rather
that margarine proved to be a great carrier for this ingredient
and this innovation revived a dormant category dominated by
Unilever globally,' city analysts JPMorgan point out in their
study of how the food industry is responding to the obesity
crisis. 'It has allowed Unilever to limit the damage of increasing
private label [i.e. supermarket own-brand] penetration at the
lower end of the market.' The Flora pro-activ fat spread sells at
a premium of over 300 per cent on standard products. It is in
other words expensive stuff.

You can see the genius of so called 'functional foods' like
plant sterols from the manufacturers' point of view. They
medicalize food so that a specific brand of product can be sold
as something you should keep taking and stick with, it becomes
something for which it is OK to charge a great deal more
than ordinary food. Unilever recommends that you eat Flora
pro.activ three times a day, and this is indeed what you need to
do to achieve the cholesterol-lowering benefits. The labelling
they use echoes the language of drugs. The leaflet I picked up
with my sample of Flora pro.activ spread followed the format

of the advice leaflets that come with medicines, covering such questions as: 'What happens if I have less than three portions a day? How long should I continue eating Flora pro.activ?' Answer, of course, stick with it for the long term. When I put this to them, Unilever and Benecol disagreed with my view that they were encouraging consumers to think of foods as medicines. Benecol's Director of Regulatory Affairs, Colette Short said, 'Benecol came about as a public health initiative in Finland, where rates of heart disease are very high and it was backed by the Finnish government. We reiterate that it should be part of a healthy diet.' But should they be promoted to those who do not have a diagnosed problem? She was reluctant to be drawn. 'They are for people who have high blood cholesterol.' And what about the general population? 'They are for health maintenance.'

Unilever's Director of External Affairs Anne Heughan was clear that the general population could benefit. 'Raised cholesterol is a very large problem in Britain, affecting about 70 per cent of the population. We talked to lots of experts who thought [adding sterols] was a very good thing. Over forty studies show they work. There is scientific consensus that with 2g you can reduce your blood cholesterol by an average of 10 per cent. Of course people also need to change their diets – pro.activ is about lowering blood cholesterol levels but there are other risk factors. On healthy diets, which are very, very important, generally people can't achieve better than a 5 per cent reduction in blood cholesterol. A 10 per cent reduction will have an effect on long-term health and the majority of experts support the idea. But I don't see this as a drug at all. It's marketed as a food.'

The worry for Dr Mike Rayner, Director of the British Heart Foundation's health promotion research group at Oxford University, is that these products not only appeal to the healthy wealthy – those who generally need them least – but are also a distraction. 'They are not something government should be encouraging. It's true that 67 per cent of the population have cholesterol levels above five, but that's what used to be considered normal in Britain until recently. These products are very expensive and you have to eat a lot of them. I don't think they do harm in themselves but if they make you think you don't have to cut down on saturated fat, which is the most important thing, they are unhelpful.'

Food manufacturers have been squeezed in the past couple of years, both by supermarkets' demands for lower prices on standard lines and by shoppers' growing wariness of processed food. Functional foods, sold at a high premium, represent a way of restoring profit margins while also wrapping brands in a glow of general health. It is no coincidence that the companies among the most active in developing functional foods are those who most want to dissociate themselves from cheap unhealthy products. Coca-Cola has developed sports drinks and waters with added minerals, while PepsiCo has been marketing Tropicana juices with a growing number of added nutrients.

I find it paradoxical to say the least to solve a problem of too much fat in the diet by adding a specialized ingredient to fat. In fact many in the food industry don't see why phytosterols shouldn't be put in other products too. Coca-Cola applied for approval to add them to fruit juices. PepsiCo is using Benecol in its Tropicana fruit juice. Others have looked at adding them to cereal bars, baked goods, meat products, and even sweets. They are already added to some dairy foods such as yoghurt drinks.

You can detect a note of alarm in some of the rulings from the expert advisory committee on such applications. It has turned down several. If everyone starts putting sterols in their processed foods, where will it end? We could end up with large daily doses of them. Who knows what the effect would be. On the other hand, why on earth should margarine and yoghurt have a monopoly on this particular neutraceutical additive?

Production of plant sterols meanwhile has been ramped up.

The companies setting up factories to make them and marketing them are our old friends – Cargill, ADM, Bunge, and the pharmaceutical companies. Cargill is supplying the sterols for Coca-Cola's new orange juice with sterols. Bunge has a new alliance with Procter and Gamble to produce sterols. And ADM makes them too. This is not surprising. It is the oil refiners who strip them out of seed oil, so it is they who have the expertise. Analysts expect the global demand for phytosterols to keep growing.

The range of industries rushing to cash in on these cholesterol-lowering additives exposes the catch in this pharmacological approach to food of course. We are told that sterols and stanols are as effective as, if not more effective than, drugs, but compounds as potent as this are usually administered under the supervision of a doctor in controlled doses, for good reason. Who will monitor the levels of those vitamins that sterols appear to compromise in the consumer who assumes that more might be better, and so buys sterols with everything? Who has checked what the long-term effects of blocking absorption of cholesterol are? What if raised cholesterol in the blood turns out to be what some sceptics suspect, evidence not of high levels of crime, but of the police force rushing to the crime?

When I asked Professor Michael Crawford some time ago whether he ate butter or margarine, his face betrayed a confusion at the irrelevance of the question, as though to even ask were the wrong thing. He hesitated, then replied, 'Both and neither. I have porridge for breakfast; if I want fat with my bread at lunch I dunk it in the olive oil of my salad . . .'

Why do we need all these industrial fats and miracle fat cures? Cooking of infinite variety has evolved over hundreds of years to use the produce of traditional farming, before industrial fats were ever thought of or heart disease much heard of. We managed without them for centuries and were healthier for it. For those whose diets have been so depleted by this industrial production that they have become deficient, we may need therapeutic doses of nutrients. But this cannot be the answer for the whole population. We need to put right what went wrong with our food in the first place. We cannot do that with hi-tech ingredients. We can only do it by looking at the power structures that control food supply and rejecting the great volumes of commodity fats and sugars they offer. Or as Professor Crawford put it: 'You abandon evolutionary nutritional principles at your peril.' Preferring to stick to evolutionary principles, I like to use butter and olive oil, and only cook with other vegetable oils very sparingly. Quite apart from anything else, they taste so much nicer.

8. Soya

Bake a soya bean and — provided you have first soaked and boiled it long enough to neutralize its toxins — you can make a dish that is cheap but cheerful. It may be slightly indigestible still and make you fart, but it is nevertheless useful for providing complete protein in inexpensive vegetable form. As a whole bean, soya has its limits, though. As well as being famous for flatulence, it tastes a little too distinctly, well, beany, unless disguised with liberal doses of tomato, sugar and salt. In China, where soya was native, it was originally grown mainly as a green manure to fix nitrogen in the soil. The Chinese regarded the mature soya bean itself as inferior food best left to the poor.

But crush a soya bean and the possibilities become infinite. A crushed soya bean can be separated into its more lucrative parts. The oil, as we have seen, can be extracted with solvents and degummed. The lecithin can be removed from the resulting sludge to be sold for a thousand and more food processing purposes. Then, deodorized and hydrogenated, the oil can be used in, or in the frying of, any number of fast foods, snacks and convenience meals. The vitamin E, which has the irritating habit of being unstable and interfering with shelf life, can be stripped out and turned to money elsewhere. So too can the sterols.

The oil removed, defatted soya bean meal full of protein can be fed to intensively farmed chicken, cattle and pigs to turn them into highly productive factory units — intensive dairy cows who can deliver ever greater yields of milk, chickens that grow to shop weight in just a few weeks, pigs and cattle that fatten faster than they ever could on grass or other forage. The soya bean's protein fraction can also be turned into defatted soya flour, or soya protein concentrate, or soya protein isolate or woven into textured soya protein, though these applications are small beer compared with the possibilities in animal feed.

Soya meal was used experimentally in animal feed in the US in the 1930s but farmers were reluctant to take it up because raw soya with the oil still in it is indigestible to chickens and pigs. The Danes led much of the development of soya protein for animal feed. When they found their wheat-based economy was being undermined by subsidized US exports of cereals, they decided to concentrate instead on export of animal products, and built up their diary, pork and chicken industries using high-protein soya feed. They turned to soya protein mainly because the growing European margarine business had begun using soya oil and that left the soya protein as a cheap by-product.

In the US meanwhile, thanks to lobbying by the American Soybean Association, import tariffs were introduced to protect the fledgling US industry, which initially was geared to producing oil rather than protein. It was ADM researchers in the mid 1930s who worked out how to heat treat the protein meal to overcome the problems of indigestibility and then started marketing new soya protein-concentrated feeds to the livestock farmers. US production was boosted during the war when other oil supplies were disrupted, so that the US emerged as the world's leading producer and exporter of soya oil and protein at the end of the conflict. US farmers had been encouraged to grow more soya for victory. The oil still had a flavour problem, but that was solved when the Americans, following the tanks advancing through Germany, managed to acquire the technology from the defeated enemy to get rid of the off flavours.

That left the way open for the US to promote the soya that suited its agricultural conditions as part of the reconstruction of Europe through the 1950s. Soya oil exports to Europe tripled under the Marshall Plan, which played such a key role in internationalizing the food system. Heavily subsidized exports of surplus US soya ensured the commodity's dominance in animal feed.

As Europe recovered, soya exports were supported by the other US food aid programmes. From 1955 to 1969 more than half of US soya oil exports came under the food aid act Public Law 480. In 1967, a staggering 86 per cent of all US soya oil exports were subsidized this way. As a result of the Kennedy round of talks for the General Agreement on Tariffs and Trade in the mid 1960s, European countries opened up to more US soya imports as the price for keeping their own protectionist agricultural subsidies. The American soya subsidies continue, with the US-based transnational trading corporations reaping huge rewards. Just as with corn, US primary producers get their taxpayers' subsidies too. Between 1998 and 2004, US soya farming received $13 billion in subsidies from the state.

The first animal factories to take off using the new concentrated soya in scientifically formulated and pelleted feeds were chicken ones. Chicken has a particular attraction for the livestock industry. The birds are referred to by producers not as flocks but 'crops' for the good reason that they grow fast and produce a return in just over a month. The US industry began to develop highly integrated, automated factory poultry units. It was a wonderful way to accumulate capital: it takes about 3kg of protein feed to produce half a kilo of poultry protein. As we have seen, for the commodity traders and processors, the livestock revolution represented the best way to move up the value chain. You can make a fine margin on trading grain and soya, especially if you are a powerful enough presence in the markets. But feed your surplus to animals and you concentrate your resources. You can even deliver meat and dairy products at cheap prices at the same time. Persuade the world to eat vast quantities of this cheap intensively-fed factory meat, consumed preferably in a highly processed way that divides the parts and separates out the 'high value' lean meat – and you make far greater margins.

Soya never looked back. Today over 60 per cent of all processed foods in Britain contain soya in some form, according to the food industry's own estimates. It may appear as soya flour, hydrolyzed vegetable protein, soya protein isolate, protein concentrate, textured vegetable protein, vegetable oil, plant sterols, or emulsifier. You have to work very hard to avoid the commodity and its derivatives. As well as being the fast food of the animals we eat, it is in factory breads and pastries, breakfast cereals and cereal bars, in cake mixes, crisps, biscuits, chocolate and confectionery, processed meats, cheeses, gravies, noodles, soups, sausage casing, sauces, sandwich spreads, ready meals, ice creams, mayonnaise and margarine. Soya ups the protein content of cheap processed meat products. It replaces them altogether in vegetarian foods. It stops industrial breads shrinking. It makes cakes hold on to their water. It helps manufacturers mix water in to oil. It is in my cat food and your dog food. Increasingly it masquerades in novel techno-foods as a health product.

But who is really driving this apparently insatiable demand for soya? It took me a journey of more than 7,000 km to the heart of the rainforest to understand the power structures in this particular food chain and their real impact.

It is only from the air that you can absorb the vastness of the Amazon. What happens to the rainforest that surrounds the world's largest river system will affect every single one of us, as experts in climate change and global warming constantly point out. But Brazil is the new agricultural frontier and land clearance, much of it for soya production, has been taking place on a scale from which the forest may not recover. Just like the palm plantations producing oil in the peat forests of Indonesia, soya in Brazil is exacting an alarming toll on the climate. The environmental group Greenpeace has been using satellite surveillance and aerial mapping to track illegal deforestation in the last few years and it agreed to take me up in its small spotter plane in 2006 just as it was launching its campaign to stop the food industry destroying the Amazon.

As we flew over mile after mile of deep green canopy, I could see how farmers might argue that taking a little more of the rainforest wouldn't hurt. Here and there a field of uniformly green soya would appear under a wing, but then the plane would move on, and the depth of the forest seemed impenetrable beneath us, its expanse limitless. In another era – when sugar plantations were being carved out by white Portuguese 'colonos' and their slaves further south, or when palm plantations were being brought to Malaysia say, cultivating such territory would have been represented as the triumph of man over the jungle, conquering the heart of darkness in the name of industrialization, progress and higher civilization. Progress then equated with ever higher yields to feed the world's growing population. But today not only have we reached our biological limits but we are also hitting the environmental buffers.

A fifth of the planet's fresh water is contained in the Amazon. Three quarters of rainfall here, 7 trillion tonnes of vapour a year, is recycled back into the atmosphere, from where it drives the world's weather. The cycle begins with the trade winds blowing off the deserts of Africa, the hot winds I had felt on the beaches of Senegal. They blow out over those warm tropical waters that once teemed with fish. Picking up moisture and absorbing vast amounts of the sun's energy, they cross the Atlantic to South America, where the jutting northern shoulder of that continent matches the jagged hollow torn out of the coast of West Africa. When the winds reach the Amazon the vapour falls as rain in great sheets. The trees of the rainforest suck up the water and give it back to the atmosphere through their leaves of infinite variety. Convection carries the mass of this moist air from the rainforest up and on to the Andes, the spine of mountains running down South America, which in turn push it higher and out of the influence of the spinning earth, from where it flows back to Africa, by now cold and dense, ready to sink back over that continent and start the trade winds again. Cut down the forests of the Amazon, and you snap a hole in the conveyor belt around the earth's middle, the system that carries rain to the most productive areas of Brazil further south, and to the grain farmers of the American Mid-West, while also influencing the ocean currents that keep Britain's warming Gulf Stream flowing.

Yet the rainforest is being cleared at an unprecedented rate. Between 2000 and 2005 an area four times the size of Belgium was destroyed in Brazil, three quarters of it cleared in illegal logging or burning, turning Brazil into the world's fourth largest climate polluter. If current trends in agriculture and livestock production go unchecked, more than half of the Amazon will be lost by 2030. The tipping point might be closer than anyone imagined.

Below us from the window of the Greenpeace plane I could see on one side the velvet folds of virgin forest, with hundreds of species of tree, some 500 years, some even 1,000 years old, thick-woven with palm, creeper and bush, all breathing out moisture.

About a fifth of the world's bird and plant species, and 10 per cent of the world's mammals, find their home in this treasure trove of biodiversity, explained Marcelo Marquesini, Greenpeace's satellite forest mapper. Where man had not ventured with chainsaw and bulldozer, the trees were transpiring, giving off the water vapour that controls the world's climate system, like a thousand puffs from a life-giving inhaler.

Then he pointed out of the opposite window: we were now flying over an enormous area recently planted with soya. A strangely luminous green carpet had appeared where the trees had been razed. It looked as though a giant industrial lawnmower had cut a swathe through the jungle, and the land below shone through a dry heat haze. This wasn't taking just a little more forest, it was plundering it.

Here, miles from any watching eyes on the ground, the trees had been cleared and great tracts of the deep red-brown earth were still being ploughed. 'So who is buying all that illegally

259

planted soya, and how on earth do they get it out?' I shouted over the roar of the engine.

The answer had to wait. A storm was blowing in and we quickly turned back through the flashes of lightning for Santarém, the frontier port built deep in the Amazon basin. Its features emerged briefly from thick black cloud, as the sun set over the river, and the sky lit to an ominous sulphurous yellow, then warmed to burnt orange, and finally darkened to a fiery red. Its shifting shades were thrown back by the floodplain, which had this year spread further than ever before, another record broken, as with so many climate statistics now.

I watched that night from the roof of my hotel in Santarém as a new storm blew great squalls hundreds of miles up the Amazon from the Atlantic. On the waterfront below, the baroque blue cathedral, built by the original colonizers, the Portuguese, came and went from view in the enveloping rain. Its twin towers and pediment still present a proud façade to anyone coming up the river's main navigation channel, but the paint was peeling and fading now. The centre of gravity had shifted. A few hundred yards up the great brown river, Cargill has built its own monument to power, an enormous soya loading and storage facility. The elevator towers of this $20 million grain terminal are testaments to the new gods of transnational trading efficiency and global economic domination. The digging of the port here has brought Brazil's soya, not just from the Amazon region but from the biggest growing states further south, closer to its main European export markets.

Just as the new railroads had been a vital part of opening up the prairies of North America, it was this newly constructed infrastructure that was driving the deforestation.

Here in Brazil you can see the other end of the livestock revolution, and all the connections in our agrochemical-based, fossil fuel-hungry food system.

Those aseptic supermarket packages of so-called prime meat, those fried chicken takeaways, those plastic-packaged soya health products, start their journey here. And in the Amazon you can see on the ground the dreadful environmental and social costs of today's food system. This is a system that has created the conditions for the return of slavery in its worst forms in Latin America where forced labour, punishment beatings and debt bondage have re-emerged in forest clearance and on soya plantations, and in Europe where appalling labour abuses are the norm for migrants working in processing the final goods. It is a system that drives climate change, threatening the planet's future, while undermining social structures and our own individual health.

The soya trading nexus is as powerful as anything seen during the days when mass consumption of sugar first emerged. It is an oligopoly whose members are the same corporations that dominate trade in corn, wheat, sugars and ethanol. Cargill, ADM and Bunge control nearly three quarters of the global market in soya. Bunge is the largest processor of bottled vegetable oils and holds a quarter of all US oilseed processing capacity. Almost half of ADM's global sales come from its oilseed products, including animals feeds, vegetable oils and emulsifiers. Cargill is the world's largest crusher of oilseed. The three companies together are estimated to control 80 per cent of the European soya bean crushing industry. Dreyfus has huge processing interests in South America. Cargill, ADM and Bunge, together with allied companies, also control about three quarters of European animal feed manufacturing. They account for 60 per cent of Brazil's soya exports.

Cargill, the builder of the Amazon terminal, is in most years the largest private company in the US, and in the world. With revenues of $88 billion in 2007, it is twice the size of its nearest competitor, ADM.

Established in 1865, Cargill has its headquarters in a mock French château outside Minneapolis in the US Mid-West. Still owned by members of its founding Cargill and MacMillan families, it is famous for being immensely secretive. It told me it did not comment on its market shares. Brewster Kneen, its unauthorized biographer and author of *Invisible Giant*, has spent decades trying to track its activities, no small feat since as a private company it does not have to publish detailed accounts. 'It is the undisputed ruler in the global grain trade and extends its tentacles into every aspect of the global food system,' he says. Or, in the words of Cargill company brochures: 'We buy, trade, transport, blend, mill, crush, process, refine, season, distribute around the clock, around the globe' and 'We are the flour in your bread, the wheat in your noodles, the salt on your fries. We are the corn in your tortillas, the chocolate in your dessert, the sweetener in your soft drink. We are the oil in your salad dressing and the beef, pork or chicken you eat for dinner. We are the cotton in your clothing, the backing on your carpet, and the fertilizer in your field.' And, as I had found on my own journeys around the food system, Cargill is also: the feed in your milk, the emulsifier and fat in your ready meal, the sterols in your margarine, the soya proteins in your veggieburger, the inulin in your prebiotic drink, the frying medium in your fried snack ... It doesn't stop there. Its financial activities, though opaque, are where much of its power resides. It is banker, and hedger, and derivatives trader too.

There has perhaps been nothing quite like it in terms of reach since the days of the first transnational corporation, the private commercial force behind the British Empire in India until eventually taken over by the Crown, the East India Company.

Cargill initially built up its power in the speculative days of that earlier agricultural frontier, the American Mid-West, when US grain along with sugar began providing the fuel for workers in an industrializing, urbanizing Britain. It began with a family of grain traders who bought up grain storage facilities in the US on strategically placed transport routes – the new railroads and the waterways of the Great Lakes and Mississippi.

Having the ability to store grain and release it to market when the price is right or withhold it when it is too low is the essence of successful commodity trading, as British eighteenth- and nineteenth-century sugar traders with their bonded warehouses on the new West India docks on the Thames well knew.

Until the early 1980s the soya trade was a North American business, with the US accounting for more than 90 per cent of global exports. But rapid expansion in Latin America has been led by companies such as Cargill and ADM. In 2003 the combined soya exports from Argentina and Brazil passed US exports for first time. The rapid growth in Latin America has driven down world prices, making it less economically viable for US farmers, even with their enormous subsidies, to grow soya. Cargill's grain terminal and presence on the new key transport route to market, the Amazon, was a crucial force in expanding production and in driving deforestation, according to Greenpeace.

Cargill and the two other giants of transnational commodity trading, ADM and Bunge, are responsible for about two thirds of the total financing of soya production in Brazil. They provide seed, fertilizer and agrochemicals to the ranchers. Monocultured soya crops have to be sprayed against pests between five and eight times a cycle. They are greedy for fertilizer too, for the fertility of the Amazon is in its biomass – the rich humus formed from its falling leaves – not its soil and once the forest has been cleared, the land is quickly exhausted. Many of the farmers further south had found that year that they could no longer cover their costs of production – with the price of crude oil rising inexorably, their input costs were going up too – and they had been blockading the roads the month before my trip. Because land could be grabbed for next to nothing or even for free in the Amazon, it was cheaper to produce here, and so speculators had been sucked in.

If you can use slaves to clear the land for soya, it is of course even cheaper. Greenpeace had gathered documentary evidence to show that the transnational companies Cargill, Bunge and the main Brazilian producer Gruppo Maggi had bought soya from large farms where slaves had been found by government inspection teams. A Dominican priest Xavier Plassat has been one of the leading campaigners against slavery in the region. He has lived under the threat of death by gunmen since he denounced slavery on a large farm in 2002, but he still sees it as his vocation to accompany the government's swat squads that go into the forest to free slaves when they hear reports of them, usually from another slave who has managed to escape. I spoke to him from Santarém down a crackly phone line to the remote town where he lives. 'Slavery and latifundia, these large-scale intensive farm operations, go together. But something new is happening,' he told me. 'Most of the cases of slavery were until recently tied up with forest clearing for cattle ranching, but now soya is taking over. Three weeks ago I was on a farm 350km from my town, it was off the road and we had to travel 60km on the farm itself to reach the people. We found over 200 workers in slavery, they were being forced to work without pay, and deprived of the freedom of movement. They were controlled by debt bondage and their documents had been taken from them by middle men. There was no clean water, they had little food. There were thirty living in one room, miles from any trace of civilization. We only found these workers because one of them had managed to escape, but what of all the other cases? Monoculture for export has created the conditions for this slavery: it is eliminating the traditional family farming that provides food for 60 per cent of Brazilians. The highest incidence of violence against the rural population and of slavery is where agribusiness is strongest.' The trading companies all condemn slavery and say they are committed to eradicating abusive labour practices in the supply chain. Cargill, for example, says: 'Cargill does not accept the use of illegal, abusive or enforced labour in any of our operations and abides by the laws in the countries in which we operate. Our contracts stipulate that we have the right to refuse deliveries of soya or refuse payment if we suspect slave or child labour was used in its production. We have signed the Brazilian National Pact for the Eradication of Slave Labour and through the soya moratorium are also supporting the Brazilian government's campaign to eradicate abusive labour practices.' But it is no coincidence that slavery has re-emerged with this new soya complex, nor is it simply the work of a few unscrupulous subcontracted rogues. From Roman days expansionist intensive agriculture has been built on such cheap labour. Slaves and exploited migrants, often dispossessed or driven into migration by the squeeze on family agriculture, are what make the economics of agribusiness work.

Cargill has a virtual monopoly on soya buying around Santarém. The other transnationals have built facilities further upriver. Cargill, ADM and Bunge have joined a consortium to provide finance to finish building a paved road, the BR 163, through the Amazon ecosystem that would connect vast acres of land to their export markets. The road infrastructure stimulates deforestation – it draws ranchers to it who speculatively grab land that may be publicly owned and clear it. Greenpeace's tracking has shown that more than three quarters of all deforestation occurs within 50km either side of roads.

Cargill's reach stretches still further than trading, shipping and processing the soya beans. It is a leading player in what it calls the 'global chicken value chain' too. Its soya goes to make animal feed in its factories in Europe that then feed crops of birds for fast food restaurants such as McDonald's, and for ready meals and cheap supermarket fresh cuts of chicken. Cargill's UK subsidiary Sun Valley processes about a million birds a week, fattening them on soya imported from Santarém. Sun Valley's biggest customer is McDonald's – it produces about half of all the chicken products such as McNuggets used by McDonald's across Europe. It also supplies chicken to leading supermarkets. Yet Cargill has no consumer face. Few people in Britain have even heard of it. Greenpeace was about to change all that.

Next morning I awoke to see the green outline of the campaign group's *Arctic Sunrise* ship framed briefly between the towers of the cathedral on the Amazon, before it chugged on up to the Cargill terminal, where it threw down anchor, and its battle line.

Cargill had built the Amazon River port for its soya exports without the full environmental assessments required by Brazilian federal law, according to a local prosecutor who had taken the company to court. Cargill insisted it had complied with all the legal and environmental requirements of the local state. A series of legal battles had been fought since; two courts had ruled against Cargill but a third had overturned the decision on appeal. Then Brazil's second highest court had decided that Cargill must carry out an environmental impact assessment not just for the port terminal but for the impact on the surrounding Amazon region. The battle was still going on while I was there. Cargill issued a statement that it was committed to sustainable development that provided income for local communities while managing the environment over time. It had also made a substantial donation to a forest conservation group to support work on protecting the Amazon and the rainforests of Indonesia.

Santarém was tense with anticipation that morning. The frontier town itself is a small grid of straight streets, where traffic lights strung from loose electric cables creak and sway in the wind, and everything points down to the main drag of the river. It was eerily quiet outside but for a few barefooted shoe shine boys and farmers in pick-up trucks cruising around with banners and stickers demanding Greenpeace get out of town.

Violence frequently erupts over land disputes here. The original white 'colonos' or colonists of the Portuguese empire raised their own armies to police their territories as they carved out the interior further south – giving us the word colonel – and today the same holds true. The writ of the state barely runs into some of the remotest areas of the rainforest. Many of the biggest landowners have their own armed security guards. Those campaigning against deforestation like those fighting slavery have to live with death threats, many of them carried out. At least thirty-seven people had been killed in land disputes the year before my visit.

The local newspapers were full of reports of a protest that had taken place a couple of days previously. Small farmers and their communities had marched on the Cargill terminal, demanding its closure. Thousands of these farmers have been displaced by soya growers. Some have been forcibly removed from their land by ranchers. Others have sold up to land speculators, thinking the money was good, only to find themselves falling into destitution, without a way of earning a living in the city and without land to grow food. Since the arrival of big soya in the area, church charities and the landless movement find themselves dealing with a rapid and intense increase in deep poverty. The outskirts of Santarém are now home to a small cardboard settlement of those who have lost their land and search the rubbish tips for food.

The big soya farmers, most of them white descendants of European immigrants of previous generations and newcomers to the region, had come out in response to the demonstrations. They had moved in to the Amazon like ranching pioneers in the style of the Wild West from Brazil's agricultural belt further south. There had been violence.

As the cloudy morning cleared to a bright blue sky, I set off to see Father Edilberto Sena, priest and director of Santarém's Catholic Radio Rural, and a leading opponent of Cargill's port. I found him composing his 'Jesus blogspot', swearing away at his primitive computer in the radio station's offices opposite the town cemetery. 'Sonofabitch machine. It's telling me I can't whistle and sing at the same time,' he cursed, welcoming me in past a larger than life plastic statue of Our Lady.

Sena, a charismatic Franciscan friar in his sixties who favours green polo shirts and traditional beads made from forest seeds

over monk's habit or dog collar, has used the airwaves to broadcast regular information about the environment, land rights and
soya's impact on the Amazon to the local population, in among
news and sports programmes and practical advice to women and
children. He is the second recipient of the Brazilian lawyers'
human rights award. Such an award was a mixed blessing, he
reminded me with a grin and a sigh. The first recipient, the
American nun and rainforest campaigner Dorothy Stang, was
shot dead in the rainforest in 2005 by gunmen allied to illegal
ranchers. Sena has received death threats too.

Sena had been a liberation theologist, part of the Latin American church movement of the 1960s and 1970s that believed that
to do God's work on earth entailed fighting poverty and social
injustice. When the movement fell foul of the war being waged
by Ronald Reagan and the then pope John Paul II against
communism in the 1980s, he had been sent to the Amazon
wilderness as parish priest to an abandoned church. There for
seven years he served a community of 20,000 people that you
could only reach by an eight-hour boat journey upriver.

He returned to Santarém in 2001 and the bishop entrusted
him with a new transmitter and the radio station. He found
Cargill building its port. He knew what impact this new infrastructure would have on the sort of communities he had served
and their environment, and so he worked out with the local
prosecutor how to challenge the terminal, using the courts
as well as his broadcasts. 'They were installing that monster
over there, so we started fighting Cargill and soya. Cargill saw
that it would be cheaper to ship their soya from here than
from the south, so they moved the frontier to the Amazon.
But they didn't do the proper environmental impact assessment. They miscalculated because we are a poor Third World
country. They thought they would get away with it. Look how
big the ships are – it takes three days to load them even with
the most advanced computer equipment and machines. If the
big companies go ahead with their plan to pave the road

through the Amazon, 300 trucks a day will start delivering soya to that monster, but all they will bring for the ordinary people here are drugs and prostitution not development.'

Sena, who studied at university in the US, was fluent in the protest language of the civil rights movement of his opponents' home country. 'I am "caboclo". Do you know what that means? I am a descendant of Negro slaves and Brazilian Indians and Europeans. We, as Amazon natives, as "caboclos", feel so indignant. This is the new colonization. It's the same as the seventeenth century, but now they call it globalization. They suck the life and wealth out of the land here, and leave nothing for us. The soya people come from outside, they don't know our ecosystem. They despise us. And when they have destroyed everything, and cut down the Brazil nut trees that have fed people here for hundreds of years, and soya is finished, they will go away. In the time of the Portuguese, they brought pots and beads to buy us, now Cargill builds a little library for the town and thinks it can take what it wants.'

I said I could see why Reagan had taken fright and branded liberation theology a Marxist threat in America's backyard. 'I've never read Marx. I read the gospel, "Blessed are the poor for they shall inherit the earth . . . I was hungry and you gave me meat, I was thirsty and you gave me drink . . ." You know, the bishop of Recife once wondered why when he fed the poor he was called a saint, but when he asked why they were poor he was called a communist.

'I do think Fidel Castro has a special place waiting for him in heaven though,' he laughed. 'But see, you British, you will suffer in the afterlife, you will be hot in hell. Your crime wasn't just building North America, but inventing mad cow disease. US agribusiness and demand for animal feed that's not made from old blood and bones, that's what's driving demand for soya. That and the Chinese, of course, but I'll let you off responsibility for China . . .'

Relieved at this slight diminution of my burden of historic

guilt, I asked what he thought of the arguments that the West, having cut down its own forests to develop during its agrarian and industrial revolutions, had no right to criticize Brazil and China for wanting to develop this way too, and that transnational companies were playing an important role by providing the means for economic progress.

For although most of the soya being shipped from Santarém was going directly to Liverpool or Amsterdam for European markets, China's soya imports from Brazil increased over 10,000 per cent in the decade to 2005. Cargill and ADM have been expanding rapidly in China. China meanwhile has been creating financial structures in Brazil to help it trade direct. As its population urbanizes, and it loses its own arable land to cities, factories and transport infrastructure, China too has been importing soya to provide protein for intensively reared animals. Its growing factory workforce is increasingly adopting the dietary patterns of the West, eating further up the food chain and consuming more processed foods. So Brazil, with its vast tracts of land, is becoming to global agriculture what China is to manufacturing, mirroring the supply relationship between nineteenth-century America and Britain in its industrial heyday. Did we have the right to say they shouldn't consume in the way that we do?

'Well, see for yourself,' Sena continued. 'Go to Belterra, my birthplace, it's near here. It used to be paradise, virgin forest. First the gringos came to plant rubber, but when the rubber didn't make them money anymore, they left; just as the forest was recuperating, the soya people arrived. Now it's mile upon mile of soya desert, it's mostly illegal, look . . .' He leant over to show me a sheaf of land documents he had somehow obtained, demonstrating that the planting around his home land was illegal. 'I stole them. I go to confession once a year, but it's like Robin Hood, if you steal to give to the poor, it's not a sin. Look at this paper, this ranch is illegal. So is this one. This is not development. This kind of development only makes a few people rich, here or in China. Go and look at Belterra, and you will see how I bleed.'

So I took a journey into the forest the next day, accompanied in a jeep by two aid workers from a local NGO, Saude & Alegria. I was hoping, though not expecting, to talk to some of the big soya farmers on their ranches and to go into the heart of the rainforest.

We drove first to Belterra town, a strange relic of the early 1930s and Henry Ford's expansionist dreams.

Wanting to control the raw materials for his car manufacturing, Ford had bought a great tract of the Amazon and established a settlement of rubber plantations called Fordlandia. His monocrop rubber had been plagued by pests and disease, however, and he found the native workers were tediously mutinous, so had uprooted and tried again further down river, at Belterra.

From 1934 Belterra plantations had been run by Ford managers who built themselves neat wooden houses with trim shutters and porches, opening on to cool verandahs and lawned gardens, like an incongruous New England resort. They are still there today in the middle of the jungle; but now the Old Rubber Tapper Palace with its mahogany-panelled walls is the town's administrative building, for when the bottom fell out of the natural rubber market, the Ford company abandoned its settlement and sold it to the local council for one dollar. This is the cycle of boom and bust that foreigners had brought, the kind of development that sucks money out but doesn't leave it behind that Father Edilberto was so forcefully rejecting.

The mayor of Belterra did not think many of the new soya planters would speak to me, with the tension running so high in Santarém. We tried calling round to their ranches but none wanted to be at home, so we drove past their fields of beans and on into the forest reserve, entering where the sign by the road declared we were coming in to a settlement called 'Revolt'. By the time you have travelled to the other side of the reserve, under the great canopy of ancient trees with their searching aerial roots, it has acquired a different name, being called simply 'Paradise'.

The forest here in the reserve is community owned. Long-eared white cattle were grazing in clearings next to patches of rice, corn, beans and manioc, circled by vines of water melon. Wild forest pigs, deer, other small mammals I had never heard of, and fish provide all the protein people need – there are still over 2,000 species of fish in the Amazon River. The trees themselves provide fruits, nuts and seeds, some of them without names in English. Yellow butterflies as large as my hand flitted past, humming birds – known as flower kissers by the locals – hovered over exotic blooms. In the centre of the settlement, around a palm-covered circular meetinghouse, we found the heart of the village – a rough dirt football pitch, a school, a church, and a water tower topped by solar panels to power the community computer and TV. They all vote to decide what they will watch together during the hour or two a day for which they have stored enough electricity. Strong social norms bind them together across the generations; I found this power-ful sense of social harmony wherever I visited communities in the forest and on the shores of the Amazon that trip. The Brazilian aid worker with me had been struck by it too in his far longer experience. He and the Amazonian people knew it was precious. I longed to take some of the simplicity of this existence and its social cohesion back to my overstimulated screen-crazed world.

We met Pedro Gama Pantoja, one of the community leaders, who lives on the river's edge. The communities all around the reserve had been selling up to soya, he said and now that they had no means of living on their own land they wanted to come into this area, even though the resources would not support so many more people. Pedro was worried that the soya industry would encroach even on his protected forest area; the land just outside is polluted with chemicals, and no longer fertile; highly mechanized agribusiness offers no seasonal employment to supplement their living; the pesticides are killing the birds. 'We detest these soya farmers. People imagine the Amazon will always be here whatever you do, but it's not true. We hold it in the palm of our hands.'

Pedro had been asked to go to a conference in the city to talk about what was happening in the forest, he said, but he couldn't get home fast enough. He found himself pining. 'I missed the calm too much. There was so much rushing and consuming. I have as much as I need here. I don't understand why people always want more.'

It was time to leave 'Paradise' and return to the frontier town. I wondered as we left what the communal TV and internet access with all the aspirational marketing it would bring would do for Pedro's neighbours and their desires. But the jeep radio diverted my thoughts. An increasingly hysterical commentator was describing the scene back in Santarém. The streets had been sealed off. Over 1,000 angry soya farmers and their supporters were roaming the town in pick up trucks, mounting a demonstration in support of Cargill and against Greenpeace. They were shooting off giant firecrackers, intimidating anyone foolish enough to be showing a Save the Rainforest car sticker or T-shirt.

That morning as a barge arrived in port to offload its tonnage of soya into Cargill's elevators, Greenpeace sent its ship's launch alongside and delivered its own cargo – a highly trained climbing team, who mounted the towers, strung up protest banners and blocked the unloading. Cargill's guards turned high-pressure hoses on to them, but a group of soya farmers took more determined action and launched a tug boat at the *Arctic Sunrise*. The soya farmers loosed a round of giant firecrackers at the parent ship, burning a photographer and forcing the captain to lock down. A distraught Cargill manager tried to urge calm. Police arrived, smashing their way on board the *Arctic Sunrise* with teargas and pepper spray and took over command. The climbers and the ship's captain were arrested. The Greenpeace activists were released later that day, but not before the lead Amazon campaigner had received new death threats.

Small farmers, the landless, and rainforest campaigners were planning yet another march on the Cargill terminal two days later; Father Edilberto would be among those leading it. I went back to find Santarém's turbulent priest. No wonder Cargill wanted to be rid of him. He said the company had written complaining about him to the bishop the month before. A delegation of business interests had asked for him to be removed; this was how agribusiness expected to pull the levers of power.

Walking through the hot night, I took the road down to the cathedral on the waterfront, where elderly matrons in black were finishing performing their quiet evening pieties. Suddenly an amplified samba version of 'Ave Maria' burst forth from the church doors. It seemed gloriously Latin, irrepressibly defiant. In the rooms over the cathedral, they had hired extra security. Sena was finishing his round of meetings for the day, planting a huge loud kiss on the bare shoulder of a devout campaign helper, asking after another parishioner's love life on the way out. 'Thank God that as a Catholic priest I have to be celibate. I could never be monogamous,' he joked. Then suddenly he was serious; he wanted to show me another document: 'We are in the middle of a battle of two ideologies: the transnational neo-liberal model of progress and the social model of development. Cargill tried to have me removed. They say I am against progress. I am against only their kind of progress. I told the bishops the church would have to take a position. It has been good at making its accommodation with power in the past. But now the bishops have written to President Lula. They have come out and said that agribusiness is making the poor poorer. Here, here's their pronouncement . . .' He handed it to me, and I read its title: 'The poor shall inherit the Earth . . .' It was signed by some 300 Brazilian bishops.

274

Before I left the Amazon, I had wanted to hear the soya farmers' point of view, however reluctant the individual soya growers might be to meet me. So although warned that I might receive a violent reception, I caught a taxi to the office of the farmers' union in Santarém, down near the Cargill terminal. I was met with perfect courtesy by the director, Adinor Batista dos Santos, who broke off from his engagements to explain their side of the soya story to me. Three other producers arrived, two young men and a middle-aged redneck, to talk. They said they had moved into the area recently from the south to plant soya and they saw themselves as hard-working pioneers, struggling to make a living, which a foreign organization, Greenpeace, acting aggressively and illegally, wanted to destroy. 'This seems to be the only place in the world where it is wrong to produce food. Many people here are re-using areas that were cleared before by others. How would you feel if Greenpeace invaded a bit of England – they have invaded private property here. If we did this in your country we would be deported.'

The director of the farmers' union had been born near Santarém and had witnessed previous cycles of boom and bust. 'Soya is very important. The whole world wants it. It brings employment; it makes money for our region. Some people think the Amazon belongs to the world, but what do you English think should happen to the 23 million people in this region. How should they live?' he challenged.

It is a fair question. And one Cargill raised in the statements it put out about its involvement in the Amazon area. 'It's important to remember that the Amazon is home to more than 23 million people. It is one of the poorest regions in Brazil and the world, and there is a recognized need for responsible economic and social development. Economic development is the long-term solution to protecting both the Amazon's peoples and the environment; poverty does not do that. The Brazilian government has wisely chosen not to prohibit soya production in the forested areas of the Amazon. Instead Brazil's Forest

Code seeks to combine strong environmental protection with limited but economically important agricultural production. In the Santarém region Cargill is working with the Nature Conservancy, the farmers' union and the farmers who sell soya to our export facility to identify and implement best management practices for environmental stewardship,' it said.

But the farmers' union idea of development assumes that companies operating in poorer regions of the world leave most of the money they make in the countries where they operate. While I was in the Amazon area, an anonymous campaigner had handed me some of Cargill's soya shipping documents. They opened a window on a phenomenon that has mushroomed with globalization. It is a phenomenon that I fear makes a mockery of the hope of farmers such as those I had met at the union by the port, that they will share equally in the prosperity that their country's agricultural resources could bring or that the poor will be raised out of poverty by soya and that therefore any environmental and social costs can be weighed against a greater long-term benefit.

What the documents showed was the records of shipments of soya from the Cargill terminal in the month before my visit. When the merchant vessel *Daphne,* for instance, set sail in April 2006 from Santarém it ploughed across the mud-laden expanse of the river heading for the deep navigation channel that weaves down to the Atlantic sea, and set course for Liverpool. Its cargo was 52,000 tonnes of Brazilian soya beans loaded from the Cargill terminal. The exporter of the soya was listed as 'Cargill Agricola Brazil'. Once the *Daphne* reached the Mersey, its load would be crushed by a Cargill subsidiary in the UK. It would be turned into the high-protein meal for factory animals reared by yet another Cargill subsidiary Sun Valley, for McDonald's and for British supermarkets Sainsbury's, Morrison and Asda, and by another poultry processor Grampian for Tesco. But first the cargo, worth $11.2 million, would make a notional journey to the offshore tax haven of the Turks and Caicos. Just like shipments before it, each worth over $11 million, it would be first imported on paper not where it actually landed but by a PO Box in the Temple Financial Centre that is the address of 'Cargill Agricola' on the tiny island of Providenciales.

The elaborate financial engineering that allows transnational companies to shift their buying and selling between subsidiaries and affiliates so that profits are relocated to havens beyond the reach of taxing government in Latin America say or in Europe, has gone hand in hand with globalization. I came across the phenomenon, dubbed the flight of capital, when looking at how the international banana trade worked.

About 60 per cent of world trade now consists of internal transfers within transnational companies, according to the OECD. Although tax havens have existed for decades, this flight of capital took off with the removal of exchange controls and the development of information technology first with the fax machine in the 1970s, and then at greatly increased speed with the internet in the late 1990s. Large corporations have been able to shift profits around between complex networks of subsidiaries and branches in different countries, choosing where to incur costs, where to allocate overheads or locate assets, where to borrow money, where to categorize transactions for duties, tariffs or quotas, where to direct money flows and where to make taxable profit. They tend to weight their costs towards countries with high rates of tax thereby reducing their taxable profits in those, and weight their profits instead towards jurisdictions with minimal or no tax.

John Christensen, a former economic adviser to the Jersey government and director of the campaign group Tax Justice Network, explained how it worked in principle. When transnational corporations trade internationally with their own subsidiaries they use a mechanism called transfer pricing. Sales between parts of the same company are meant to take place at the open market price, at an arm's length price. A whole accountancy industry has grown up around determining them and justifying them to the tax authorities. In practice, however, it can be very difficult to determine an open market price, especially when trade in a particular sector is highly concentrated in a few companies.

Transnationals have also developed ways of bundling up parts of their business such as shipping or financial expertise, insurance, intellectual property, and marketing, and owning them offshore. In this way an agricultural product may be sold by one subsidiary of a group in the country where it was grown to another group subsidiary offshore at little more than the cost of production in the originating country. The company makes little taxable profit in that first country. The product can then on paper follow a circuitous trail through the world's tax havens, with further subsidiaries charging royalties at each point for the use of brands, distribution networks, insurance, finance and marketing services. The profits from these royalties accrue to the subsidiaries based offshore in low tax areas. By the time the product reaches the final destination country, on paper its cost may be close to what the onshore subsidiary is able to sell it for, so it can make little money there either.

The result of this flight of capital has been that corporation tax worldwide is falling as a percentage of profits, and the burden of tax has been shifted away from companies in the last thirty years and on to the consumer and to workers. Governments in poorer producing countries are deprived of the revenue they need for development and governments in richer countries find their tax base for services eroded. In a double blow to the workers at the bottom of the scale who produce agricultural commodities and labour in the factories that process them, the fall in tax as a percentage of profits paid by large corporations has coincided with a determined driving down of wages.

All this is legal. Many companies argue that they have a duty to their shareholders to manage their tax as efficiently as possible like this. In fact, since this has become standard practice for transnationals, the trading company that was not doing it would be aberrant, was the view of John Christensen.

Cargill was an early pioneer in this form of financial engineering. More than three decades ago, the bible on the grain trade, Dan Morgan's *Merchants of Grain*, recorded how the US Internal Revenue Service tracked some of its highly complex trades through subsidiaries in which grain moving from America to Holland passed on paper through a completely different route that took in the tax haven of Panama where some of its profits were booked and the low tax jurisdiction of Switzerland where Cargill's trading subsidiary Tradax was based. The information came out in a senate committee hearing on Multinational Corporations and US Foreign Policy in 1976.

Since Cargill is a private company and not obliged to file detailed accounts, tracking its current activity is almost impossible. I asked it why its soya shipments were routed on paper through a subsidiary in the Turks and Caicos where the rate of corporation tax is zero and where else they passed through before reaching Britain. It told me that the branch in the Turks and Caicos played an operational role for its Brazilian businesses and provided 'flexibility and agility' to support its customers' requirements.' When I asked what this meant, it said it gave 'operational benefit that maximises internal efficiencies'. It added that the operations in the Turks and Caicos provided no fiscal or tax-related benefits as no transfer pricing or charging for services was taking place through the Turks and Caicos branch and the transactions ended up on the balance sheet of Cargill Brazil, where all taxes were paid by the company in accordance with Brazilian law.

So I do not know what exactly Cargill's business in the tax haven of the Turks and Caicos is, and it has no obligation to tell me.

Whatever the nature of Cargill's offshore operations, it seemed unlikely to me that many of the type of farmers I met on the new agricultural frontier in Brazil would get rich out of this system, which gives such advantage to those operating transnationally.

The Greenpeace campaign in 2006 did however achieve a remarkable outcome. McDonald's, fearful of a public relations disaster that would reopen its old wounds over the McLibel case in which two environmental activists had put out leaflets saying the company was guilty of animal cruelty and rainforest destruction in the making of its burgers, had reacted swiftly. They said they wanted nothing to do with any production that involved rainforest destruction or slavery. They put intense pressure on Cargill, as did the supermarkets. Those transnationals with a public face could no longer afford not to take notice of their customers' objections to the environmental and social impact of their activities. Asda–Walmart, Lidl, Marks & Spencer, McDonald's, Morrisons, Sainsbury's, Tesco, Waitrose and Alpro, makers of soya milk, all made their concerns known to their suppliers. The big soya traders, Cargill, ADM, and Bunge, when faced with the threat of business being lost from such key customers and on such a scale, quickly agreed to negotiate a moratorium on buying soya from illegally deforested areas. A year later Amazon deforestation was the lowest in twenty years. The moratorium, along with a downturn in the global economy, seemed to be having an effect.

It was not to last. As thousands of US soya farmers switched into growing corn for ethanol production, much of it to be processed with subsidies from the US government by the same transitional corporations, the price of soya rose significantly. Stimulated by the prospect of greater returns, deforestation in the Amazon once again increased sharply, despite the corporations' continuing commitment to the moratorium and to supporting responsible soya production. The deeper rooted problems of the economic order remained unchanged.

At the time of writing the legal case over the Cargill port in Santarém was still dragging on. Cargill had finally been forced to close it in March 2007 by the Brazilian environment agency.

But it had appealed once more and a month later was given permission to open it again and keep it running while it conducted a full environmental impact assessment. Then in January 2008, the Brazilian National Institute for Space Research, which monitors rainforest loss from satellite images, sounded a new alarm. Deforestation in the Amazon was once again taking place, this time at a rate it had never seen before.

In the stockbroker belt of Surrey where Cargill has its European headquarters at Cobham, they are far removed from the frontline battles of Brazil's agricultural frontier. This is where Cargill's 300 or so staff organize the shipping of Brazilian soya to Europe and where the company pursues its latest strategy, of becoming the 'premier provider of solutions to our food and agricultural customers', that is to the leading food manufacturers and retailers.

Nevertheless the Cargill executives were finding it a little harder than usual to get to work the week the fight over its Amazon port was coming to a head. Greenpeace activists had dumped nearly four tonnes of soya beans at the entrance to their secluded offices. Over in France activists had closed down a Cargill-owned Sun Valley factory where chickens are produced each week for Tesco, KFC and other household names.

The contrast of sedate Surrey and a large volume of dumped crude bean drew out the curious disconnect at the European end of the soya market. Instead of seeing soya for what it mostly is, a raw agricultural commodity controlled by a handful of powerful trading corporations, that is the essential prop of a livestock industry geared up to extract maximum production from animals before slaughter, and a key ingredient in the fried and oiled junk food market, consumers have bought into soya as the latest miracle health food. Soya protein, sold as soya milk or as a special ingredient in juices or cereals, has become the latest fashion, with the health conscious lapping up skinny soy lattes in their coffee shops.

The leading suppliers of these soya proteins are of course the major transnational trading corporations. ADM and Cargill promote soya protein isolates and soya isoflavones as new functional foods for the food industry. Bunge supplies soya protein concentrates and isolates through a joint venture with agrochemical company DuPont.

The attraction in these hi-tech developments is that soya sold this way, although a small sector compared to animal feed and oil trading, becomes an even higher-value product.

The rise of the specialized soya protein is of course no happenstance. The American soya industry spends about $80 million every year, raised from a mandatory levy on producers, to research and promote the consumption of soya around the world. It began an intensive marketing effort for soya in the late 1970s and 1980s. A raft of industry sponsored scientific studies began to emerge.

These suggested that plant oestrogens, or phyto-oestrogens, the commonest of these being a group of compounds found in soya protein called isoflavones, could produce biological effects in humans. Food manufacturers began variously marketing soya foods as an antidote to menopausal hot flushes and osteoporosis, and as a protective ingredient against hormone-related cancers. The hypothesis behind the claims is that rates of heart disease and certain cancers such as breast and prostate cancer are lower in East Asian populations with soya-rich diets than in Western countries, and that the oestrogens in soya therefore might have a protective effect.

The real boom in specialist soya protein was started by a division of DuPont when it petitioned the US Food and Drug Administration in 1998 to permit a claim on food labels that soya protein could help reduce the risk of heart disease. The FDA agreed. All might have continued swimmingly for the industry but for a dogged New Zealander.

For Dr Mike Fitzpatrick the saga of soya began in Monty Python style with a dead parrot. Or hundreds of dead parrots to be precise. His investigations into the ubiquitous bean started in 1993 when a rich American lawyer called Richard James turned up at the laboratory where he was working as a consultant toxicologist. James was sure that soya beans were killing his rare birds. He and his wife Valerie had been breeding exotic birds as a retirement dream and had been feeding the chicks a high-protein soya-based feed that had been marketed in the US as a miracle food, formulated with all the scientific nous of the country that had put men on the moon. The result had been a catastrophic breeding year with many of the birds being infertile, dying prematurely and ageing abnormally fast. 'We thought he was mad, but he had a lot of money and wanted us to find out what was going on,' Fitzpatrick recalled.

Over the following months, Fitzpatrick carried out an exhaustive study of soya and its effects. He was particularly struck by the accelerated rate at which the male parrots had reached sexual maturity. 'We realized that there was some sort of hormonal disruption going on but we'd eliminated other possible hormone-disrupting chemicals such as pesticides from the inquiry.' From his review of the scientific literature Fitzpatrick quickly discovered that soya's plant oestrogens were powerful enough to disrupt women's menstrual cycles in experiments. They also appeared damaging to the thyroid. 'My next thought was, what about the children who are fed soya milk?' He calculated that babies fed exclusively on soya formula could receive the oestrogenic equivalent, based on body weight, of five birth control pills a day. Thanks to James' lobbying, the information that emerged eventually forced governments to take notice.

In 2002 the UK government's expert Committee on the Toxicity of Food was asked to conduct a full inquiry into the safety of plant oestrogens, mainly from soya proteins in modern food. It concluded that in general the health benefits claimed for soya were not supported by clear evidence and judged that there could be particular risks from high levels of consumption for certain age groups.

Mass exposure to isoflavones in the West has only occurred in the past thirty years due to the widespread incorporation of soya protein into processed foods, a fact noted by the Royal Society in its expert report on 'Endocrine Disrupting Chemicals' in 2000. When the independent experts on the scientific Committee on Toxicity (CoT) trawled through all the scientific data, they concluded that soya milk should not be recommended for infants even when they had cow's milk allergies, except on medical advice, because of the high levels of oestrogenic isoflavones it contains.

On breast cancer, they decided that 'despite the suggested benefits of phyto-oestrogens in lowering risk of developing breast cancer, there is also evidence that they may stimulate the progression of the disease'. The lower risk of certain cancers among Asian populations might be due to other factors – their high consumption of fish, for example. They advised caution. On the effects on menopause symptoms, the evidence was inconclusive, the experts ruled. On bone density, the committee thought there might be some protective effects, but the data was unclear. The evidence on prostate cancer was mixed. Since isoflavones cross the placenta, the implications of pregnant women eating large quantities of soya were unclear. There was some evidence that soya-based products had a beneficial effect on the good HDL cholesterol but they were not sure that was down to the isoflavones. On the other hand – reassuringly – they judged that fears raised by one study that high consumption might be linked to increased dementia were not convincing.

What the UK toxicity committee also pointed out was that the way soya was processed affected the levels of phyto-oestrogens. Traditional fermentation reduces the levels of isoflavones two- to three-fold. Modern factory processes do not. Moreover, modern American strains of soya have significantly higher levels of isoflavones than Japanese or Chinese ones because they have been bred to be more resistant to pests. (One way to tackle pests is to stop them breeding by making them infertile. Unfermented soya did play one role in traditional Asian diets – it was eaten by monks to dampen down their libido.)

Sue Dibb, a former food policy expert at the National Consumer Council, was a member of the CoT working group that compiled its final report. She questions whether infant soya milk should still be on public sale and is troubled by the latest marketing of soya. 'We looked in detail at the claimed health benefits for adults for soya consumption and concluded there was not sufficient evidence to support many of them. There may be benefits but there are also risks. The groups of adults of particular concern are those with a thyroid problem and women with oestrogen-dependent breast cancer. It worries me that soya is being pushed as a health food by a big soya and supplements industry. We ought to be taking a more cautious approach.'

The Food Standards Agency advice is that soya's potential to have an adverse effect on babies' hormonal development is still controversial, but that soya formula should only be given to infants under twelve months old in exceptional circumstances.

Professor Richard Sharpe, head of the Medical Research Council's human reproductive sciences unit at Edinburgh University, was also a member of the CoT's working group on phyto-oestrogens in food. He has been studying the decline in male fertility in the past half-century. He recently completed studies on the effects of soya milk on young male monkeys which showed that it interferes with testosterone levels. 'In the first three months after birth, baby boys have a neonatal testosterone rise. The testes are very, very active in hormone production at this point and there is a lot of cell activity going on that will determine sperm count in adults and will affect the developing prostate. If you introduce a phyto-oestrogen, which can, in large amounts, alter these changes, you may predispose children to later disease. Soya formula milk is a [recent]

Western invention. There is not the historical evidence to show it is safe.'

Manufacturers, however, argue that soya infant formula has been widely used without problems. 'The industry has said that if the CoT comes up with clear science, we will take note, but the case is not proven,' says Roger Clarke, director general of the industry's Infant Dietetics Food Association. 'A lot of the work it looked at was based on experimental work with animals. There does not seem to be clear evidence of adverse effects, and there is demand for it. There are some markets, such as vegan usage, where soya is the only alternative.'

While 30–40 per cent of all infants in the US are raised on soya formula – not least because it is given away in welfare programmes – and it has been suggested as a possible factor in the growing phenomenon of early puberty in girls, soya milk for babies has always been confined to a small minority in the UK. So did Sharpe think exposure to soya from other sources – vegetarian soya proteins, the soya flour in factory bread, the hydrolyzed proteins added as flavourings, for example – has a cumulative effect that might be worrying to other age groups? He told me he was not concerned about people who eat soya foods in moderation or in the way they are traditionally used in oriental diets, although there should be no presumption that what was all right for Asian populations was automatically all right for Western ones – Asians have may adapted genetically over many generations to the oestrogenic properties of soya. But when it comes to modern processed foods, which use soya proteins in different ways, he preferred to turn the question round. 'If someone said they were adding a hormone to your foods, would you be happy with that? There may be lots of effects, some of them may be beneficial, but would you be happy with that? I am not a fan of processed foods, full stop. And these quick fixes for protecting against ill-health – you know they can't be true,' he added.

Much of the marketing-led Western fad for soya is based on

misconceptions about the traditional oriental diet. Fitzpatrick looked into historic soya consumption in Japan and China and concluded that Asians did not actually eat that much. What they did eat tended to have been fermented for months and was nothing like the form of soya used in modern Western diets. 'If you look at people who are into health fads here, they are eating soya steaks and veggie burgers or veggie sausages and drinking soya milk – they are getting over 100g a day. They are eating tonnes of the raw stuff.'

Soya is used in traditional oriental diets but generally only after cultures, moulds or precipitants have achieved a bio-chemical transformation. The young green beans, now sold as a fashionable snack, edamame, are lower in oestrogens and compounds that block the absorption of nutrients, though not free of them. But raw mature soya beans contain phytates that prevent mineral absorption and enzyme inhibitors that block the key enzymes we need to digest protein.

Christopher Dawson, who owns the Clearspring brand of organic soya sauces, lived in Japan for eighteen years and his Japanese wife, Setsuko, is a cookery teacher. 'I never saw mature soy beans on the table in Japan – they're indigestible.'

He explained that traditionally soya sauces are made in a process that takes eighteen months, during which time the soya bean is transformed through fermentation, so that its valuable amino acids become available but its antinutrients are tamed. The end result is an intensely flavoured condiment in which the soya's chemical composition has been radically altered.

Most soya sauces (and misos) are not made this way any more, however. Instead of using the whole bean, manufacturers short-cut the fermentation by starting with defatted soy pro-tein meal given accelerated ageing at high temperatures. The cheapest grades are made by mixing defatted soya flour with hydrochloric acid at high temperatures to create hydrolyzed vegetable protein. This rapid hydrolysis method uses the enzyme glutamase as a reactor and creates large amounts of the unnatural form of glutamate that is found in MSG. Soya veggie burgers and sausages generally use the same chemically extracted fraction of the bean.

Most commercial soya milk today is made from soya isolates, although not all; some of the pioneers of soya foods as health products in Europe avoid the chemical extraction process and use whole beans to make their milk. The key selling points for both types of soya milk are that they contain complete proteins and the oestrogenic isoflavones.

Bernard Deryckere, president of the European Natural Soyfood Manufacturers Association, says that his members' products, made using natural processes rather than soya isolates are a healthy alternative to dairy products. 'A lot of people in Europe are lactose-intolerant. Soya milk was invented in China 4,000 years ago and today it's consumed by all types of people as a cholesterol-free source of quality protein.'

Most soya milk in Asia was, however, until recently made not to drink, except in times of famine, but as the first step in the process of making tofu. After the long, slow boiling of soya beans in water to eliminate toxins, a curdling agent was added to the liquid to separate it. The curds would then be pressed to make tofu and the whey, in which the nutrient blocking substances were concentrated, would be thrown away.

Dibb points out that if you are drinking non-dairy milk because you want calcium without cow's milk, there are plenty of other sources such as green leafy vegetables and nuts. And only those eating extremely limited diets in the West are likely to be short of protein as adults.

Dawson, a lifelong vegetarian, does not drink soya milk and only eats tofu in moderation. 'I will only use a product for my family if there is 200 years of tradition behind it. You are asking for trouble if you take an isolate from soya – yet so much effort seems to go into taking industry's waste and turning it into new food.'

It was however 2005 before the soya health food bandwagon

began to come off the rails. Then another expert government panel, this time in the US, found unclear or insufficient evidence that soya can prevent heart disease, or osteoporosis or relieve menopausal symptoms. The industry withdrew its petition to the FDA asking to be allowed to label foods in the US with the claim that soya protein prevents cancer. And in 2006 the American Heart Association dissociated itself from claims about soya protein and heart disease and other protective effects. 'The direct cardiovascular benefit of soya protein or isoflavone supplements is minimal at best,' its expert nutrition committee ruled, although there could be indirect effects if eating soya made people cut down on the saturated fats in meat and dairy products. It too found no benefit from soya protein consumption in preventing cancer of the breast or prostate.

The rise and fall of soya products, and the rise and rise of the soya bean from which they are made, brings today's food system in to sharp focus. So much about the trade in soya is extreme – the explosive rise in volumes of a commodity we barely ate half a century ago; the way it has displaced with its ubiquity a diverse food supply for one of increasing homogeneity; the extra-ordinary impact of its production on the environment and on climate change; its contribution to the re-emergence of slavery; its role in the damage we appear to be inflicting on our own biology, from changing the very architecture of our brains to affecting our fertility, even as it claims to offer miracle promises of health.

But if the saga of soya is extreme, it also reflects what has happened more widely with our food. We have been swept up in a system in which a few transnational corporations have been able to capture the value of the chain. Half the world's population depends on agriculture for at least part of its living, but today's food system is pushing all but the largest farmers off the land, driving migration as it does so. It wreaks havoc with the environment and hastens climate change while destroying precisely the sort of sustainable farming we will need in the years ahead as the impact of that climate change is felt. We have come to depend on industrial processing of food that adds commercial value to it while stripping it of the nutrition we need to be healthy. We have eaten our way through a period of post-war American economic power, but we are in a period of rapid transition. Having inflicted this dysfunctional food on us in the West, agribusiness is now bringing it to the emerging economies of India and China. The question is: will we keep following the road that hurtles on down this destructive path, or we can take a different route?

9. Food for Tomorrow

I am quite often asked to give talks around the country about various aspects of today's food system. The range of people who invite me is enormous: aid and development organizations, farming interests, schools and parents' associations, church groups, foodies, special interest campaigners from those fighting the loss of local shops or traditional social structures to those campaigning over particular health problems to those opposing slavery. The origins of concern are as diverse as they could be, and cover the political spectrum from right to radical left, but I am nearly always asked the same questions towards the end of any debate. Am I optimistic that our food will get better? And what advice would I give people about shopping? What do I eat myself?

It may seem curious, but I am in fact optimistic that the food system will be transformed, and sooner rather than later. I don't believe it will be overhauled by shopping alone. Shopping cannot meet such a political challenge. It will take wider collective action to do that. I do however think that the enormous shift in consumer attitudes to food that we have seen in just a few years is playing a part in the transformation.

One of my reasons for optimism paradoxically is just how much is wrong with our industrialized diets. Things will have to change if only because they simply cannot go on. We are in fact already in a period of what is likely to be rapid transition. With oil prices soaring, the impact of climate change already being felt, the rising economies of China and India putting pressure on supplies, and obesity and related illnesses gobbling health budgets around the globe, it is inevitable that the way food is produced and traded will look very different in the near future. Even if the short-termism that plagues governments prevents them taking the tough, co-ordinated action that is needed for these interrelated crises, events will force the pace.

When you look back at the origins of much of today's consumption, you can seeing the ebb and flow of empire: of the British empire that turned its slave-produced sugar into the engine of mass consumption, of the pre-war European powers that controlled fats, of the post-war American model, a privatized form of empire that has reached into every corner of world food supply in the second half of the twentieth and early twenty-first century. History shows too that empires rise and fall, and the fall, when it comes, tends to be fast. Food empires are likely to be no different. We have been living through a period of US-led food Fordism, fed a production-line diet that is homogenized and bolted together from standard commodity parts. People are now in revolt. The seeds of a global food revolution have been planted.

I do not expect the food industry or agribusiness to reform itself. Some food manufacturers may be willing but when they try they come up against an ineluctable problem: they operate within a market system that puts no price on environmental and social costs. They cannot make the same sort of return from plain wholesome food that they can from their industrialized production. City analysts JPMorgan expressed their quandary neatly in a detailed report in 2006 on how the food industry was responding to the obesity crisis: 'The profitability of the vast majority of food and beverage categories usually regarded as healthy (for example, water, dairy, fruit/vegetables) is below industry average. This certainly creates a dilemma for companies who enjoy above-industry-average margins (e.g. confectionery, hot beverages, snack producers) and would like to enter the healthier segments of the market.' The simple unprocessed foods we need to eat more of – the staples such as fruit, vegetables, wholegrains, pulses – only give manufacturers and processors a 3–6 per cent operating margin. You don't make big margins selling humble oats in a plain package for porridge. Relatively simple processed foods like cheese or plain yoghurt give 9–12 per cent margins. Highly processed cereals, snacks, biscuits, soft drinks and confectionery on the other hand give brand manufacturers more than 15 per cent margins. Even higher margins can be gained from specialist nutrition products such as baby food and sports drinks. There's little incentive in other words for manufacturers to move into selling products that are less processed. They have to stay high up what industry describes as the 'value chain' by developing new products within their existing categories which can command premium prices because they claim to be healthier. That's why in the three years to the beginning of 2006 two thirds of product launches within the food industry fell into the category of foods that were 'light', 'diet', 'better for you', 'enriched with', or made other health claims. These can be priced at a premium of up to 400 per cent, according to the analysts. But what the rest of us need is for these unhealthy categories simply to wither. We need to return to whole foods and eat less processed food, full stop. We need a redistribution of the money made in the food chain, away from the transnational traders and manufacturers and back towards the primary producers.

Supermarkets have shown themselves susceptible to the consumer backlash against their growing dominance and the environmental and social impacts of their way of doing the food business. They have made some moves that would have been unthinkable even five years ago. Many of the retailers, including Tesco, Asda and Marks & Spencer, have launched plans to become more 'green'. Their dilemma, however, is that their economic model is also built on the inherently unsustainable. They are locked into meeting shareholders' constant demand for ever more growth from greater efficiencies of scale. They are still rationalizing and centralizing even as the oil runs out and climate change calls for more localized, less environmentally damaging production and a radical rethink of what sort of food system we need. To change meaningfully would require them to abandon the globalized systems of sourcing, just-in-time production and distribution that they have invested billions in creating over the last few decades.

Nor do I have much hope that the regulators who are supposed to oversee our food will do what is needed for real change. Bound by the political vision of their Western governments, whether they like it or not they are committed to the food status quo, that is the food of the deregulated global market and a flexible labour force, a status quo that illogically and unfairly keeps agricultural protections in place for developed countries while imposing the so-called free market on everyone else. Food regulators as a result are mandated only to see the quality of food through a hopelessly narrow prism – one that looks at food safety obsessively yet almost ignores food quality and nutrition, one that daren't advise people to eat less processed food, one that ends up putting industry's needs before consumers', and one that takes no account of the environmental, social and developmental considerations that are so important. They have no influence over the economic drivers that shape our food supply – the distorting subsidies and trade rules, nor the concentrations of agribusiness power. They say that they can move only on the basis of science but the science they depend on is all too often corrupted – not in a narrow pecuniary sense, but in that industry so often frames the questions science asks and shapes the mindset with which results are approached.

There was a good example of this recently, when a substantial piece of research, based on rigorously conducted tests whose methodology the Food Standards Agency had itself been involved in setting up, found an inconvenient result. It showed that certain artificial colourings and a preservative, widely used in food and under suspicion for decades as a cause of hyperactivity, did in fact make children behave badly. The effect was seen in ordinary children, not just those suffering from hyperactivity, and the cocktail of additives tested induced precisely the sort of problem behaviour schools complain is on the rise and disrupts education. The artificial colourings used in two mixtures in the study were sunset yellow (E110), tartrazine (E102), carmoisine (E122), Ponceau 4R (E124), quinoline yellow (E104) and allura red (E129). The preservative was sodium benzoate (E211). As regulator, the FSA turned first to its expert advisory committee, the Committee on Toxicity of Chemicals in Food. Half the scientists on this committee have links to agribusiness and the pharmaceutical industry, in the form of collaborations or research funding or consultancies. That is not to impugn their personal integrity – that is the way science is these days: in the absence of public funding, researchers must bring in the money where they can. But it does little to reassure us that consumer interests will come before commercial ones. The CoT decided it could not draw conclusions on the implications of the additives study for the population as a whole, which appeared to contradict the published science, since the effects were seen in the study in the general population of children. The Committee also said it was not possible to extrapolate from the additives used in this particular research to others; in fact several other additives in common use have similar chemical structures to those used in the study. Regulators have applied the opposite assumption when approving them for use – if tests showed that one additive was safe, they happily extrapolated to additives with a similar structure. From a consumer point of view, taking a precaution-ary approach and getting rid of these additives would seem to be a no-brainer, especially since the colourings are purely cosmetic, and these mixtures of additives are used by and large to disguise sugars and fats in junk foods and drinks. Instead the FSA advice to parents was simply that they might consider avoiding these additives by reading food labels if they thought their children were suffering from hyperactivity. There was no advice to schools, no mention of what to do about all the foods containing these additives that are sold unlabelled, no questioning of why on earth they are used anyway. It was advice so impractical that Gordon Brown was moved to say that parents shouldn't have to root around supermarket shelves reading all the small print to check if food is going to harm their children. The FSA's lawyers advice had been that there was not enough evidence to impose a unilateral ban on the additives. They may make ordinary children behave badly, but they did not meet the requirement of EU law that an additive 'endangers health' before an individual government can take action. The European Food Safety Authority later came to a similar conclusion. Not for the first time, industry interests ended up coming before consumers'.

The regulators, to be fair, have not been without their triumphs. The FSA's policy of naming and shaming manufacturers until they removed excess salt that causes high blood pressure from their foods has finally made manufacturers address this particular aspect of our industrialized diets. Targets such as these to reduce salt, fat, and sugar in processed foods are well and good, but raise a different dilemma. You may get industry to respond on these narrow negatives (and to have done so is no small achievement), but you cannot make them move from there to positive nutrition. The more fat, salt and sugar come out, the more they are replaced by other cheap, empty ingredients. The economics of the food business have not changed. So the trend now is towards bulking agents, notably starch and water. We will be no better off in terms of nutrition.

Food cannot in any case be reduced to such confined compartments for reform. Half the world's population depends on farming for some part of its income. The quality of food we eat and how that food is produced go to the heart of health, both physical and mental, educational achievement, criminal justice, trade, development, the sustainability of communities and the survival of ecosystems, as I hope the previous chapters have shown.

That is not to say that the way people shop makes no difference. Demand for organic food is growing rapidly; farmers' markets that achieve a different distribution of the money in the food chain are flourishing, as are vegetable box schemes and new ways of getting good food to consumers direct. There has been a revival in cooking. The microwave is in decline. The rise of these alternatives has given the intensive farming industry and retailers pause for thought. It has sent powerful messages to government that we are not happy with the system as it is. This fledgling rebellion has achieved more than I dared hope when I gave a list of ways people could use their purchasing power in *Not on the Label* four years ago.

Shopping decisions have their limitations, however. You can buy organic where possible, assuming you have the money; you can support local food and small shops, assuming you have the time; you can choose to invest a larger proportion of your time and money in good food you cook from scratch and avoid industrialized processed foods; you can refuse packaging and demand fair trade, you can consume in a way that reduces your own carbon footprint, and I believe passionately we should do all these things as much as we can, but this only takes us so far. We have not yet built a healthy food system in to the structure of our lives and until we do so our children will still be exposed to the junk that continues to predominate in schools. We will still have little idea where the food we eat when we are out, in our work canteen or in cafés and restaurants, comes from. Most of what we buy will not tell us how the workers producing it were treated or what environmental toll was taken in its production.

Modern food production involves processes that quite apart from having little care for real nutrition, drive people off the land, stimulate migration, increase inequalities and the depth of poverty, are corrosive of society, and depend on extravagant use of natural resources, from water to oil to land, that are running out. The politics of food is in other words not the art of shopping but the politics of modern globalized capitalism itself. Any solution to the current dysfunctional food system requires us to think about how we frame our political ideologies. Can we continue to measure success in a warming world and planet of shrinking resources by the usual economic measure of endless growth? How far should the state intervene and what are the boundaries of individual responsibility? How will we devise a way of re-regulating the markets so that the losses from the industrialized food system are not externalized and socialized as now, the bill left to be picked up by the taxpayer, but paid by those who do the damage and make profits from it? What institutions do we need to draw up those regulations and how and with what resources will we enforce them? How do we limit corporate power, support our agriculture, shape our communities, determine our migration policies, collect our taxes? Which, if any, political parties are addressing these sorts of questions?

This is why ethical consumption cannot be left to personal choice, as politicians, supermarkets and agribusiness would have us believe. So often the reality is that there is no real choice anyway, just an illusion of it, but even were there a choice, if we are not careful, we shall find the burden of behaving decently has been thrown back to the disempowered shopper. We will be offered a choice of one shelf full of more expensive goods for those affluent enough to take their morals and eco-fears shopping and a far larger shelf next door of bargain goods, produced without regard for the planet or for the rights of its peoples, for those who don't care or simply can't afford to care. Then the supermarkets will be able to say: 'Ethics? We just do what our customers want.' This cannot be the answer. If we want to tackle these issues, we have to change the system root and branch. We have to mobilize, engage politically, and take collective action.

One of the other reasons I am optimistic that the food system will get better is that I can see people already engaging in so many different areas. The soya protests on the Amazon, for example, represented one such turning point. The campaign there marked a new kind of asymmetric engagement between non-governmental organizations and agribusiness giants, in which active consumers and citizens whose resources are dwarfed by those they take on have nevertheless found a real power to bring about change. The soya campaigners were harnessing the same tools that transnational corporations have used to build up their control. Activists made use of advances in technology, of the internet and an instant globalized media, to bring together shared interests around the world in a focussed series of actions that challenged the established order. The charismatic 'caboclo' priest in furthest Brazil can now connect simultaneously with the French activist outside a chicken factory in Northern Europe and the ordinary supermarket meat shopper in Britain. Moreover the campaigners have found ways to turn the troubling integration of the food system to their advantage. The trading giants may have managed to be faceless in the past but they can no longer remain so when we as ordinary consumers are shown how their control of the food chain connects with what ends up on our plates. Amazon soya after the 2006 campaign was no longer an abstract, a bulk commodity from a remote, unknown region, but the base material that feeds the chickens and provides the fat that ends up processed into the brands that we have all heard of. As McDonald's well knew, global brands may conquer the world, but they can still lose in the court of public opinion. McDonald's responded immediately to Greenpeace's Amazon campaign and wanted to work co-operatively to stop the destruction of the rainforest. It and the supermarkets were able to apply the pressure to the trading giants that brought them to a groundbreaking agreement. Greenpeace, the commodity processors and the leading retailers all acknowledged that the moratorium on soya from the Amazon represented an unprecedented initiative among opposing interests. The currency of power had changed. The destruction has not ended but agribusiness is under scrutiny as never before.

The fair trade campaign group Banana Link and its partners around the world have pioneered a new way of highlighting the global injustice in the food system too. They have done it by focussing on a particular sector with which we can all identify. Bananas are highly profitable. They are the largest single item by volume sold in British supermarkets and the third largest in value, so most of us have a stake in how they are produced and sold.

Three transnational corporations dominate the banana trade. Dole, Chiquita, and Fresh Del Monte account for more than two thirds of the global market between them and source mainly from large industrial plantations in Latin America and West Africa.

Banana Link's strategy has involved recording and then publicizing the business practices of the global banana chain that would otherwise be opaque, since neither supermarkets nor traders are keen to reveal who is buying what, where, and at what price. By doing this it has been able to trace the connection between British supermarket price wars over bananas and a sharp deterioration in working conditions for those on plantations in Latin America.

Thanks to Banana Link's campaigning over a decade, all three companies now acknowledge the need for corporate social responsibility in their businesses. They are working with Latin American unions and say they support freedom of association.

By turning the spotlight on a particular product in the food chain, and enabling us as consumers to connect with workers on the ground in producing countries, Banana Link has managed to mobilize support from British shoppers for a different way of doing trade and has had real impact. Bananas have become one of the largest sectors for fair trade sales. This new kind of globalized campaigning has achieved a sea-change in attitudes. There's still lots to be done, and further progress to make sure there is a fairer distribution of the money made in the trade will have to involve new international agreements, since one of the biggest issues still facing the sector is beyond the reach of individual governments. The big corporations have created elaborate structures to move profits through subsidiaries to offshore centres such as the Cayman Islands, Bermuda and the British Virgin Islands to minimize the money they hand over to tax collectors in the countries where their goods are produced and in those where they are consumed. As proof of the power and influence consumer engagement can have, though, Sainsbury's took the brave decision in 2007 to buy all, not just some, of its bananas from fair trade sources. I say brave decision, because it will still have to match the prices of its competitors who are able to procure their supplies more cheaply from other sources. If that battle can be won, why not the next one? If we fight for it, how and where companies pay their tax, and how much they put back into the economies where they generate their products and their sales, could become as much a subject of scrutiny as other forms of corporate social responsibility.

It is not just transnational non-governmental organizations that I see bringing about change. Plenty of the different groups I meet when giving talks have found their own ways of making a difference. Parents' groups have realized that if they make sufficient determined fuss they can break through the complacency that characterizes so much school food catering and make councils improve what their children eat. In the London borough of Merton, Jackie Schneider, a parent inspired by the Jamie Oliver TV series on school meals, decided to set up an action group to improve food in her local schools. She contacted me when endless obstacles were thrown in her way, including private finance initiatives that meant schools were being built without kitchens in which to cook properly. We ran a piece about it in the *Guardian,* other press followed, and thanks to Jackie's indefatigable organizing, the campaign mushroomed. As well as transforming food in their education area, the Merton parents now help other groups set up their own action groups. Their website, www.mertonparents.co.uk, is a model of how new networks of activism can spread.

With the plight of dairy farmers, it has been the National Federation of Women's Institutes that has held supermarkets and processors to account for pushing so many milk producers into bankruptcy. Despite the conservative image many people hold of it, the WI has been a radical organization from its earliest days. It chose to mobilize its national network to put pressure on the industry to pay dairy farmers more because its members could see not just farmers but the very fabric of their rural life being destroyed. The Church of England too has challenged the Competition Commission inquiry into supermarkets to put an end to practices that put stress on farming communities, with profound implications for us all. What strikes me most about the change in attitudes to food in the last few years is that people and organizations from so many different spheres have learned to connect.

The late-twentieth-century deregulation of markets also saw the weakening of the institutions that have traditionally mediated between the excessive power of those markets and the individual. Gradually some of those institutions are finding renewed strength. The summer of 2005 saw the first agricultural workers' strike in Britain since the 1920s. Eastern European migrant workers walked out of an intensive strawberry farm in Herefordshire that supplies leading supermarkets and sat down on the old Hereford to Leominster road in protest at their conditions. I first interviewed Polish farm workers in the area in 2004. Back then it was local church groups that had become involved in taking up their cause and in providing emergency accommodation to migrants who found themselves homeless. Whether the migrant workers had just cause for their 2005 protest has been the subject of dispute between the farm owners and the unions. What is not in dispute is that by taking collective action, migrants were able to exert pressure not just on the farm owners but on the big supermarket chains. It was perhaps no coincidence that these strikers were Poles. With their recent history of Solidarność, they know better than most that it takes collective action to change political systems. The Transport and General Workers' Union, later absorbed into the new superunion Unite, took up the cudgels for the Herefordshire agricultural workers again in 2006. It took its protest about conditions for strawberry pickers to the high street and supermarket doors. It found that by connecting directly with shoppers, it could elicit a swift response from supermarkets and their suppliers. Unite has done enormous work in the last few years to organize migrant workers and tackle abusive employment in food and agriculture.

Migrant workers have revitalized many parts of the international union movement too. In 2003 I visited the horticultural areas of southern Spain that supply much of northern Europe with vegetables such as broccoli, peppers, tomatoes and salads through the winter months. About 70,000 migrants by official estimates but probably more, from northern and western Africa, and eastern Europe, were working there illegally. Without them the supermarket supply system would collapse. They were living in appalling squalor, mostly without sanitation or water in make-shift plastic and cardboard housing. An illegal Senegalese worker called Spitou had been one of those who explained the work and conditions to me. A highly educated former teacher, he was being used as sweated labour on the tomato harvest, paid a pittance, and living miserably and in fear, without proper housing and without papers. He had risked everything to come to Europe because the collapsing Senegalese economy made it impossible for him to support his family at home. Then three years later, when this sort of routine exploitation of migrants had at last made it on to the political agenda, I was invited to talk to members of the European Parliament about my research. To my surprise and delight I found myself sharing a platform with Spitou among others. With the public growing increasingly uneasy at conditions among illegal migrants, the Spanish government had granted a series of enlightened amnesties for those who had already worked in the country for several years. Spitou had been able to acquire legal status. As soon as he had his papers, he began devoting his time to helping other migrants improve their conditions through a rural workers' union and it was this work that brought him to the parliament. Spitou and so many of the other union activists whom I have met working on the ground remind me of the early-nineteenth-century British factory workers. They often take great personal risks to help organize fellow workers so that they can collectively take on the system that crushes them as individuals. They are engaged in what they know will be a long struggle.

Dozens of local campaign groups have adopted a form of opposition to agribusiness whose activities may be more humdrum but are just as important. Several have contacted me as they try to stop the building of new supermarkets which they fear will hollow out their towns and communities. For them political engagement has meant enduring hours of tedious planning meetings, footslogging around the streets to drum up support from neighbours, pitting themselves with painstaking study in unequal engagement against industry's top planning consultants and lawyers. They have won some and lost some. But with every campaign, it becomes just a little bit harder for supermarkets to ride roughshod over the wishes of local communities, and just a little bit easier for beleaguered council planning departments to take a stand.

It is at local, grass roots level too that the Transition Town movement has found a way to overcome inertia and paralysis on energy and climate change. Rob Hopkins, who gave the talk on peak oil in Lampeter, can now boast of over forty transition towns that have joined him in his energy descent. In each of these there has been the same public-minded pooling of interests, inspired by a belief that individuals can make a difference by coming together. They are prepared to trade giving up some material things for acquiring the new comforts of long-term security and community spirit. More like a party than a protest march, the harnessing of hope rather than guilt, of optimism instead of fear – these are some of the descriptions written of these transition town launches.

How then should we shop and eat? My efforts, not always successful, are still focussed where they were four years ago – organically, more locally, more seasonally, more directly from producers and independent retailers, more fair trade, less meat and animal produce, more wholegrains, pulses, fresh fruits and vegetables, few highly processed foods, nothing with ingredients on a label you cannot recognize, nothing that claims to be a new or techno food, nothing highly packaged. Follow these principles and by and large you will find you are buying less from production that damages the environment or threatens ecosystems and you are less likely to be eating the fruits of exploited labour. You will also be supporting the sort of small-scale domestic production that will be vital to our future security. It requires effort, and though it is not fashionable to say it, it requires giving up things we like. See it as a first urgent step in a new political engagement.

Notes and References

Chapter 1: Cereals

Additional research for this chapter was conducted by Susannah Osborne.

Much of my information about processing methods and their history has come from technical experts within the industry who wish to remain anonymous. The regulators, the Food Standards Agency and broadcasting watchdog Ofcom, provided background briefings on the process of introducing controls on advertising foods to children.

The Kellogg's Cereal City museum of cereal history in Battle Creek is a treasure trove of information and history. Professor Edward Wheatley and Mary Mackay were generous companions, both during my trip there and in Chicago. Kellogg's kindly hosted my trip to its Manchester factory, and communications director Chris Wermann has been an unfailingly open and thoughtful interlocutor on food processing and marketing even when we have disagreed with each other.

The websites of the leading cereal manufacturers, *The Oxford Companion to Food*, edited by Alan Davidson (OUP, 1999), *The Cambridge World History of Food*, edited by Kenneth Kiple (CUP, 2000), and *The Encyclopaedia of Food and Culture*, edited by Solomon Katz (Thomson Gale, 2002) all provide detailed accounts of cereal history. Scott Bruce and Bill Crawford's *Cerealizing America: The Unsweetened Story of American Breakfast Cereal* gives a highly entertaining and informative alternative account. Vance Packard's 1950s' classic on the advertizing and marketing industry, *The Hidden Persuaders* (Ig Publishing reissue, 2007), remains a classic source.

Jack Thurston of farmsubsidy.org in the UK, and Ken Cook of the Environmental Working Group explained agricultural subsidies to me. The EWG's farm subsidy database is the source for the US subsidy figures. Oxfam provided many background briefings on the wider impact of subsides on developing countries and commodity prices.

I am very grateful to David Goodman, Emeritus Professor of Environmental Studies at the University of California Santa Cruz, for comments on US policy in this and other chapters.

p. 4 *Babies retain a liking* ... Julie A. Mennella, Cara E. Griffin and Gary K. Beauchamp, 'Flavor Programming During Infancy', *Pediatrics*, vol. 113, no. 4 (April 1, 2004).

p. 5 *When the first National Food Survey* ... as cited in *Plenty and Want: A Social History of Food in England from 1815 to the Present Day*, John Burnett (Routledge, 1989).

p. 6 *as* The Oxford Companion to Food *puts it* ... *The Oxford Companion to Food*, ed. Alan Davidson (OUP, 1999).

p. 6 *Today, instead, the British and the Irish are* ... Figures from Datamonitor, per capita consumption in kg 2000–2005, personal communication.

p. 8 *some of the best insights into his motivations* ... *Man the Masterpiece*, J. H. Kellogg (London, 1890).

p. 12 *they typically have glycaemic index scores* ... GI scores taken from K. Foster-Powell, *et al*, 'International Table of Glycemic Index and Glycemic Load Values', *American Journal of Clinical Nutrition*, vol. 76 (2002), pp. 5–56.

p. 13 *in fact very highly milled starches can be worse than sugar* ... personal communication, Aubrey Sheiham, Emeritus Professor of Dental Public Health, University College London.

p. 13 *The Kellogg company however held back* ... *Cerealizing America*, Scott Bruce and Bill Crawford (Faber and Faber, 1995).

p. 14 *Companies are also looking at adding omega-3 fatty acids* ... *Food Manufacture*, September 16, 2005.

p. 16 *Acrylamide contribution from home-cooked food is in general relatively small* ... The Heatox (heat toxicology) Project report , November 2007, www.heatox.org; The CIAA Acrylamide 'Toolbox',

September 2005, p. 24; *Food Manufacture*, April 2006, p28; FSA, 'Study of Acrylamide in Food: Background Information and Research Findings', May 17, 2002; 'A Prospective Study of Dietary Acrylamide Intake and Risk of Endometrial, Ovarian and Breast Cancer', Janneke G. Hogervorst *et al,* Maastricht University, 'Cancer Epidemiol Biomarkers' Prev 2007; 16 (11) November 2007; FSA, 'Analysis of Total Diet Study Samples for Acrylamide', food survey information sheet, January 2005.

p. 17 *A US congressional hearing into breakfast cereal . . . Time*, August 3, 1970.

p. 20 *The UK market for those cereal boxes was worth over £1.27 billion in 2005 . . .* Mintel, 'Breakfast Cereals', UK, February 2006.

p. 20 *Or as Kellogg's European president Tim Mobsby put it to MPs . . .* House of Commons Health Select Committee inquiry into Obesity, oral evidence, November 2003.

p. 23 *a survey published by the independant consumer watchdog Which? . . . Which?* 'Cereal Reoffenders', July 2006

p. 24 *it takes 7,000 kilocalories . . .* 'Fuelling a Food Crisis: The impact of peak oil on food security', Caroline Lucas MEP, Andy Jones and Colin Hines, The Greens/ European Free Alliance in the European Parliament, December 2006.

p. 25 *Nearly three quarters of the market value of US corn . . .* 'Truth or Consequences: Why the EU and the USA must Reform their Subsidies', Oxfam Briefing Paper No 81, Liz Stuart, Oxfam International, November 2005.

p. 25 *US agricultural subsidies totalled $165 billion . . .* Environmental Working Group farm subsidy database.

p. 28 *The Marshall Plan . . . Merchants of Grain*, Dan Morgan (BackinPrint.com, 2000); *The American Business Community and their European Recovery Program 1947–1952*, W. F. Sandford (Garland Publishing, 1987).

p. 29 *the US moved on to new ways of using its agricultural surplus . . .* 'The History of America's Food Aid', USAID, http://www.usaid.gov/ our_work/humanitarian_assistance/ffp/50th/history.html.

p. 30 *The commodity traders that get the contracts . . .* Bids for sales of US surpluses through food aid may only be made by US-based companies on a limited list. The companies that win the bids tend to be a handful of dominant US grain traders. For example in March and April 2003, the contracts for grain for food aid worth more than $28 million were shared by just four US-based companies: Cargill, Dreyfus, ADM and an export company that is 45 per cent-owned by ADM. Oxfam Briefing Paper No 71, 'Food Aid or Hidden Dumping?', Gawain Kripke, Oxfam International, March 2005.

p. 31 *Moore Lappé founded a think tank* . . . Peter Rosset, 'Giving Away the Farm', Food First/Institute for Food and Development Policy, Backgrounder, vol. 8, no. 3, (summer 2002).

p. 32 *Cargill . . . was said in testimony to the US senate* . . . President of National Farmers' Union testimony to US Senate Agriculture Committee January 1999, quoted in Bill Vorley Food, Inc (UK Food Group, 2003); Forbes.com; Cargill press office, personal communication.

p. 32 *ADM . . . controls about 30 per cent of global grain trade* . . . Bill Vorley, Food, Inc; revenues from Forbes.com.

p. 33 *Two other grain and oilseed giants* . . . see websites for Bunge www.bunge.com/ and Louis Dreyfus www.louisdreyfus.com/; revenues from Forbes.com.

Chapter 2: Meat and Vegetables

I am very grateful to Patrick Holden, director of the Soil Association, for making my trip to Lampeter and stay in Wales such an enjoyable and inspiring one. Patrick, together with Rob Hopkins and Rosie Boycott, provided many hours of stimulating debate about all aspects of the food system.

Green MEP Dr Caroline Lucas has a habit of being several steps ahead of the rest of us in her understanding of what's wrong with today's industrialized farming and what needs to change. My interest in the impact of peak oil on food security was stimulated by her report 'Fuelling a Food Crisis', co-authored with Andy Jones and

Colin Hines (The Greens/European Free Alliance in the European Parliament, December 2006).

Lester Brown is the guru on global food security and incredibly generous with his knowledge. His *Plan B 2.0: Rescuing a Planet Under Stress and a Civilization in Trouble* (New York: W.W. Norton & Co., 2006, also available to download free from the Earth Policy Institute, www.earth-policy.org/) is required reading. David Pimental, Professor of Ecology and Agriculture at Cornell University has published extensively on energy use in food and biofuel production.

Joyce d'Silva and her colleagues at Compassion in World Farming provided detailed research to back up the call to eat less meat and briefed me on the history of intensive livestock farming. Professor John Webster's *Limping Towards Eden* (Blackwell Publishing, 2005) is the bible on animal husbandry and welfare. Dr James LeFanu was a sounding board on reductionist chemistry and the history of fertilizer. Colin Tudge, author of *So Shall We Reap* (Penguin, 2003), and Graham Harvey, author of *The Killing of the Countryside* (Vintage, 1998) and *We Want Real Food* (Constable, 2006) have provided further inspiration.

I am grateful to Dan Basse of AgResource analysts for patiently explaining the workings of the Chicago Board of Trade, commodity trading, hedge funds and financial derivatives to me as a novice. The essential reference work for the grain trade is Dan Morgan's seminal *Merchants of Grain*, originally published by Viking and now reissued by BackinPrint.com. William Cronon's history of Chicago and the American West, *Nature's Metropolis*, (W.W. Norton, 1992) is also indispensable.

p. 35 *it takes three quarters of a gallon of oil* . . . 'The End of Cheap Oil', *National Geographic*, June 2004.
p. 35 *turning itself into a Transition Town* . . . for more information on Transition Towns see the movement's website, http://transitiontowns.org/. Rob Hopkins has distilled his knowledge and experience into the newly published *The Transition Handbook: From oil dependency to local resilience* (Green Books, 2008).

p. 37 *The Intergovernmental Panel on Climate Change had just published* ... IPCC Fourth Assessment Report: 'Climate Change 2007', www.ipcc.ch/ipccreports/assessments-reports.htm.

p. 37 *The Australians ... were having national second thoughts ...* 'Drought Threatens Crop Catastrophe, Australian PM Says', *Guardian*, April 20, 2007.

p. 38 *Biofuels looked ... like a quick way to exacerbate climate change ...* 'The Most Destructive Crop on Earth', George Monbiot, *Guardian,* December 6, 2005; *Heat,* George Monbiot (Penguin, 2006); 'Fuels Gold', *New Scientist*, September 23, 2006; 'Impact of Biofuels – Transport Fuels from Crops', Soil Association, Background Briefing, February 2007.

p. 39 *Just where all the oil goes ...* 'Fuelling a Food Crisis', Caroline Lucas, Andy Jones and Colin Hines (The Greens/European Free Alliance in the European Parliament, December 2006).

p. 40 *You can make the same sorts of calculations for ...* see 'Oil and Food: A Rising Security Challenge', Danielle Murray, Earth Policy Institute, May 9, 2005.

p. 40 *Justus von Liebig was the first to show ... Justus von Liebig: The Chemical Gatekeeper,* William H. Brock (CUP, 2002).

p. 41 *Guano imperialism had emerged ...* 'Liebig, Marx and the depletion of soil fertility: relevance for today's agriculture', John Bellamy Foster, *Monthly Review,* 1998.

p. 42 *the Haber-Bosch process ... Enriching the Earth: Fritz Haber, Carl Bosch, and the Transformation of World Food Production,* Vaclav Smil (MIT Press, 2004). See also *So Shall We Reap*, Colin Tudge (Penguin, 2003) and *We Want Real Food*, Graham Harvey (Constable, 2006).

p. 42 *World fertilizer use ...* www.fertilizer.org/ifa/statistics/IFADATA/summary.asp.

p. 42 *The global fertilizer market is dominated by Cargill, ADM and Bunge ... Invisible Giant,* Brewster Kneen (Pluto Press, 2002); Stocks, US, full descriptions, Reuters.com; and company websites.

p. 42 *nitrous oxide ... has also soared ...* Danielle Murray, as above.

p. 42 *There is a chart farmers can use* ... personal communication, Gundula Azeez, Policy Manager, Soil Association.

p. 44 *By spring 2007 ... the lid had blown off* ... 'Consumers set to feel the bite as fears grow over food price inflation', *Financial Times*, May 24, 2007.

p. 46 *livestock farming had remained relatively unchanged, as John Webster ... Limping towards Eden*, John Webster (Blackwell Publishing, 2005).

p. 47 *Global meat production quintupled* ... 'Reducing Meat Consumption, The Case for Urgent Reform', Compassion in World Farming, 2004.

p. 47 *Up to three quarters of the animal feed production in Europe* ... Food, Inc, as above.

p. 47 *Cargill's subsidiary Sun Valley produces* ... 'Eating Up the Amazon', Greenpeace, April 2006.

p. 48 *the Indian environmental activist Vandana Shiva ... Stolen Harvest, The Hijacking of the Global Food Supply*, Vandana Shiva (South End Press, 2000).

p. 49 *China was a net exporter of grain* ... 'The Global Benefits of Eating Less Meat', Mark Gold, Compassion in World Farming, 2004.

p. 49 *Intensively reared animals are an inefficient way* ... 'The Global Benefits of Eating Less Meat', as above.

p. 49 *If you look at it purely in terms of meeting people's protein needs* ... FAO's Protein Advisory Group.

p. 50 *changes the composition of meat* ... Professor Michael Crawford, personal communication; 'Healthy Chicken Piles on the Fat', *Sunday Times*, April 3, 2005.

p. 51 *Cutting down on meat significantly reduces the risk of cancer* ... 'Food, Nutrition, Physical Activity and the Prevention of Cancer', Second Expert Report, World Cancer Research Fund, November 2007.

p. 51 *Most adults in the UK eat more protein than they need* ... Food Standards Agency, http://www.eatwell.gov.uk/asksam/healthydiet/meatq/.

p. 52 *The UN's Food and Agriculture Organisation produced a report* . . . 'Livestock's Long Shadow', FAO, 2006.

p. 52 *Researchers at the University of Chicago* . . . 'Vegan Diets Healthier for Planet and People than Meat Diets', Gidon Eshel and Pamela Martin, University of Chicago press release, April 13, 2006.

p. 52 *Cows produce prodigious quantities of methane* . . . http://www.guardian.co.uk/science/2007/jul/10/ruralaffairs.climatechange.

p. 53 *you could take it from the Hirsh report* . . . Summary at http://www.energybulletin.net/4673.html; for full report, see http://www.projectcensored.org/newsflash/the_hirsch_report.pdf.

p. 55 *the cookery writer Elisabeth Luard* . . . *European Peasant Cookery*, Elisabeth Luard (Bantam 1986).

p. 58 *Patrick told me of his struggle* . . . The story of Patrick's carrots was originally published in the *Guardian*, 'Sainsbury's giant carrot washer, and the rejected royal roots', June 26, 2007.

p. 62 *The futures and options markets* . . . A futures contract is an agreement to make or take delivery of a given commodity at a set place at a specified time in the future at the price agreed at the time of trade. Physical delivery seldom takes place. Only one bushel of soya beans for example is actually produced for every thirty-one that are traded (Food, Inc, Vorley). Buyers and sellers can offset their obligation by taking another futures position that is the opposite, that is by hedging against changes in price and transferring the risk to a speculator.

p. 63 *growth in speculative trading in grains* . . . The volume of US futures traded in commodities for example went from 13.6 million lots to 159 million lots between 1970 and 1985; 'Grain crossing borders', *The Food System: A Guide*, Geoff Tansey and Tony Worsley (Earthscan, 1995).

p. 64 *world reserve stocks of grains have been reduced* . . . Lester Brown, as above.

p. 64 *President Bush, in a speech* . . . 'President Discusses Biodiesel and Alternative Fuel Sources', The White House, news release, May 16, 2005.

p. 66 *the Department for Environment, Food and Rural Affairs slipped* out ... 'Food Security and the UK: An Evidence and Analysis Paper', Food Chain Analysis Group, DEFRA, December 2006.

p. 66 *The Ministry of Defence does its own thinking ahead* ... The DCDC Global Strategic Trends Programme, 2007–2036, DCDC, December, 2006.

Chapter 3: Milk

The Milk Development Council and the National Farmers' Union provided much of the statistical analysis and background information on the dairy industry in this chapter. I am particularly grateful to their expert economics departments. Kemble Farms and Richard Joyce gave up valuable time to make me feel welcome on their dairy farms, for which many thanks. Sir Don Curry has shared his extensive knowledge with me in the course of several meetings. Professor Tim Lang pointed me in the right direction on subsidies and health.

Joyce d'Silva of Compassion in World Farming explained the welfare issues to me. Conversations with film-maker Molly Dineen, whose documentary *The Lie of the Land* was broadcast on Channel 4 in May 2007, kept me going.

Supermarket milk buyers and experts from the leading processing companies kindly spoke to me about market shares and prices in the dairy chain but preferred to remain unidentified.

The work on EU subsidies was first published in the *Guardian* at the end of 2005, and built on research under Freedom of Information legislation originally carried out by my colleagues there, David Hencke and Rob Evans. Jack Thurston of farmsubsidy.org and officials at the Rural Payments Agency gave many hours of their time to explain the mechanisms and history of subsidies to me. Susannah Osborne conducted additional research.

David Thomas kindly made his research on mineral contents of food available. Thanks too to officials at the Food Standards Agency for background briefing on dairy products.

p. 68 *There were 35,000 dairy farmers in the UK* ... This and other statistics are drawn from 'Dairy Statistics: An Insider's Guide', Milk Development Council, 2006.

p. 74 *The price we pay for fresh milk in the shops has risen* ... It went from just over 44p per litre in 2002 to just over 53p in 2007. The supermarkets' margin on fresh milk increased more than five-fold in the last decade from about 3p a litre a decade ago to about 16p a litre in 2007. During that decade the share of the price we pay for milk that went to the processors, the companies that collect, pasteurize and bottle milk, stayed about the same, but the farmers' share kept going down. It actually fell by more than 6p a litre. It was 24.5p per litre ten years ago and had fallen to 18p per litre in 2007. Statistics on prices and margins from National Farmers' Union.

p. 74 *The supermarkets, Tesco, Asda, Sainsbury's, Waitrose and M&S, have each reduced the number of suppliers they use to just one or two companies* ... In 2007 Tesco was getting about 60 per cent of its milk from Wiseman, and 40 per cent from Arla. Sainsbury's was supplied half by Arla and half by Dairy Crest, and Dairy Crest was supplying all of Waitrose and all of M&S milk. Personal communication, various industry sources.

p. 75 *Such concentration of market power carries its dangers, as Adam Smith* ... *The Wealth of Nations*, Adam Smith, Book I, Chapter X.

p. 75 *The Office of Fair Trading accused* ... 'OFT Welcomes Early Resolution Agreements and Agrees Over £116m penalties', OFT Press Release December 7, 2007; OFT clarification, press release, December 13, 2007.

p. 75 *the farmers' unions said farmers had seen little benefit* ... personal communication, Richard MacDonald, NFU.

p. 77 *Thousands of WI members* ... 'The Great Milk Debate', the WI's campaign on milk prices, featured 100 debates and actions around the country in April/May 2007, www.thewi.org.uk/standard.aspx?id=10883.

p. 77 *the supermarkets agreed to increase the price they paid* ... 'Tesco to pay dairy farmers more', BBC News April 3, 2007; Sainsbury's

Justin King pledges further support for UK dairy farmers, talkingretail.com, April 26, 2007.

p. 82 *Across all OECD countries in the year 2000, subsidies accounted for* ... Food, Inc, Vorley, as above.

p. 83 *The global market in dairy processing* ... Revenues and market shares from Rabobank International 2006 for the Danish Dairy Board.

p. 83 *The turnover of the top twenty global dairy corporations* ... Food, Inc, Vorley, as above.

pp. 83–4 *who exactly was getting the money from the CAP* ... 'Multinationals, Not Farmers, Reap Biggest Rewards in Britain's share of CAP Payouts', Felicity Lawrence, *Guardian*, December 8, 2005. Figures based on information from RPA on subsidies paid 2003–4. www.farmsubsidy.org later published more comprehensive lists and links to other European researchers looking at payments in their countries.

pp. 86–7 *Describing the now reformed EU sugar regime, an Oxfam report* ... 'Dumping on the World, How EU sugar policies hurt poor countries', Oxfam Briefing Paper No 61, Kevin Watkins, March 2004.

p. 87 *Much of dairy cow feed in the UK now depends* ... 1.8 million tonnes of soya were imported for animal feed from the Americas in 2005, and about 800,000 tonnes of corn gluten was imported for feed from the US in 2005. Together with imported soya, these materials made up about 20 per cent of the animal feed used by British farmers. 'GM material in animal feed', Food Standards Agency, May 15, 2006.

p. 88 *companies advertising 'zero grazing' for dairy herds* ... www.zeroagri.co.uk/.

p. 88 *None of this is much fun for the cow* ... *Limping Towards Eden,* John Webster (Blackwell Publishing, 2005); personal communication, CIWF.

p. 89 *intensively produced milk appears to be nutritionally depleted* ... 'The Mineral Depletion of Foods Available to Us as a Nation (1940–2002)', David Thomas, *Nutrition and Health,* vol. 19 (2007), pp. 21–55.

p. 90 *other studies that have found a marked difference in levels of the omega-3 essential fatty acids* ... 'Comparing the Fatty Acid Composition of Organic and Conventional Milk', K Ellis *et al, Journal of Dairy Science 89:1938–1950,* American Dairy Science Association, 2006.

p. 92 *Nestlé's head of nutrition summed up the trend in 2003* ... 'Fancy that, healthy ketchup', *The Economist,* December 13, 2003, quoted in Food Ethics Council 'Getting Personal' report 2005, www.foodethicscouncil.org.

p. 94 *Thanks to a detailed submission by Danone's advertising agency* ... 'Danone Actimel, From Hampstead to Hartlepool: Turning Live Bacteria into Popular Culture', IPA submission 2006, Rebecca Moody, RKCR Y&R.

p. 95 Details from label on product bought at Sainsbury's, February 2008, £1.37 for 4 pots of 100g each. 'Suitable for the family, from aged 3 upwards'. The label elaborates as follows: 'What you may not realize is that the majority of the bad bacteria that get into your system enter through your gut. That's why an essential part of your body's natural defences is the billions of good bacteria that naturally exist there! Actimel, with its unique bacteria L. casei Imunitass can help top up these good bacteria, which makes life tougher for bad bacteria. Better still Actimel can benefit everyone, mums and dads, grans and granddads, big and little kids from the age of three. So take Actimel every day★ and help support your body's natural defences. (★As part of a balanced diet.)'

p. 96 *When I first looked at their labels* ... 'Should We Swallow This?' Felicity Lawrence, *Guardian,* February 8, 2006.

p. 96 *Which? looked at a range of probiotics in 2006* ... 'Probiotics', *Which?,* January 5, 2006.

p. 96 *depended on the refined carbohydrates that feed bad gut flora* ... 'Do We Really Need a Daily Dose of Bacteria?' The Food Commission, August 25, 2006, www.foodcomm.org.uk/.

p. 96 *The independent Drug and Therapeutics Bulletin* ... *Drug and Therapeutics Bulletin* vol. 42 (2004), pp. 85–88; *Drug and Therapeutics Bulletin* vol. 43 (2005), pp. 6–8; 'Probiotics', *Which?* January 5, 2006.

p. 96 *It commissioned a technical report* ... Final Technical Report for

FSA Project G01022, 'An Evaluation of Probiotic Effects in the Human Gut: Microbial Aspects', G. R. Gibson *et al,* 2005.

p. 97 *When I asked what advice it would give* . . . personal communications, FSA, August 16, 2007, February 12, 2008.

p. 98 *Proposals to prevent food companies selling products with health claims unless they have first proved them* . . . personal communications, Sue Davies; *Which?*, February 2008; FSA, February 2008.

Chapter 4: Pigs

Thanks to Digby Scott, editor of *Pig World*, and the National Pig Association, who between them have supplied much of the background information on market shares and the state of pig farming.

Miles Hubbard, of Unite the union, and Thelma Paines helped me on trips to Thetford. Many others from Unite (or the T&G union as it used to be called) have dedicated hours to supporting migrant food and agricultural workers and have shared their experiences and knowledge with me. Don Pollard is my original hero in this work. Thanks too to Jack Dromey, Pauline Doyle, and to two late and much missed campaigners Mick Cashman and Nuno Guerreiro.

Mark Boleat and the Association of Labour Providers are a constant source of help. A special thanks too to 'Dan' who keeps me informed about gangmasters.

Professor John Salt of University College London generously gave me an invaluable tutorial on migration statistics at the beginning of my research. Many thanks also to academic experts Ben Rogaly of Sussex University and Bridget Anderson of Compas, Oxford University. Paul Farrelly and Jon Cruddas, MPs, have offered insights in to the impact of migration in their constituencies.

Duncan Swift and Grant Thornton have helped with economic background.

Marek Kryda was a fascinating and tireless guide on my trip to Poland.

The story of the Polish workers in Devon was originally published in the *Guardian* in 2005, and I am grateful to the editors and legal department for support with it. My piece on Polish agriculture at the time of EU accession appeared in the paper in 2004.

p. 103 *Danish Crown and its subsidiaries* . . . Subsidy figures from farmsubsidy.org and its international partners.

p. 103 *Half of new jobs created since 1997* . . . 'Half of New Jobs Go to Migrants', BBC News, October 30, 2007.

p. 104 *A year later, there had been hours of violent rioting* . . . BBC News, July 29, 2005.

p. 105 *Large numbers of Portuguese workers* . . . *the numbers, like all migration statistics, were disputed* . . . Interview with Thelma Paines, May 2, 2007. Thelma gave me an estimate of the number of migrants of all nationalities absorbed into Thetford as up to 10,000, and this was the figure I used in an article in the *Guardian* on September 24, 2007. *Guardian* columnist Ian Jack was given different numbers later, of about 6,000 Portuguese and Eastern Europeans, 'How many migrants does it take to change a Norfolk Town', *Guardian*, September 29, 2007. Most migration statistics are necessarily guesstimates as I should have made clear, since many migrants are undocumented. Drs Becky Taylor and Ben Rogaly conducted research in 2003/4 for Norfolk County Council which found data suggested 6,000 Portuguese migrants were living in Thetford and nearby Swaffham.

p. 109 *Tulip* . . . *said in a statement* . . . May 10, 2007.

p. 113 *I was called late one night to visit a group of Poles* . . . 'Polish Workers Lost in a Strange Land', Felicity Lawrence, the *Guardian*, January 11, 2005.

p. 119 *The GLA's first inspection, carried out in 2007, was on* . . . *Bomfords* . . . GLA Press Release, 'Operation Scallion', March 7, 2007; 'Firm Closed as Licence Revoked', BBC News, March 8, 2007.

p. 120 *common knowledge* . . . *that Bomfords offered its gangmasters hourly rates* . . . 'Bomfords knowingly paying below minimum wage, says ALP', *Farmers Weekly*, March 20, 2007.

p. 121 *the new pack house burned down one night* . . . 'Firefighter Dies

Tackling Blaze', BBC News, November 3, 2007; 'Bodies found in Fire Crew Search', BBC News, November 6, 2007.

p. 122 *Dawn Meats ... told workers ... that most of them would have to accept a pay cut ...* 'Bedford Meat Firm Urged: Don't Rat on Your Workers', T&G News release, April 13, 2007.

p. 123 *at a microeconomic level, migration has clearly affected ...* 'Immigration and its Effect', Martin Weale and Rebecca Riley, *National Institute Economic Review*, October 2006.

p. 123 *sharp increase in ... unemployment accounted for by those under twenty-four ...* Professor David Blanchflower in Bernard Corry Memorial lecture, May 2007.

p.125 *The British Brands group submission ...* Competition Commission Inquiry, British Brands Group letter to inquiry, March 16, 2007. The BB group pointed out that two thirds of manufacturers and processors said that their gross margins had decreased in the last five years, with operating margins showing a decline of 17 per cent in two years to 2005 and the trend for profits continued downwards. It added that the current state of the market 'has all the hallmarks of the *Titanic* tragedy where everything was serene above decks while the bridge failed to spot an iceberg, 90 per cent of which was submerged'.

p. 127 *For most Poles, joining the EU marked ...* For a brilliant account of recent Polish history see Norman Davies' *Heart of Europe: The Past in Poland's Present* (OUP, 2001).

p. 130 *The EU plans for agricultural reform assumed ...* 'Poles fear the yoke of agri-giants', Felicity Lawrence, *Guardian,* April 29, 2004.

p. 132 *Smithfield Foods is the largest and most profitable pork processor in the world ...* Statistics from Smithfield Foods' annual report, 2006.

p. 132 *Its Polish acquisitions were a bargain ... Smithfield bought 70 per cent of ... Animex ...* 'Poles Fear Yoke of Agri-Giants', *Guardian,* April 29, 2004 as above; 'Polish Farmers Raise a Stink over US Agribusiness Giant', *Washington Post*, February 2, 2004; 'US Pig Farmer Raises Almighty Stink with Invasion of Poland Countryside', *Independent*, November 18, 2003; 'US Pork Producer Hogtied in Polish Venture', *Washington Post*, July 3, 2000.

p. 133 *Denmark which has only 5.4 million humans raises 24 million pigs a year, which produce enough slurry* ... 'Denmark's Pigs: Too Many, Too Smelly', *The Economist*, August 9, 2003.

p. 135 *The company has however been at the centre of bitter disputes* ... Human Rights Watch 2005, www.hrw.org/reports/2005/usa0105/6.htm; Union of Food and Commercial Workers Fact sheet: Smithfield Foods, September 2002; BBC *Food Programme*, 27 August, 2006.

p. 135 *Smithfield won notoriety* ... *largest ever environmental fines* ... EPA Environmental News, August 8, 1997 – 314.

p. 136 *In a 400-page ruling* ... *one US judge* ... National Labour Relations Board Division of Judges, before John H. West, Administrative Law Judge, Smithfield Packing Co, Tar Heel Division and United Food and Commercial Workers Union, Decision, December 5, 2000. A Court of Appeal in May 2006 upheld previous judgments.

p. 138 *Cargill began legal proceedings against the Polish government* ... 'Cargill Sues Poland', *The Times*, January 7, 2004.

Chapter 5: Sugar

Aubrey Sheiham, Emeritus Professor of Dental Public Health at University College, London, has shared his lifetime of insights and experience on sugar with unfailing generosity. I am also grateful to curator Tom Wareham and staff at the Museum of Docklands, London, for sharing their encyclopaedic knowledge of the sugar trade and slavery with me. The museum's new galleries on the subject are a moving exposition of the way the history of sugar still affects our lives. The classic study of the politics of sugar through the ages is Sidney Mintz's *Sweetness and Power: the Place of Sugar in Modern History*, (Penguin, 1985). Jane Landon of the National Heart Forum gave me detailed briefing papers on modern sugar production and supply. Special thanks to all the researchers at East Malling.

p. 141 *'Sugar is as dangerous as tobacco [and] should be classified as a hard drug . . .'* 'No Sweet Surrender', Imre Loefler, *BMJ*, vol. 330, no. 853 (9 April, 2005).

p. 141 *A whole science has grown up* . . . see Julie Mennella, as above.

p. 143 *the Thai government introduced a proposal* . . . 'EU and US Block Thailand's Proposal to Reduce Sugar in Baby Foods', International Baby Food Action Network, November 3, 2006.

p. 151 *In Britain we consume about 2.25 million tonnes of sugar a year* . . . www.defra.gov.uk/farm/crops/sugar/index.htm.

p. 152 *Production of sucrose in the UK* . . . Sugar market shares, UK and global, Food, Inc: 'Corporate Concentrations from farm to consumer', Bill Vorley, UK Food Group, 2003.

p. 153 *In 2001 Cargill also acquired the French sweetener and starch processing company* . . . 'Cargill Incorporated and Cerestar SA: A report on the Merger', Competition Commission, May 2002.

p. 154 *The largest recipient of CAP payments* . . . 'Multinationals, Not Farmers, Reap Biggest Rewards in Britain's share of CAP Payouts', Felicity Lawrence, *Guardian*, December 8, 2005; farmsubsidy.org as above.

p. 155 *Sugar refiners and growers in the US have benefited to the tune of $2 billion a year* . . . US Congress General Accounting Office, quoted in 'Sweet deals: Big Sugar fights threats from free trade and a global drive to limit consumption', *Financial Times*, February 27, 2004.

p. 156 *The EU sugar regime was finally reformed in 2005* . . . *Guardian*, November 26, 2005.

p. 157 *Boys and girls aged four to fourteen* . . . National Diet and Nutrition Survey, 1995, 2000 and 2004; National Heart Forum Briefing Paper on sugar production and supply.

p. 158 *British children are the gluttons of Europe in this* . . . Datamonitor press release, January 26, 2007.

p. 158 *The managing director of Tate & Lyle, Clive Rutherford, had already articulated* . . . Address to ISO November 1997, quoted in Sustain report 'Sweet and Sour', 2000.

p. 158 *Big sugar was having none of it* . . . 'US Government Rejects WHO's Attempts to Improve Diet', *BMJ*, vol. 328, no. 185 (2004);

'Sugar Industry Threatens to Scupper WHO', Sarah Boseley, *Guardian*, April 21, 2003.

p. 160 *British teenagers take in nearly half their sugars each day* ... National Diet and Nutrition Survey; National Heart Forum Briefing paper.

p. 160 *Researchers at the Boston children's hospital* ... 'Relationship between Consumption of Sugar-Sweetened Drinks and Childhood Obesity', Ludwig D *et al*, *Lancet*, vol. 357, issue 9255 (February 17, 2001), pp. 505–508.

p. 160 *We have no physiological need for refined sugar* ... *Seeds of Change*, Henry Hobhouse (Shoemaker and Hoard, 2005).

p. 161 *Stimulant drinks such as tea, coffee and colas or caffeinated sports energy drinks help lift the blood sugar* ... For an excellent guide to the effect of sugars and refined carbohydrates on health and behaviour see Dr Alex Richardson's *They are What You Feed Them* (Harper Thorsons, 2006).

p. 161 *Intriguing evidence is also beginning to emerge* ... C. Colantuoni *et al*, 'Evidence That Intermittent, Excessive Sugar Intake Causes Endogenous Opioid Dependence', *Obesity Research*, vol. 10 (2002), pp. 478–488.

p. 161 *Others have linked sugar consumption to* ... A. N. Westover *et al*, 'A cross-national relationship between sugar consumption and major depression', *Depression and Anxiety*, vol. 16, issue 3 (2002), pp. 118–120; L. Lien *et al*, 'Consumption of Soft drinks and Hyperactivity, Mental Distress and Conduct Problems among Adolescents', *American Journal of Public Health*, vol. 96, issue 10, (October 2006), pp. 1815–20.

p. 161 *they give you a feeling of fullness* ... personal communications, Professor Aubrey Sheiham.

p. 162 *This was vividly illustrated by a survey of pre-school children in 1997* ... S. Gibson 'Non-milk extrinsic sugars in the diets of pre-school children, association with intakes of micronutrients, energy and fat and NSP', *British Journal of Nutrition*, vol. 78 (1997), pp. 367–378, quoted in Sustain report on 'Sugar'.

p. 163 *About 800,000 tonnes of artificial sweeteners were used around the world in 2007* ... Leatherhead Food International Sweeteners Trends and Forecasts 1998–2007.

p. 163 *A British Liberal Democrat MP* ... Adjournment Debate, House of Commons, December 14, 2005, Hansard Column 491WH and following, http://www.publications.parliament.uk/pa/cm200506/cmhansrd/vo051214/halltext/51214h05.htm; 'Safety of artificial sweetener called into question by MP', Felicity Lawrence, *Guardian*, December 15, 2005.

p. 166 *When its expert scientists gathered at a press conference in Rome* ... http://www.flyonthewall.com/FlyBroadcast/efsa.eu.int/Aspartame PressConference/.

p. 166 *Dr Herman Koëter adopted an unusual opening gambit* ... 'Food safety authority says aspartame not linked to cancer', Felicity Lawrence, guardian.co.uk, May 15, 2006.

p. 170 ... *commissioned a huge review of studies* ... B. A. Magnuson et al, 'Aspartame: A Safety Evaluation Based on Current Use Levels, Regulations, and Toxicological and Epidemiological Studies', *Critical Reviews in Toxicology*, vol. 37, no. 8, pp. 629–727.

p. 170 *In the early 1900s Robert McCarrison* ... See McCarrison Society website, www.mccarrisonsociety.org.uk/, for Cantor Lectures by Robert McCarrison.

p. 172 *As Sidney Mintz describes* ... *Sweetness and Power: The Place of Sugar in Modern History*, Sidney Mintz (Penguin, 1985).

p. 174 *In 1848 the philospher and political economist John Stuart Mill wrote* ... *Principles of Political Economy 1848*, Book 3, Chapter 25, John Stuart Mill (Longman edition).

p. 176 *the quayside warehouses that all that nineteenth-century sugar passed through* ... Now home to the Museum in Docklands, www.museumindocklands.org.uk/. 'London, Sugar and Slavery' is a new permanent exhibition on the trade.

p. 177 *In his report, 'The Sweetening of the World's Diet'* ... Barry Popkin et al, *Obesity Research*, vol. 11, no. 11 (November 2003) p. 1325ff.

Chapter 6: Fish and Tomatoes

There are two books that are essential reading for anyone interested in the future of fish: Professor Callum Roberts, leading expert in marine conservation, has written *The Unnatural History of the Sea* (Gaia Thinking, 2007), which manages to be comprehensive, erudite and wonderfully readable at the same time. Charles Clover's *The End of the Line* (Ebury Press, 2004), a powerful and equally readable polemic on the state of fish stocks, is being made into a documentary film.

For explaining the role of essential fatty acids in health over an extended period, I owe a debt to Professor Michael Crawford. Jo Hibbeln at the National Institute on Alcohol Abuse and Alcoholism in Bethesda was an equally patient instructor. Alex Richardson, Bernard Gesch and Professor John Stein have all made themselves endlessly available to my inquiries.

I am very grateful to ActionAid, which facilitated my trip to Senegal, and in particular to Hannah Crabtree in London, and Moussa Faye and Papa Gora Ndiaye in Dakar.

Médecins sans Frontières made possible my visit to find out about migrants in Calabria, and I am grateful to all the team there who were working in difficult circumstances but made it so memorable. I was accompanied for the *Guardian* by the brilliant photographer Christian Sinibaldi whose pictures of the workers and conditions can be seen at www.christiansinibaldi.com/.

p. 180 *Wild seafood will be gone in fifty years* . . . 'Impacts of Biodiversity Loss on Ocean Ecosystem Services', Boris Worm *et al*, *Science*, vol. 314 (3 November, 2006).

p. 181 *Professor Callum Roberts* . . . *The Unnatural History of the Sea: The Past and Future of Humanity and Fishing*, Professor Callum Roberts (Gaia Thinking, 2007).

p. 181 *launch a campaign to turn 40 per cent of the world's seas into marine reserves* . . . Greenpeace Roadmap to Recovery, www.greenpeace. org/international/campaigns/oceans/marine-reserves/roadmap-to-recovery.

p. 182 *a certification scheme for sustainable fish* ... Marine Stewardship Council, www.msc.org/.

p. 183 *as Charles Clover points out* ... *The End of the Line: How Overfishing is Changing the World and What We Eat*, Charles Clover (Ebury Press, 2004).

p. 187 *his beautifully written study* ... *The Unnatural History of the Sea*, as above.

p. 187 *As much as a third of tuna* ... *is now flushed with carbon monoxide* ... Reading Scientific Services Ltd briefing http://www.rssl.com/OurServices/FoodENews/Newsletter.aspx?ENewsletterID=120#3; also S. Otwell, http://oregonstate.edu/~templee/additives_in_aquaculture.html; 'Tuna's Red Glare', *New York Times*, October 5, 2004, http://www.ewg.org/node/16724.

p. 188 *the largely unregulated and previously unknown fleet of Spanish ships* ... 'A preliminary Investigation on Shelf Edge and Deepwater Fixed Net fisheries to the West and North of Great Britain, Ireland around Rockall and Hatton Bank', Nils Roar Hareide *et al*, Irish Sea Fisheries Board, Fiskeridirektoratet and others, October 2005.

p. 189 *The skippers of almost the whole of Whitby's fishing fleet* ... Martin Wainwright, *Guardian*, December 2, 2005.

p. 189 *as many questions are raised by fish farming* ... For an authoritative brief summary of the issues including fish farming, see Sustain's report 'Like Shooting Fish in a Barrel: the Collapse of World Fisheries in the 21st century and What We Can Do to Prevent it from Happening', Benjamin Wielgosz and Jeanette Longfield, August 2005, Sustain, www.sustainweb.org.

p. 191 *fish farms certified as organic* ... See Soil Association Fish Farming and Organic Standards Information Sheet, November 11, 2005, www.soilassociation.org/. For the debate over whether salmon farming should be classified as organic at all, see 'Supermarkets Accused over Organic Foods', *Guardian*, October 5, 2006.

p. 192 *vegetarian fish do not grow so well* ... personal communication, Professor Michael Crawford.

p. 192 *The UK government's Scientific Advisory Committee on Nutrition* recommends ... 'Advice on fish consumption: benefits and risks', SACN, Committee on Toxicity, 2004.

p. 193 *New research however has suggested that ... even above these intakes of fish there is a greater health benefit to foetal brain development ...* 'Maternal Seafood Consumption in Pregnancy and Neurodevelopmental Outcomes in Childhood' (Avon Longitudinal Study of Parents and Children): an observational cohort study, Hibbeln *et al*, *Lancet*, vol. 369 (2007), pp. 578–85.

p. 195 *Dr Alex Richardson had conducted clinical trials ...* For a full list of scientific papers by Richardson and others on food and behaviour, and learning disabilities such as dyspraxia and dyslexia, see the charitable Food and Behaviour website that Dr Richardson runs, www.fabresearch.org/.

p. 196 *a randomized trial in the maximum-security Aylesbury prison ...* 'Influence of supplementary vitamins, minerals and essential fatty acids on the antisocial behaviour of young adult prisoners', Gesch *et al*, *British Journal of Psychiatry*, vol. 181 (2002), pp. 22–8.

p. 200 *scientists are finally catching up with several millennia of cultural wisdom ...* 'Cultural Symbolism of Fish and the Psychotropic Properties of Omega-3 Fatty Acids', L. C. Reis, J. R. Hibbeln, *Prostaglandins, Leukotrienes & Essential Fatty Acids* (2006).

p. 200 *Hibbeln's most recent study ...* For a full list of Hibbeln's scientific papers and references, see www.fabresearch.org/.

p. 203 *As humans we eat two kinds of essential fatty acids ...* The position of the first double bond in the carbon chain determines to which family of unsaturated fatty acids the molecule belongs. If the first double bond is at the third carbon from the end of the chain, it is an omega-3 fatty acid; if the first double bond is six carbons from the end it is an omega-6 fatty acid.

EPA is eicosapentanoic acid (from the Greek for 20 and 5, having 20 carbons and 5 double bonds) and DHA is docosahexaenoic acid (from the Greek for 22 and 6, having 22 carbons and six double bonds).

p. 205 *Over 80 per cent of the fish we now eat ...* Seafish, www. seafish.org.

p. 206 *as the African delegation was preparing to go to the ministerial summit of the WTO* . . . The WTO ministerial summit Moussa Faye was about to attend ended in stalemate. Meanwhile the WTO had ruled that the preferential tariffs Europe granted its old colonies would be illegal, unless they were made reciprocal by the end of 2007. So a series of economic partnership agreements between some of the world's least developed countries and the EU have been pushed ahead, under which African states were required to implement yet more liberalization of their markets as the price of keeping their favoured access to Europe.

p. 207 *But in the 1970s American interests shifted* . . . For a detailed account of the grain trade through this period see *Merchants of Grain*, Dan Morgan (Backinprint.com, 2000) as above.

p. 208 *Senegal had become a net food-importing country* . . . Statistics on Senegal from World Bank, Senegal data at a glance, http://web.worldbank.org/WBSITE/EXTERNAL/COUNTRIES/AFRICAEXT/SENEGALEXTN/; and 'Debt and Destruction in Senegal: A study of twenty years of IMF and World Bank policies', Demba Moussa Dembele, World Development Movement, November 2003.

p. 210 *Before liberalization, tomato production had thrived* . . . 'Liberalization and Interactions with the Market', Meenakshi Raman, *International Journal of Rural Studies*, vol. 14, no. 1 (April 2007).

p. 210 *There is not much free trade about EU tomato production* . . . 'Domestic Support and Border Measures for Processed Agricultural Products', B. Rickard and D. Sumner, University of California, *American Journal of Agricultural Economics* (April 2007).

p. 211 *Maps of fish densities off West Africa* . . . 'Trends in Fish Biomass off NorthWest Africa 1960–2000', Villy Christensen, Fisheries Centre, University of British Columbia. The crisis in fishing here is reflected in the figures for fish stocks globally. The UN's Food and Agriculture Organization has calculated that over half of the world's commercial fish species are now fully exploited. Nearly a fifth are overexploited and in trouble, 8 per cent are depleted.

'Review of the State of the World Marine Fishery Resources,' FAO, Rome, 2005, p. 12.

p. 213 *The Environmental Justice Foundation, together with Greenpeace, tracked vessels fishing illegally off West Africa* ... 'Pirate Fish on Your Plate: Tracking Illegally Caught Fish from West Africa to the European market', EJF, 2007.

p. 218 *Médecins sans Frontières* ... *became so concerned* ... 'Migrants Employed in Agriculture in Southern Italy Work and Live in Deprivation', MSF, January 30, 2007.

Chapter 7: Fats

Susannah Osborne carried out much of the original research for this chapter, and both she and I have been helped by several experts in fat processing and health who have been generous with their knowledge. Some wish to remain anonymous. Ray Cook explained many of the technical aspects and was kind enough to read parts of the text – any mistakes that remain are mine. Kurt Berger shared his technical expertise and gave a fascinating overview of the fats industry acquired over a lifetime of experience. Craig Sams was the first to point out the connections between US policy and fat consumption to me and offered many other insights. Tim Lobstein pointed me in the right directions on health. Jane Landon provided briefing materials on fats and health. Many thanks too to Trevor Gorin in the Unilever press office for all his cheerful help with my questions. Charles Wilson's encyclopaedic *History of Unilever* was published by Cassell in 1954.

p. 222 *The largest sources of fat in our diets, contributing* ... 'National Diet and Nutrition Survey, Adults aged 19–64', vol. 2, 2003, Chapter 5: Fat and Fatty acid intake.

p. 223 *In the US, soya oil accounted for only 0.02 per cent of all calories available in 1909, but by 2000* ... 'Increasing homicide rates and linoleic acid consumption among five Western countries, 1961–2000', J. R. Hibbeln *et al*, *Lipids*, vol. 39, pp. 1207–1213.

p. 223 *cardiovascular disease is still the UK's largest cause* ... Statistics on heart and circulatory diseases from British Heart Foundation Heart Stats, http://www.heartstats.org/.

p. 223 *Those risk factors are widely accepted to be* ... See British Heart Foundation website, http://www.bhf.org.uk/keeping_your_heart_ healthy/preventing_heart_disease.

p. 224 *the WHO 916 report* ... 'Diet, Nutrition and the Prevention of Chronic Diseases', Report of the joint WHO/FAO expert consultation,WHO Technical Report Series, No. 916, 2003.

p. 224 *in the 1950s, cholesterol in the diet was said to be part of the problem* ... For a detailed account of early misconceptions about diet and heart disease and the politics of the issue, see *The Rise and Fall of Modern Medicine*, James Le Fanu (Little Brown, 1999).

p. 226 *Then in 1993 Professor Walter Willett* ... 'Intake of trans fatty acids and risk of coronary heart disease among women', W. C. Willett *et al, Lancet,* vol. 341 (1993), pp. 581–585; see also Interview Walter Willett, 'Frontline Diet Wars', Public Broadcasting Service, January 9, 2004.

p. 226 *the Harvard Nurses Study* ... The Nurses' Health Study, www. channing.harvard.edu/nhs/.

p. 227 *Margarine was originally developed* ... For histories of margarine, and legislation on margarines, see the National Association of Margarine Manufacturers' website www.margarine.org.uk/ and *Margarine, an Economic, Social and Scientific History, 1869–1969,* J. H. van Stuyvenberg (Liverpool University Press, 1969).

p. 228 *It was 1906 before vegetable oils were first substituted* ... *Time,* September 8, 1924.

p. 230 *Lever Brothers had come to an agreement* ... Unilever gives a detailed history of the origins of its company on its website. It also commissioned the two-volume history from the Cambridge historian Charles Wilson which was published by Cassell in 1954.

p. 231 *'Quaint was Mr. Lever's presentation to King Leopold II ...' Time,* August 6, 1928.

p. 233 *Unilever found itself with major interests on both sides* ... For a fascinating and detailed account see Ben Wubs, *International Business and National War Interests: Unilever Between Reich and Empire,*

1939–45' (Routledge, to be published June 2008), which explores the tensions during wartime between the interests of international business and those of national states and Wub's paper 'Decartelisation and Deconcentration Policy in Germany: A Post-War Threat to Unilever's Interests 1945–1950' is available at www.ehs.org.uk/conference 2004. See also Neil Forbes, *Multinational Enterprise, 'Corporate Responsibility' and the Nazi Dictatorship: The Case of Unilever and Germany in the 1930s*, Cambridge European History, 2007, 16: 149–167.

p. 233 *the US is the largest producer of oils and fats* . . . For statistics, see USDA and Fediol websites.

p. 234 *Flora was launched* . . . Unilever website.

p. 234 *fats and spreads have depended on heavy spending on advertizing* . . . 'Mintel Yellow Fats Market'; Leatherhead Functional Foods report.

p. 235 *The names dominating the world markets in refining and primary processing will be familiar* . . . Food, Inc, Vorley as above.

p. 235 *Tropical fats have followed the same trajectory* . . . personal communication, Kurt Berger, who is also principal contributor on palm oil to the *Cambridge World History of Food*. Statistics on palm consumption from Fediol, 2005 Annual Statistics.

p. 238 *a congressional hearing into tropical fats* . . . US 100th Congress, June 21, 1988 and following, Subcommittee on Health and Environment Hearing H R 2148.

p. 238 *adverts for a new 'Whole Earth Superspread'* . . . *Food Magazine*, 1993, personal communication Craig Sams.

p. 240 *I put the figures and this account . . . to Unilever* . . . personal communication, Anne Heughan, Unilever, January 19, 2006.

p. 241 *now produces Flora by interesterificaiton* . . . personal communication, Jacqui Morrell, dietician, consultant to Unilever, meeting February 23, 2006 at Cohn and Wolfe PR.

p. 243 *Unilever's highly expert research laboratories* . . . For example, 'Interesterification of fats in margarine: effect on blood lipids, blood enzymes, and hemostasis parameters', G. W. Meijer *et al*, European Journal of Clinical Nutrition, vol 51, no. 8 (August 1997), pp. 527–534.

p. 243 A *recent study, however, has suggested that interesterified fats* ...
K. Sundram *et al*, 'Stearic acid-rich interesterified fat and trans-rich
fat raise the LDL/HDL ratio and plasma glucose relative to palm
olein in humans', *Nutrition and Metabolism*, vol. 4, issue 3, (2007).

p. 245 *as refining techniques developed* ... I am grateful to Ray Cook and
technical experts at Aarhus for descriptions of modern refining and
its recent history. See also Fediol (The EU Oil and Proteinmeal
Industry) website.

p. 246 *the European Commission did commission a study of the metabolism
of trans fatty acids formed this way* ... 'Dietary trans alpha-linolenic
acid from deodorised rapeseed oil and plasma lipids and lipoproteins in healthy men: the TransLinE Study', Vermunt *et al*,
British Journal of Nutrition, vol. 85, issue 3, (2001).

p. 247 *The latest advance is the addition of* ... *plant sterols* ... For an
account of the regulatory process of approval for phytosterols see
Food Politics, Marion Nestle (University of California Press, 2002).

p. 247 *The two have since fought a long legal dispute, which was only settled
at the end of 2007* ... Raisio plc, Press Release, December 21, 2007.

p. 248 *The UK government's expert committee on novel foods also concluded*
... The Advisory Committee on Novel Foods and Processes, Fact
Sheet 6, 'Foods with Added Plant Sterols', February 2002, revised
April 2005.

p. 249 *'It cannot be said that Unilever developed this product* ...' 'Obesity:
Re-Shaping the Food Industry', JPMorgan, Global Equity
Research, January 24, 2006.

p. 251 *You can detect a note of alarm* ... Advisory Committee on Novel
Foods and Processes, 'Plant Sterols and Sterol Esters, Other
Applications', 71986, for example.

p. 251 *Production of plant sterols has been ramped up* ... 'Functional
Ingredients', *Nutrition Business Journal* (April 2005); www.function
alingredientsmag.com.

Chapter 8: Soya

I am grateful to Greenpeace for facilitating my trip to the Amazon in 2006. Many thanks to John Sauven in London and all the team in Brazil, without whom I could not have written this chapter. The awe-inspiringly polyglot Natalia Truchi translated from several languages for me, on occasion late into the night. The staff of Saude e Alegria gave additional support and helped on my trip into the rainforest. Much of the information on soya production, climate change, and rainforest destruction comes from the Greenpeace report 'Eating Up the Amazon' (April 2006) and I am grateful to them for allowing me to use it here.

Additional research for this chapter, in particular on the history of soya production and consumption, and trade statistics, was carried out by Susannah Osborne.

Sue Dibb generously shared her expert knowledge of the health aspects of soya consumption. The story of soya proteins originally appeared in the *Guardian* on 25 July 2006.

p. 254 *The Chinese regarded the mature soya bean itself* . . . 'Fermentations and Food Science', vol. 6, Huang Hsing-Tsung, *Science and Civilisation in China*, ed. J. Needham (CUP, 2000). See also *The Cambridge World History of Food*, as above.

p. 255 *The Danes led much of the development* . . . For a comprehensive technical history of soya, see W. Shurtleff and A. Aoyagi, *History of Soybeans and Soyfoods Past Present and Future* (Lafayette, CA, Soyinfo Center, www.soyinfocenter.com/).

p. 255 *It was ADM researchers in the mid 1930s who worked out how to heat treat the protein meal* . . . W. Shurtleff, as above.

p. 256 *soya exports were supported by the other US food aid programmes* . . . Oxfam 'Food Aid or Hidden Dumping' report, as above.

p. 256 *US soya farming received $13 billion in subsidies* . . . Environmental Working Group subsidy database, as above.

p. 256 *Soya never looked back* . . . In 1965, Chicago Board of Trade figures record global soya bean production was 30 million tonnes.

By 2005, the world was consuming nine times that amount at 270 million tonnes a year, with some of the steepest growth in consumption coming in the 1980s and 1990s.

p. 256 *over 60 per cent of all processed foods in Britain contain soya* ... Committee on Toxicity of Chemicals in Food, Consumer Products and the Environment, 'Phytoestrogens and Health' report, May 2003.

p. 258 *A fifth of the planet's fresh water* ... 'Eating up the Amazon', Greenpeace, April 2006.

p. 259 *more than half of the Amazon will be lost* ... *Nature* magazine warned a couple of years ago that if agricultural expansion continues, 40 per cent of the Amazon rainforests will have been wiped out by 2050, releasing into the atmosphere the equivalent in carbon of four years' worth of all current annual global emissions. By 2007, the predictions had become even more depressing. As billions of tonnes of carbon dioxide are released into the atmosphere by burning and logging they contribute to global warming, producing a multiplier effect so that if current trends in agriculture and livestock production go unchecked, more than half of the Amazon will be lost by 2030. *Nature*, March 2006; World Wildlife Fund report, D. Nepstead, December 2007.

p. 261 *Cargill, ADM and Bunge control nearly three quarters of the global market in soya* ... Food Inc, Vorley, as above; 'Eating up the Amazon', Greenpeace, as above; company websites.

p. 261 *Bunge is the largest processor of bottled vegetable oils* ... Bunge website; Bunge revenues in 2006 were $26 million, Forbes.com.

p. 261 *Almost half of ADM's global sales* ... Forbes.com. ADM sales were worth $44 billion in 2006/7.

p. 261 *Cargill is the world's largest crusher of oilseed* ... Cargill website.

p. 261 *The three companies together are estimated to control 80 per cent of the European soya bean crushing industry* ... Food Inc, Vorley, as above.

p. 261 *Dreyfus has huge processing interests in South America* ... Louis Dreyfus website.

p. 261 *They account for 60 per cent of Brazil's soya exports* ... 'Eating up the Amazon', Greenpeace, as above.

p. 261 *Cargill . . . With revenues of nearly US$88 billion in 2007 . . .*
Cargill personal communication; Forbes.com.

p. 262 *Brewster Kneen, its unauthorized biographer . . . Invisible Giant:
Cargill and its Transnational Strategies*, Brewster Kneen (Pluto Press,
1995, 2nd edition, 2002).

p. 263 *the US accounting for more than 90 per cent of global exports . . .*
Statistics on soya markets from USDA National Agricultural
Statistics Service and USDA/ERS 2005.

p. 263 *responsible for about two thirds of the total financing of soya production
in Brazil . . .* 'Eating up the Amazon', as above; J. M. Dros,
'Managing the Soy Boom', WWF.

p. 263 *Because land could be grabbed . . .* Brazilian land law is chaotic and
many of the small farmers have rights but no title deeds, having
been settled in previous military government programmes to
populate its northern border areas.

p. 265 *It is a leading player in . . . the 'global chicken value chain' . . .*
'Eating up the Amazon', as above.

p. 270 *. . . China's soya imports from Brazil increased . . .* Brazil now has
the largest agricultural trade surplus in the world, overtaking the
US. It is the third largest agricultural producer in the world,
accounting for 40 per cent of global chicken exports, over a quarter
of world beef exports and 14 per cent of global pork exports. This
is where Europe finds much of its processed meats and animal feed
and China sources its increasing demand for feed.

p. 278 *More than three decades ago the US Internal Revenue Service tracked
some of its highly complex trades through subsidiaries . . .* Documented in
Dan Morgan's *Merchants of Grain*, as above, p. 203 ff and p. 371.
The information about the international operations of Tradax was
brought out in Multinational Corporations and United States
Foreign Policy – International Grain Companies, hearings before
the Senate Subcommittee on Multinational Corporations, June 18,
23 and 24, 1976.

p. 281 *The leading suppliers of these soya proteins are . . .* 'The Food
Additives Market, Global Trends and Developments', Leatherhead
Food International, June 2005.

p. 281 *The American soya industry spends about $80 million every year* . . . 'What is the Soybean Checkoff?', United Soybean Board, www. unitedsoybean.org/.

p. 282 *DuPont when it petitioned the US Food and Drug Administration* . . . *Food Politics*, Marion Nestle, as above.

p. 282 *For Dr Mike Fitzpatrick* . . . personal communications; *Guardian*, August 14, 2006; *BMJ*, vol. 331, no. 254 (30 July, 2005), and rapid responses following.

p. 282 *Richard James* . . . Richard and his wife Valerie now run the campaigning Soy Information Service, www.soyonlineservice. co.nz.

p. 283 *the UK government's expert committee on the Toxicity of Food was asked to conduct a full inquiry* . . . 'Phytoestrogens and Health' report, May 2003, as above.

p. 283 *a fact noted by the Royal Society in its expert report* . . . 'Endocrine Disrupting Chemicals', Royal Society, June 2000.

p. 286 *Soya is used in traditional oriental diets* . . . *after cultures, moulds or precipitants* . . . 'On the Domestication of the Soybean', T. Hymowitz, *Economic Botany*, vol. 24, no. 4 (October–December 1970).

p. 287 *The cheapest grades are made by* . . . For detailed descriptions of modern soya production processes, see *The Whole Soy Story*, Kaayla T. Daniel (New Trends Publishing, 2007).

p. 288 *It was however 2005 before the soya health food bandwagon began to come off the rails* . . . For an overview of the latest scientific thinking, see 'Soyonara? Tough Times for the "Miracle Bean"', Center for Science in the Public Interest, Health Letter, vol. 33, no. 8 (October, 2006).

p. 288 *another expert government panel, this time in the US* . . . 'Effects of Soy on Health Outcomes', US Department of Health and Human Services, Agency for Healthcare Research and Quality, Evidence Report, no. 126, August 2005.

p. 288 *the American Heart Association dissociated itself from claims about soya protein* . . . 'Soy Protein, Isoflavones, and Cardiovascular Health', An American Heart Association Science Advisory for Professionals from the Nutrition Committee, January 17, 2006.

337

p. 292 *city analysts JPMorgan expressed their quandary* ... 'Obesity: Reshaping the Food Industry', JPMorgan, Global Equity Research, 24 January 2006.

p. 294 *It showed that certain artificial colourings and a preservative* ... Food additives and hyperactive behaviour in 3-year-old and 8/9-year-old children in the community, McCann *et al*, *The Lancet*, 2007; 370:1560–1567.

p. 295 *The regulators* ... *advice to parents* ... Food Standards Agency T07040: 'Chronic and acute effects of artificial colourings and preservatives on children's behaviour', Thursday 6 September 2007; Agency advice on certain artificial colours, Food Standards Agency, September 11 2007 ; http://www.food.gov.uk/news/newsarchive/2007/sep/foodcolours

p. 299 *McDonald's responded immediately to Greenpeace's campaign* ... 'McVictory: Victory as fast food giant pledges to help protect the Amazon', Greenpeace, July 26 2006, www.greenpeace.org; McDonald's press release, Greenpeace report, July 24 2006, www.mcdonalds.co.uk

p. 299 *the commodity processors and leading retailers all acknowledged that the moratorium on soya* ... Soy Moratorium in the Amazon Biome, ABIOVE (Brazilian Vegetable Oil Industry), July 2007 www.abiove.com.br/english/sustent/ms_relatorio1ano_24jul07_us.pdf.

p. 300 *The fair trade campaign Banana Link* ... www.bananalink.org.uk/

p. 301 *Sainsbury's took the brave decision to buy all of its bananas from fair trade sources* ... 'Saving St Lucia, UK Supermarket sweeps up 100m bananas', *Guardian* February 26 2007.

p. 302 *the Merton parents now help other groups set up their own action groups* ... www.mertonparents.co.uk/

p. 302 *the National Federation of Women's Institutes that has held supermarkets to account* ... WI, 'The Great Milk Debate', press release, April 24 2007.

p. 302 *The Church of England too has challenged the Competition*

Commisssion . . . Church of England press release, 'Church proposes independent ombudsman to stop supermarkets squeezing farmers', November 5 2007.

p. 302 *the first agricultural workers' strike since the 1920s* . . . 'Fruit pickers stage pay protest', BBC News, August 18 2005; 'Stop exploitation picket outside S&A strawberry farm', T&G press release, July 17 2006.

p. 304 *sharing a platform with Spitou among others* . . . Public hearing, 'Exploitation of Migrant Workers in Europe', October 24 2006, European Parliament, Strasbourg. Socialist, Liberal Democrats, Greens Alliance.

p. 304 *the Transition Town movement* . . . www.transitiontowns.org/

He just wanted a decent book to read ...

Not too much to ask, is it? It was in 1935 when Allen Lane, Managing Director of Bodley Head Publishers, stood on a platform at Exeter railway station looking for something good to read on his journey back to London. His choice was limited to popular magazines and poor-quality paperbacks – the same choice faced every day by the vast majority of readers, few of whom could afford hardbacks. Lane's disappointment and subsequent anger at the range of books generally available led him to found a company – and change the world.

'We believed in the existence in this country of a vast reading public for intelligent books at a low price, and staked everything on it'
Sir Allen Lane, 1902–1970, founder of Penguin Books

The quality paperback had arrived – and not just in bookshops. Lane was adamant that his Penguins should appear in chain stores and tobacconists, and should cost no more than a packet of cigarettes.

Reading habits (and cigarette prices) have changed since 1935, but Penguin still believes in publishing the best books for everybody to enjoy. We still believe that good design costs no more than bad design, and we still believe that quality books published passionately and responsibly make the world a better place.

So wherever you see the little bird – whether it's on a piece of prize-winning literary fiction or a celebrity autobiography, political tour de force or historical masterpiece, a serial-killer thriller, reference book, world classic or a piece of pure escapism – you can bet that it represents the very best that the genre has to offer.

Whatever you like to read – trust Penguin.